The FLASH
THE ROAD TO FLASHPOINT

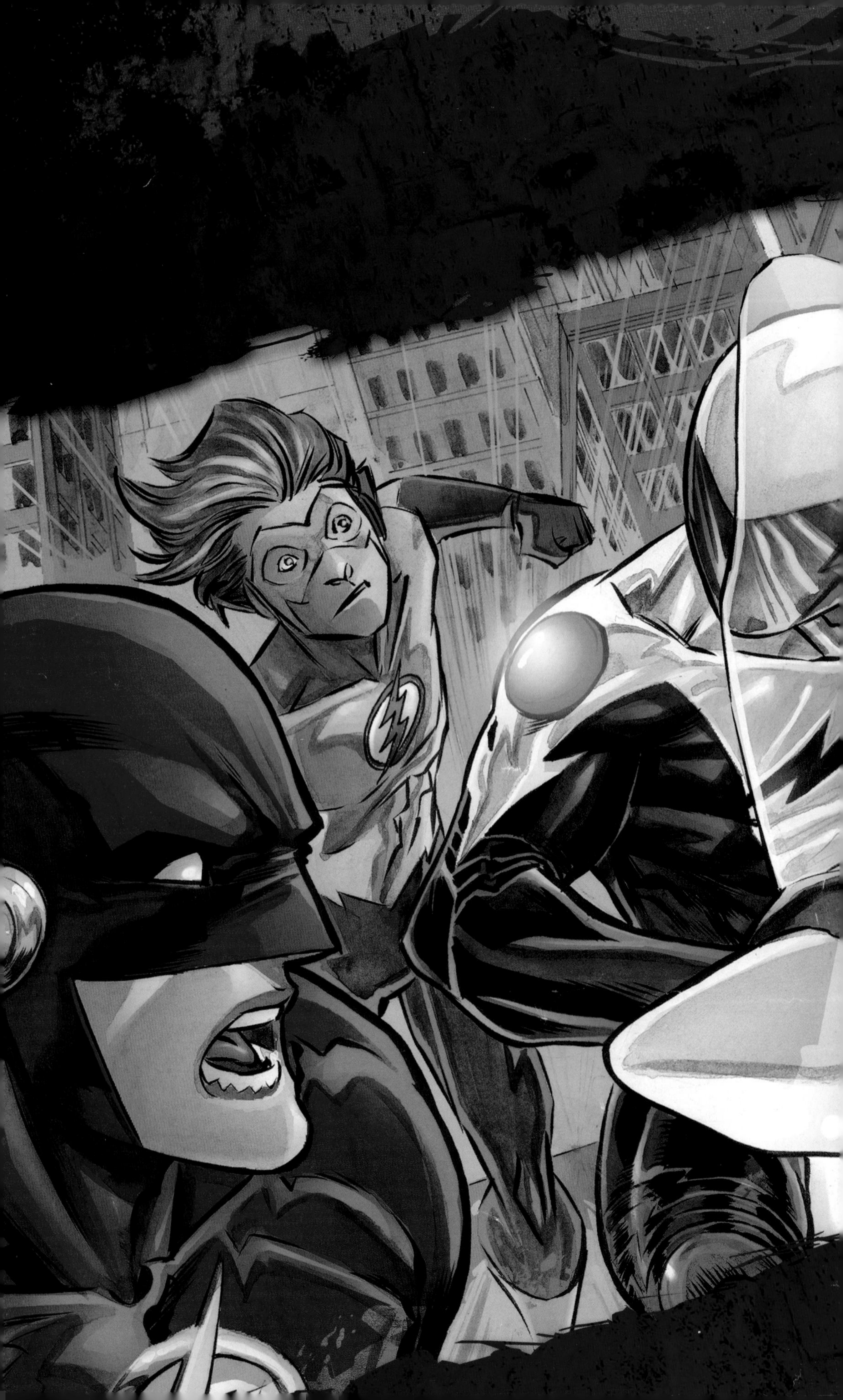

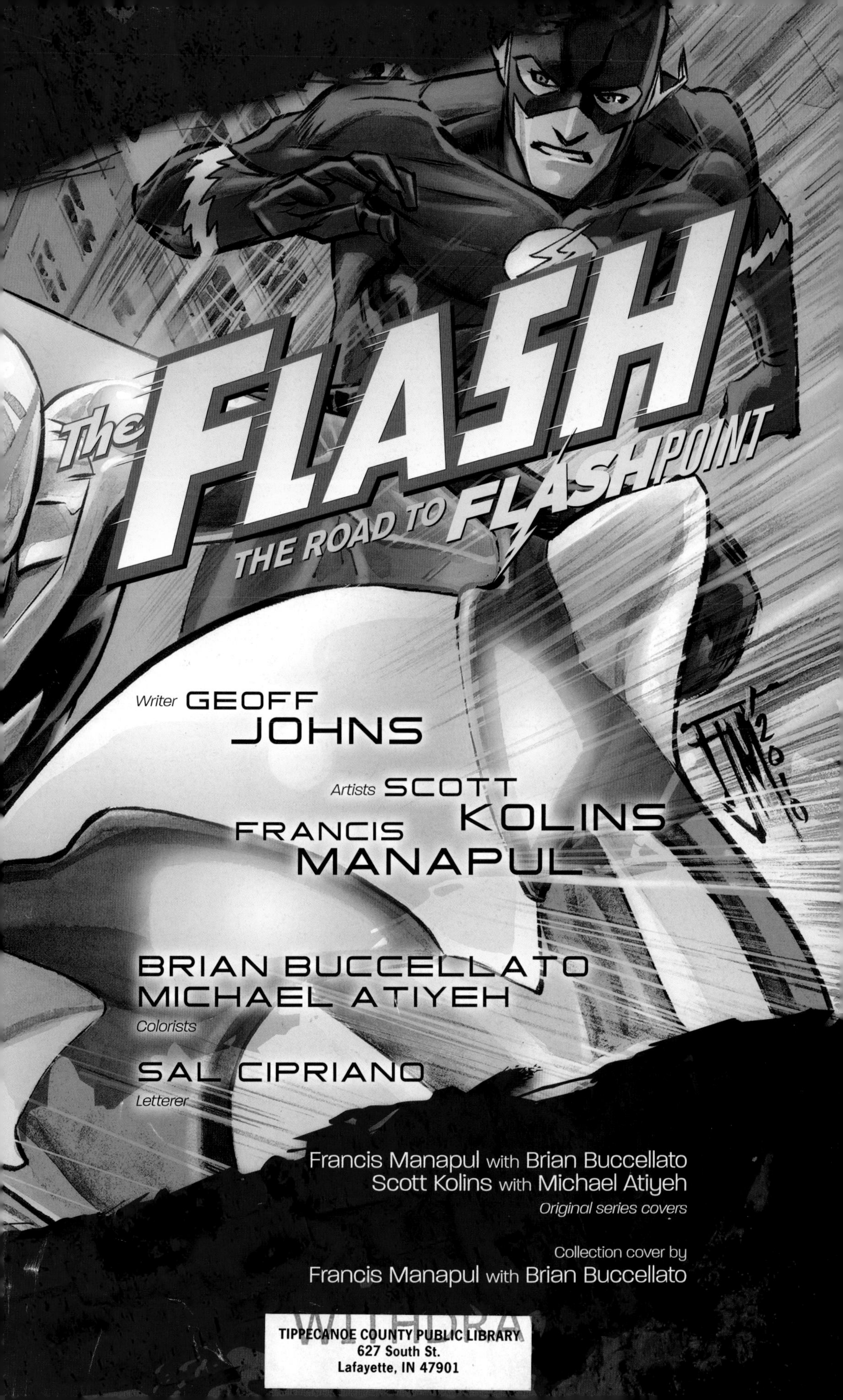

The FLASH
THE ROAD TO FLASHPOINT

Writer GEOFF JOHNS

Artists SCOTT KOLINS
FRANCIS MANAPUL

BRIAN BUCCELLATO
MICHAEL ATIYEH
Colorists

SAL CIPRIANO
Letterer

Francis Manapul with Brian Buccellato
Scott Kolins with Michael Atiyeh
Original series covers

Collection cover by
Francis Manapul with Brian Buccellato

BRIAN CUNNINGHAM
ADAM SCHLAGMAN
EDDIE BERGANZA
Editors – Original Series

DARREN SHAN
Assistant Editor – Original Series

IAN SATTLER
*Director – Editorial, Special Projects
and Archival Editions*

ROBBIN BROSTERMAN
Design Director – Books

BRAINCHILD STUDIOS/NYC
Publication Design

EDDIE BERGANZA
Executive Editor

BOB HARRAS
VP – Editor in Chief

DIANE NELSON
President

DAN DIDIO and JIM LEE
Co-Publishers

GEOFF JOHNS
Chief Creative Officer

JOHN ROOD
*Executive VP – Sales, Marketing
and Business Development*

AMY GENKINS
*Senior VP – Business
and Legal Affairs*

NAIRI GARDINER
Senior VP – Finance

JEFF BOISON
VP – Publishing Operations

MARK CHIARELLO
VP – Art Direction and Design

JOHN CUNNINGHAM
VP – Marketing

TERRI CUNNINGHAM
VP – Talent Relations and Services

ALISON GILL
*Senior VP – Manufacturing and
Operations*

DAVID HYDE
VP – Publicity

HANK KANALZ
Senior VP – Digital

JAY KOGAN
*VP – Business and Legal Affairs,
Publishing*

JACK MAHAN
VP – Business Affairs, Talent

NICK NAPOLITANO
VP – Manufacturing Administration

SUE POHJA
VP – Book Sales

COURTNEY SIMMONS
Senior VP – Publicity

BOB WAYNE
Senior VP – Sales

THE FLASH: THE ROAD TO FLASHPOINT

DC Comics, 1700 Broadway, New York, NY
A Warner Bros. Entertainment Company
Printed by RR Donnelley, Salem, VA, USA.
9/23/11. First Printing.

HC ISBN: 978-1-4012-3279-5
SC ISBN: 978-1-4012-3448-5

SUSTAINABLE
FORESTRY
INITIATIVE
Certified Chain of Custody
Promoting Sustainable
Forest Management
www.sfiprogram.org

Fiber used in this product line meets the
sourcing requirements of the SFI program.
www.sfiprogram.org SGS-SFI/COC-US10/81072

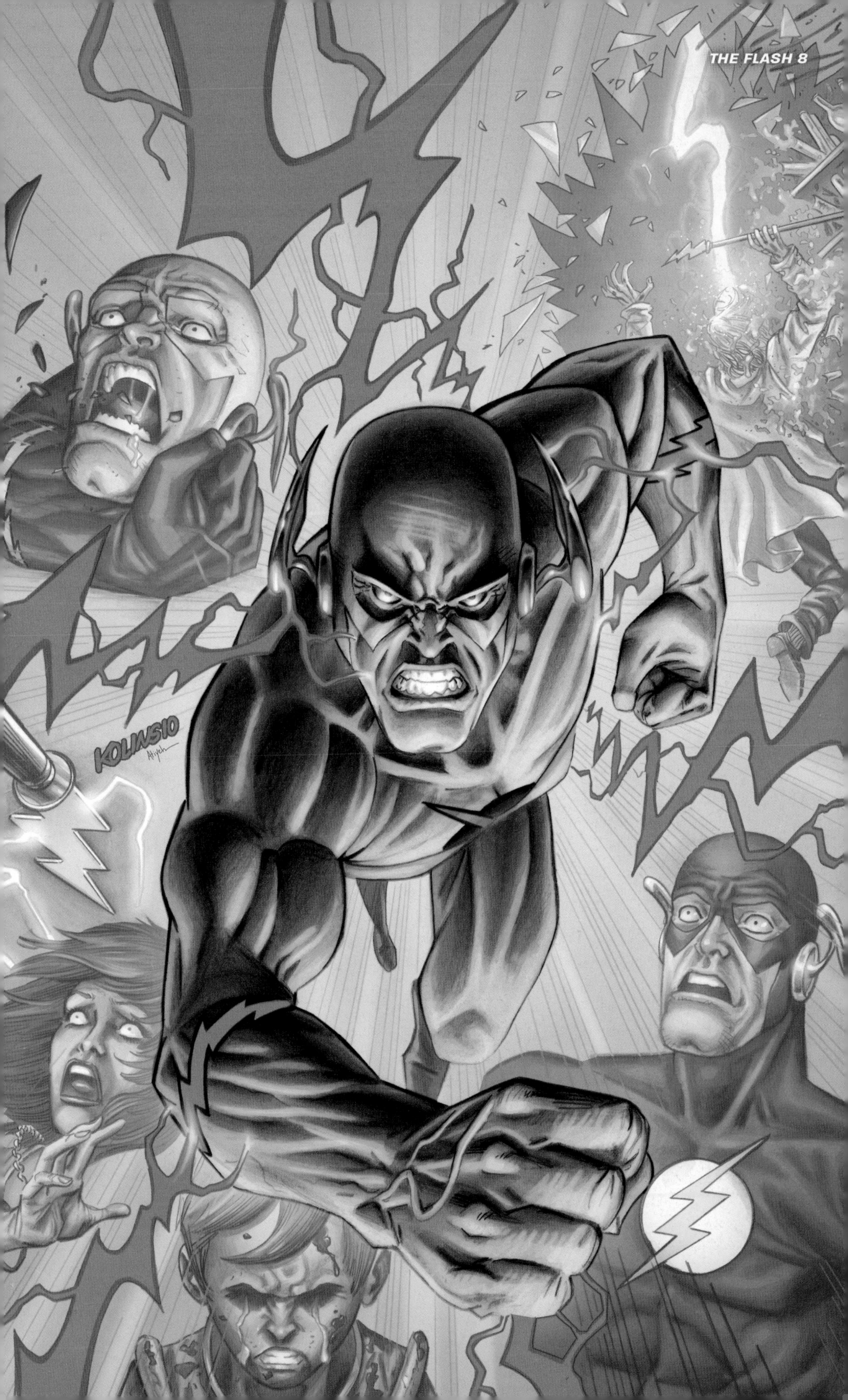
KOLINS10

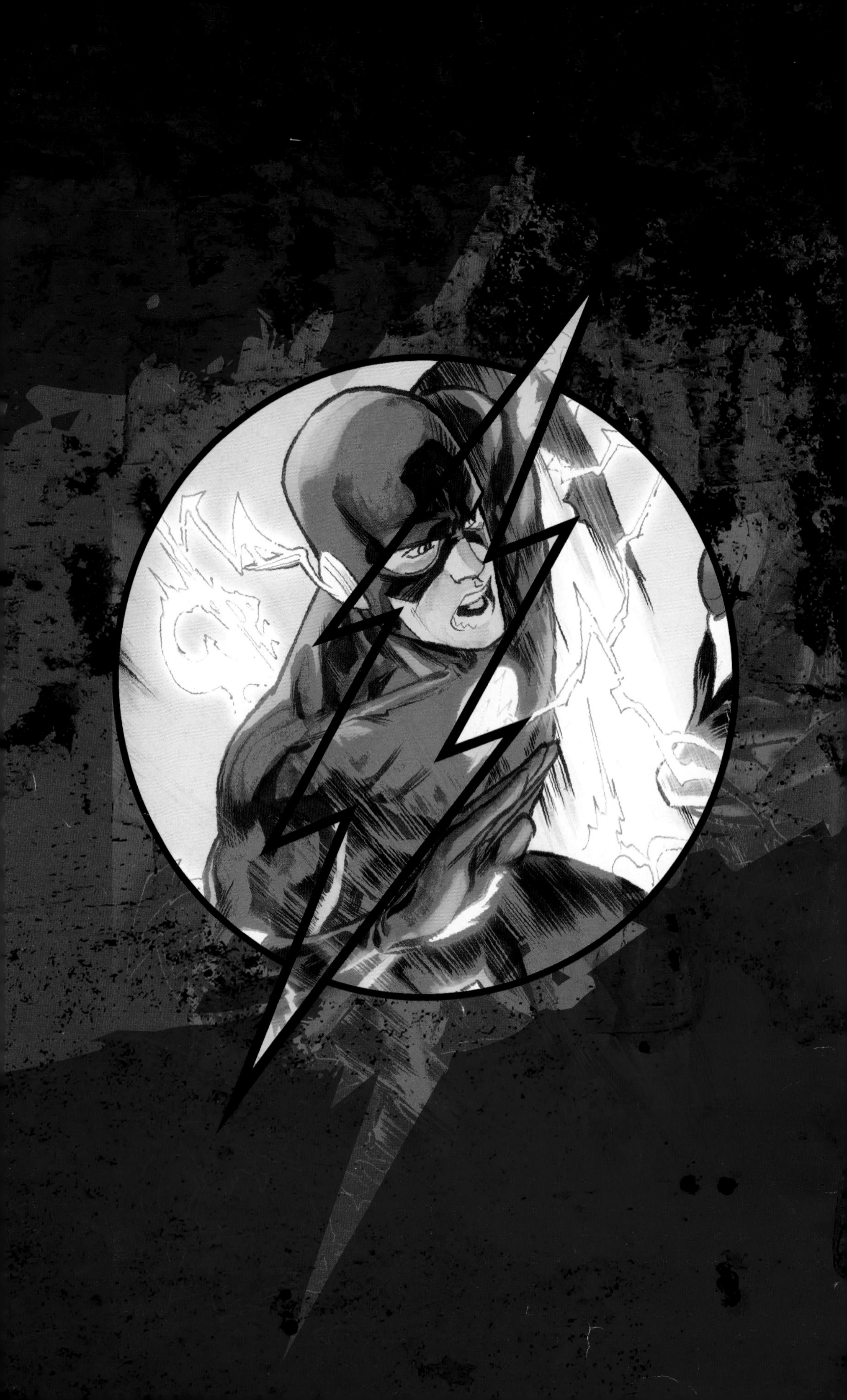

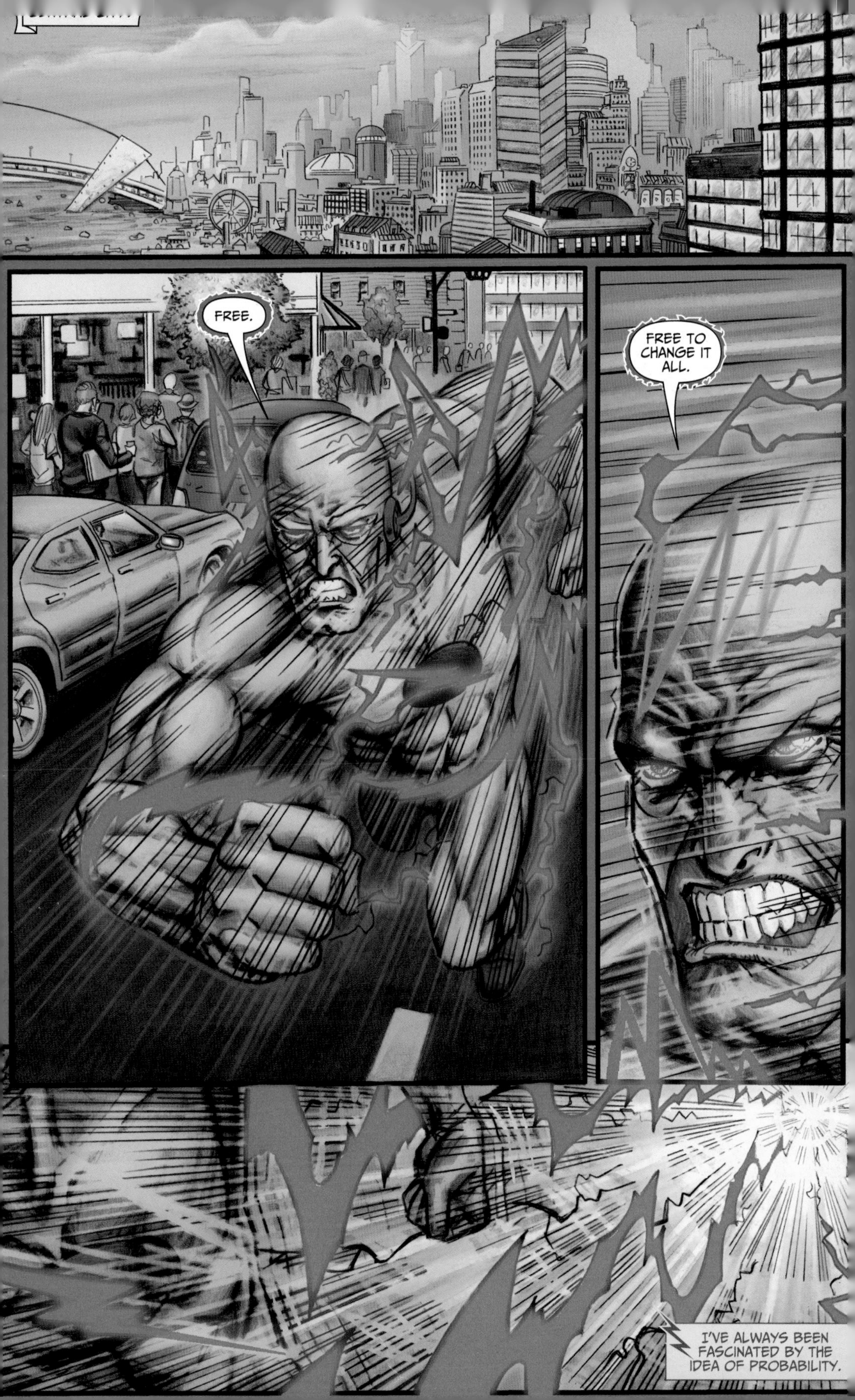
FREE.
FREE TO CHANGE IT ALL.
I'VE ALWAYS BEEN FASCINATED BY THE IDEA OF PROBABILITY.

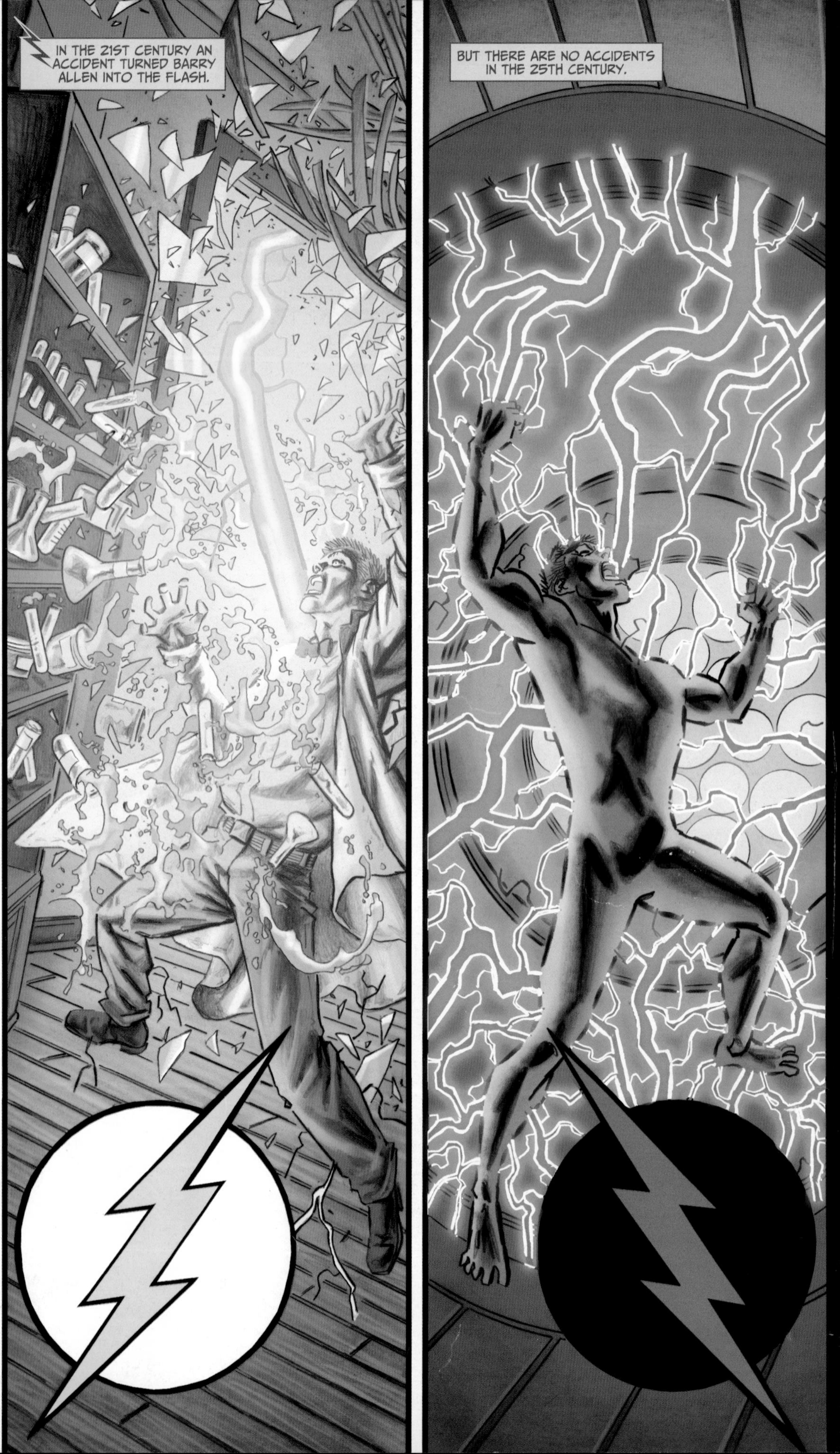
IN THE 21ST CENTURY AN ACCIDENT TURNED BARRY ALLEN INTO THE FLASH.
BUT THERE ARE NO ACCIDENTS IN THE 25TH CENTURY.

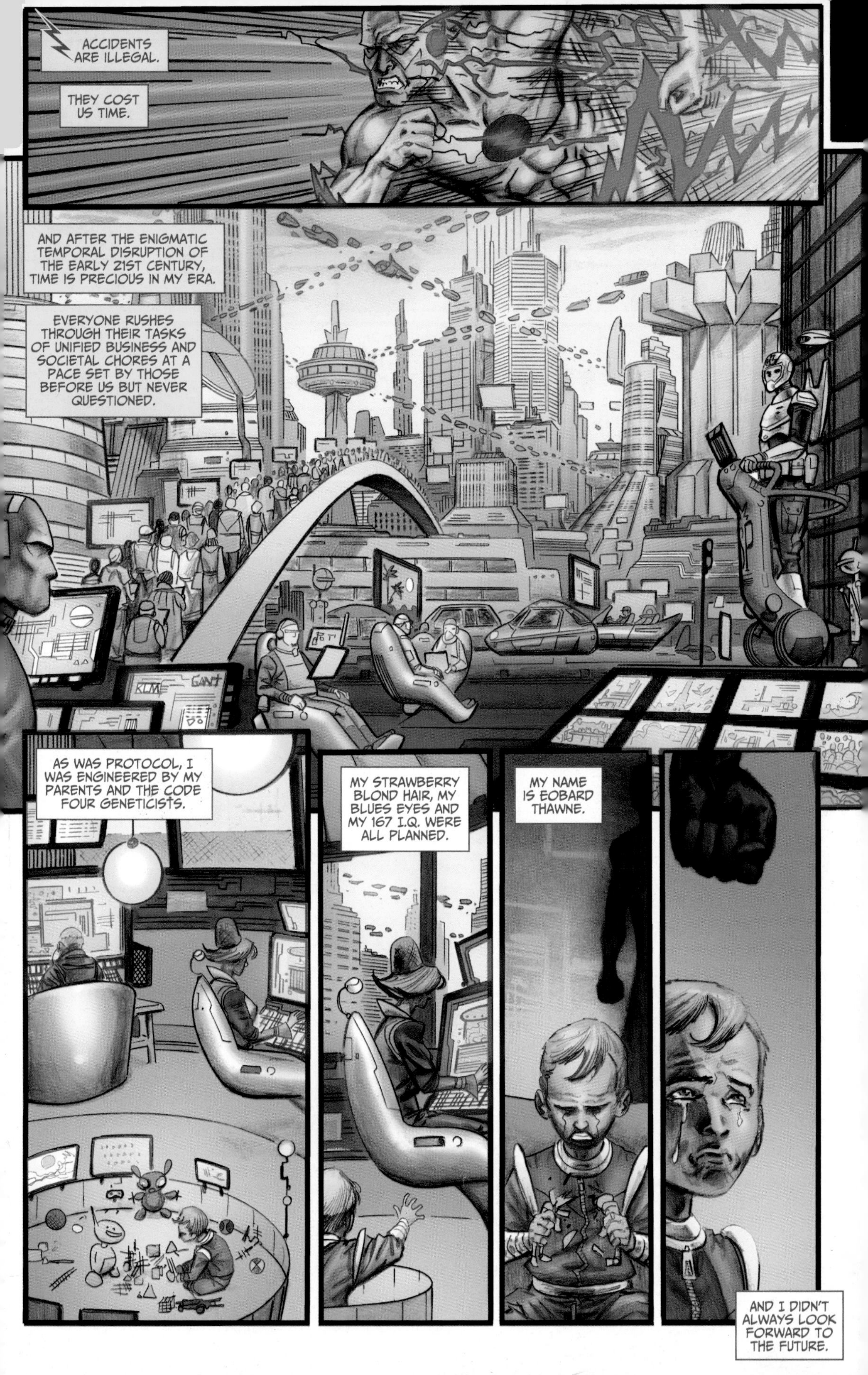
ACCIDENTS ARE ILLEGAL.
THEY COST US TIME.
AND AFTER THE ENIGMATIC TEMPORAL DISRUPTION OF THE EARLY 21ST CENTURY, TIME IS PRECIOUS IN MY ERA.
EVERYONE RUSHES THROUGH THEIR TASKS OF UNIFIED BUSINESS AND SOCIETAL CHORES AT A PACE SET BY THOSE BEFORE US BUT NEVER QUESTIONED.
AS WAS PROTOCOL, I WAS ENGINEERED BY MY PARENTS AND THE CODE FOUR GENETICISTS.
MY STRAWBERRY BLOND HAIR, MY BLUES EYES AND MY 167 I.Q. WERE ALL PLANNED.
MY NAME IS EOBARD THAWNE.
AND I DIDN'T ALWAYS LOOK FORWARD TO THE FUTURE.

DESPITE MY ACADEMIC ACHIEVEMENTS, IT WAS DEEMED THAT I SHOULD HAVE A BROTHER.

A BROTHER WOULD CREATE A FAMILY QUOTA THAT WOULD EASE OUR TAX BRACKET AND GIVE MY MOTHER A QUOTIENT AMENABLE TO THE YMA AND, MORE IMPORTANT TO MY PARENTS, IT WOULD INCREASE MY SOCIAL ABILITIES.

...NEXT EIGHTEEN DAYS, YOU WILL CREATE YOUR THESIS ON THE USELESSNESS OF "DWELLING" ON THE PAST BOTH *HISTORICALLY* AND *PERSONALLY* AND THE *NEGATIVE* TIME COSTS ASSOCIATED WITH IT...

ETIC LIFE DYNAMICS.

AMICS.

KINETIC

HEY, THAWNE, HAVE FUN IN YOUR BONDING LESSONS WITH YOUR BROTHER WHILE WE PRACTICE FOR THE COGNIZANT TIMING TEAM. I'D SAVE YOU A SPOT, BUT IT'S FIRST COME FIRST--

EOBARD.

VAANCE

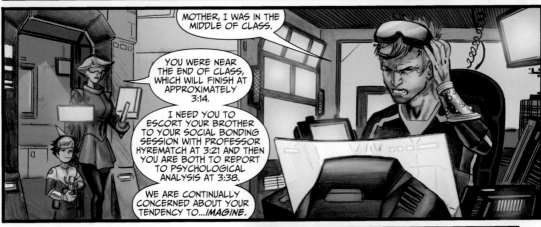

MOTHER, I WAS IN THE MIDDLE OF CLASS.

YOU WERE NEAR THE END OF CLASS, WHICH WILL FINISH AT APPROXIMATELY 3:14.

I NEED YOU TO ESCORT YOUR BROTHER TO YOUR SOCIAL BONDING SESSION WITH PROFESSOR HYREMATCH AT 3:21 AND THEN YOU ARE BOTH TO REPORT TO PSYCHOLOGICAL ANALYSIS AT 3:38.

WE ARE CONTINUALLY CONCERNED ABOUT YOUR TENDENCY TO...*IMAGINE.*

YES, MOTHER.

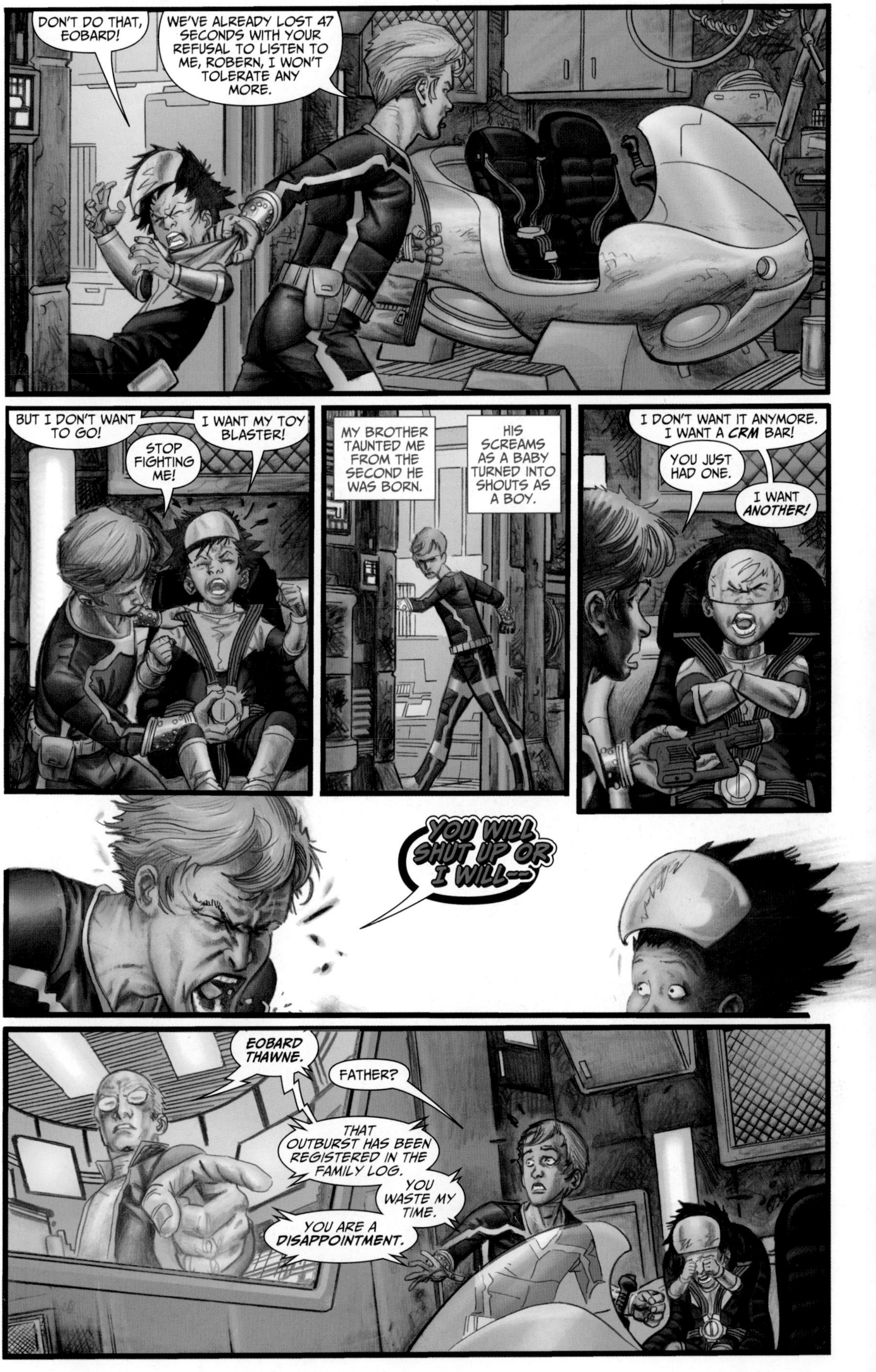
DON'T DO THAT, EOBARD!
WE'VE ALREADY LOST 47 SECONDS WITH YOUR REFUSAL TO LISTEN TO ME, ROBERN, I WON'T TOLERATE ANY MORE.
BUT I DON'T WANT TO GO!
STOP FIGHTING ME!
I WANT MY TOY BLASTER!
MY BROTHER TAUNTED ME FROM THE SECOND HE WAS BORN.
HIS SCREAMS AS A BABY TURNED INTO SHOUTS AS A BOY.
I DON'T WANT IT ANYMORE. I WANT A CRM BAR!
YOU JUST HAD ONE.
I WANT ANOTHER!
YOU WILL SHUT UP OR I WILL--
EOBARD THAWNE.
FATHER?
THAT OUTBURST HAS BEEN REGISTERED IN THE FAMILY LOG.
YOU WASTE MY TIME.
YOU ARE A DISAPPOINTMENT.

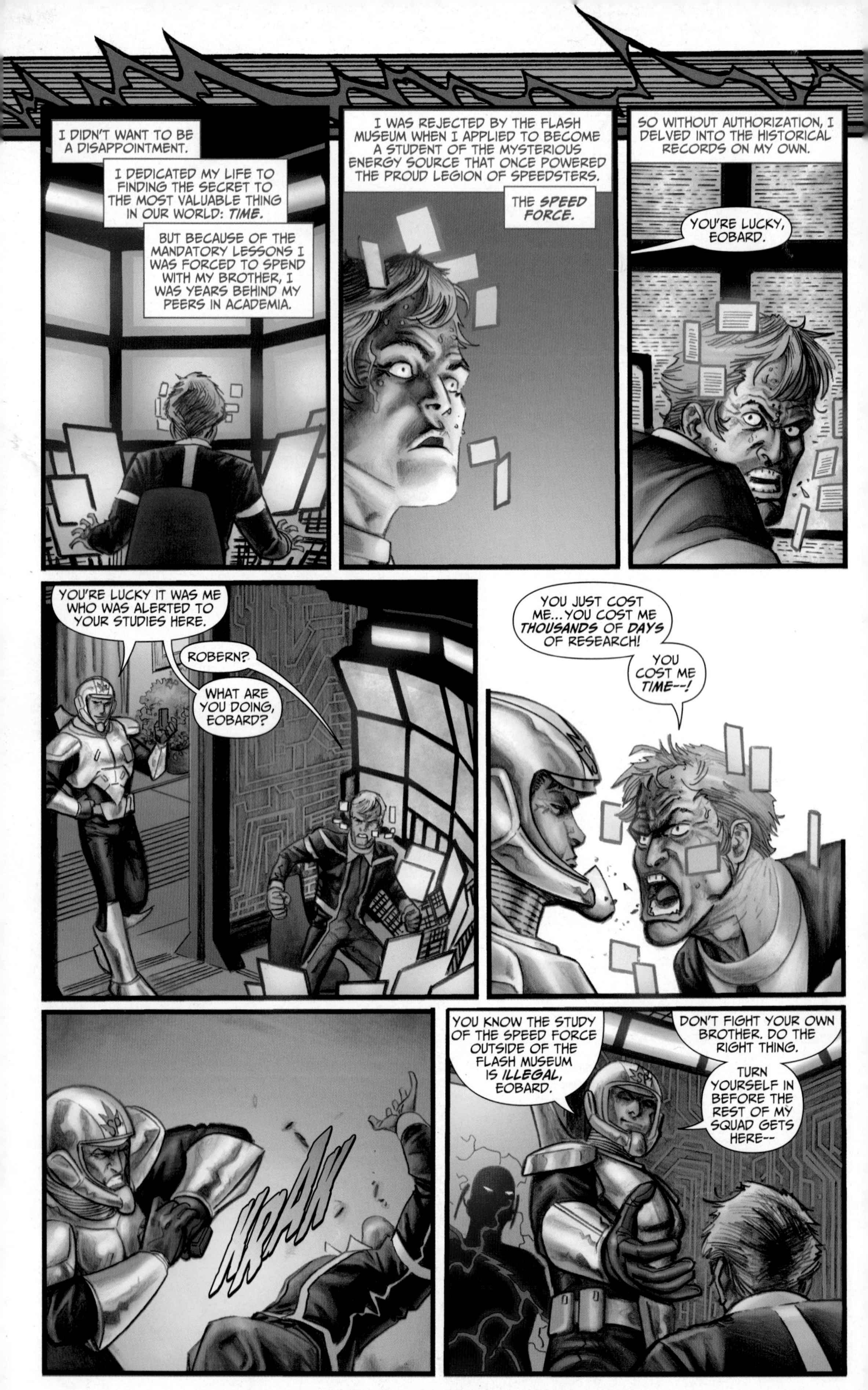
I DIDN'T WANT TO BE A DISAPPOINTMENT.
I DEDICATED MY LIFE TO FINDING THE SECRET TO THE MOST VALUABLE THING IN OUR WORLD: TIME.
BUT BECAUSE OF THE MANDATORY LESSONS I WAS FORCED TO SPEND WITH MY BROTHER, I WAS YEARS BEHIND MY PEERS IN ACADEMIA.
I WAS REJECTED BY THE FLASH MUSEUM WHEN I APPLIED TO BECOME A STUDENT OF THE MYSTERIOUS ENERGY SOURCE THAT ONCE POWERED THE PROUD LEGION OF SPEEDSTERS.
THE SPEED FORCE.
SO WITHOUT AUTHORIZATION, I DELVED INTO THE HISTORICAL RECORDS ON MY OWN.
YOU'RE LUCKY, EOBARD.
YOU'RE LUCKY IT WAS ME WHO WAS ALERTED TO YOUR STUDIES HERE.
ROBERN?
WHAT ARE YOU DOING, EOBARD?
YOU JUST COST ME...YOU COST ME THOUSANDS OF DAYS OF RESEARCH!
YOU COST ME TIME--!
HRAAAH
YOU KNOW THE STUDY OF THE SPEED FORCE OUTSIDE OF THE FLASH MUSEUM IS ILLEGAL, EOBARD.
DON'T FIGHT YOUR OWN BROTHER. DO THE RIGHT THING.
TURN YOURSELF IN BEFORE THE REST OF MY SQUAD GETS HERE--

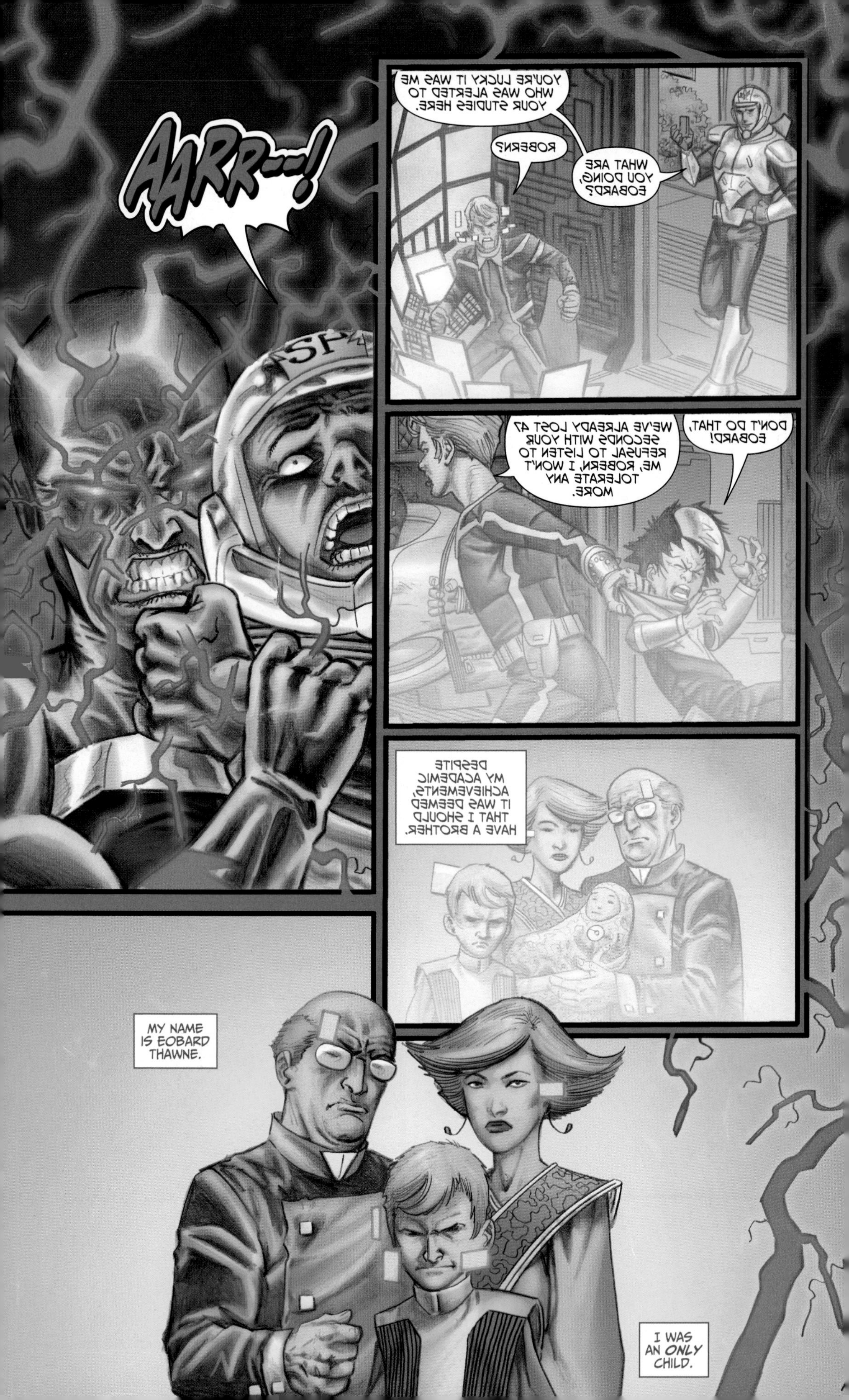
AARR--!
WHAT ARE YOU DOING, EOBARD?
ROBERN?
YOU'RE LUCKY IT WAS ME WHO WAS ALERTED TO YOUR STUDIES HERE.
DON'T DO THAT, EOBARD!
WE'VE ALREADY LOST 47 SECONDS WITH YOUR REFUSAL TO LISTEN TO ME, ROBERN, I WON'T TOLERATE ANY MORE.
DESPITE MY ACADEMIC ACHIEVEMENTS, IT WAS DEEMED THAT I SHOULD HAVE A BROTHER.
MY NAME IS EOBARD THAWNE.
I WAS AN *ONLY* CHILD.

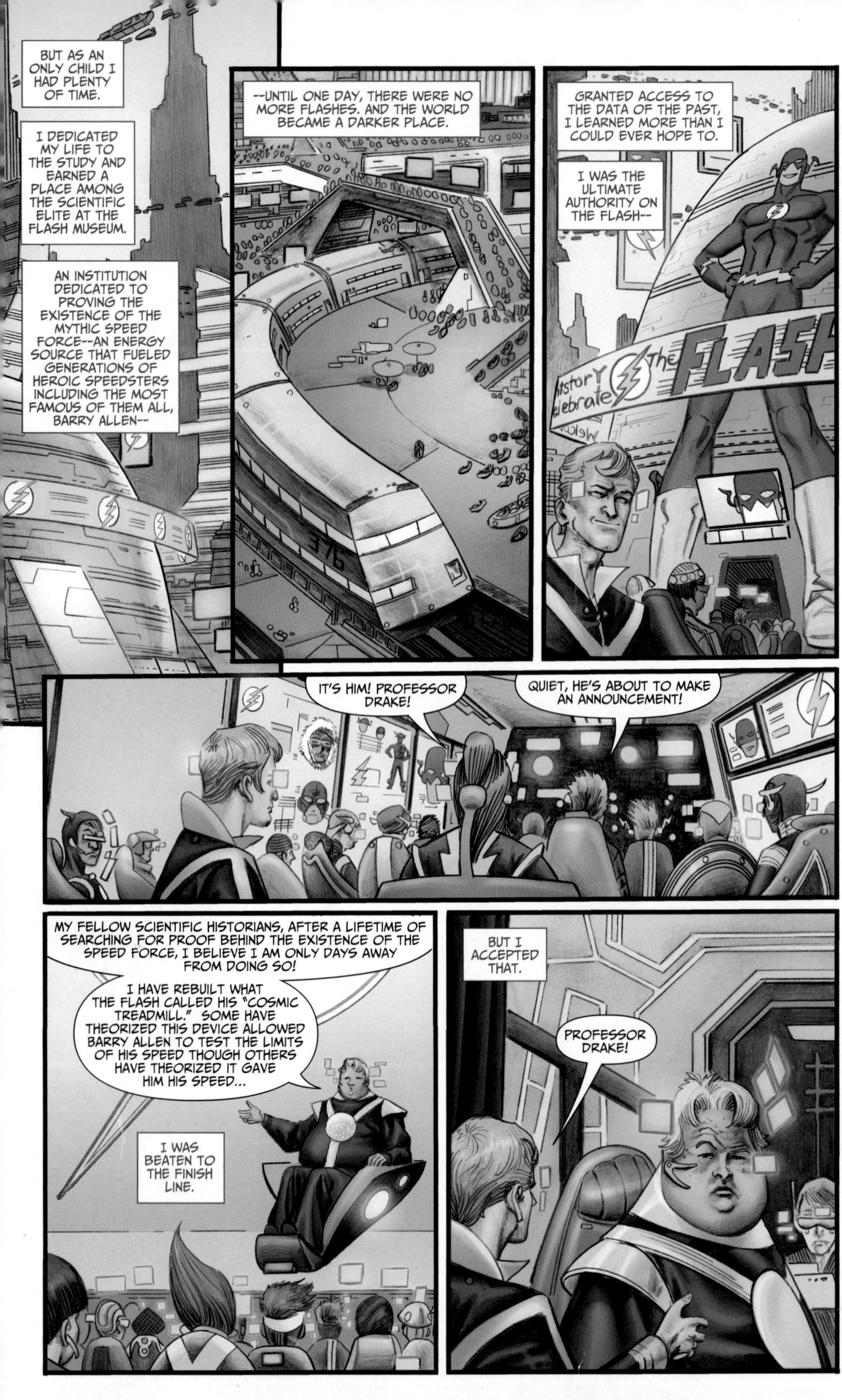
BUT AS AN ONLY CHILD I HAD PLENTY OF TIME.
I DEDICATED MY LIFE TO THE STUDY AND EARNED A PLACE AMONG THE SCIENTIFIC ELITE AT THE FLASH MUSEUM.
AN INSTITUTION DEDICATED TO PROVING THE EXISTENCE OF THE MYTHIC SPEED FORCE--AN ENERGY SOURCE THAT FUELED GENERATIONS OF HEROIC SPEEDSTERS INCLUDING THE MOST FAMOUS OF THEM ALL, BARRY ALLEN--
--UNTIL ONE DAY, THERE WERE NO MORE FLASHES. AND THE WORLD BECAME A DARKER PLACE.
376
GRANTED ACCESS TO THE DATA OF THE PAST, I LEARNED MORE THAN I COULD EVER HOPE TO.
I WAS THE ULTIMATE AUTHORITY ON THE FLASH--
The FLASH
IT'S HIM! PROFESSOR DRAKE!
QUIET, HE'S ABOUT TO MAKE AN ANNOUNCEMENT!
MY FELLOW SCIENTIFIC HISTORIANS, AFTER A LIFETIME OF SEARCHING FOR PROOF BEHIND THE EXISTENCE OF THE SPEED FORCE, I BELIEVE I AM ONLY DAYS AWAY FROM DOING SO!
I HAVE REBUILT WHAT THE FLASH CALLED HIS "COSMIC TREADMILL." SOME HAVE THEORIZED THIS DEVICE ALLOWED BARRY ALLEN TO TEST THE LIMITS OF HIS SPEED THOUGH OTHERS HAVE THEORIZED IT GAVE HIM HIS SPEED...
I WAS BEATEN TO THE FINISH LINE.
BUT I ACCEPTED THAT.
PROFESSOR DRAKE!

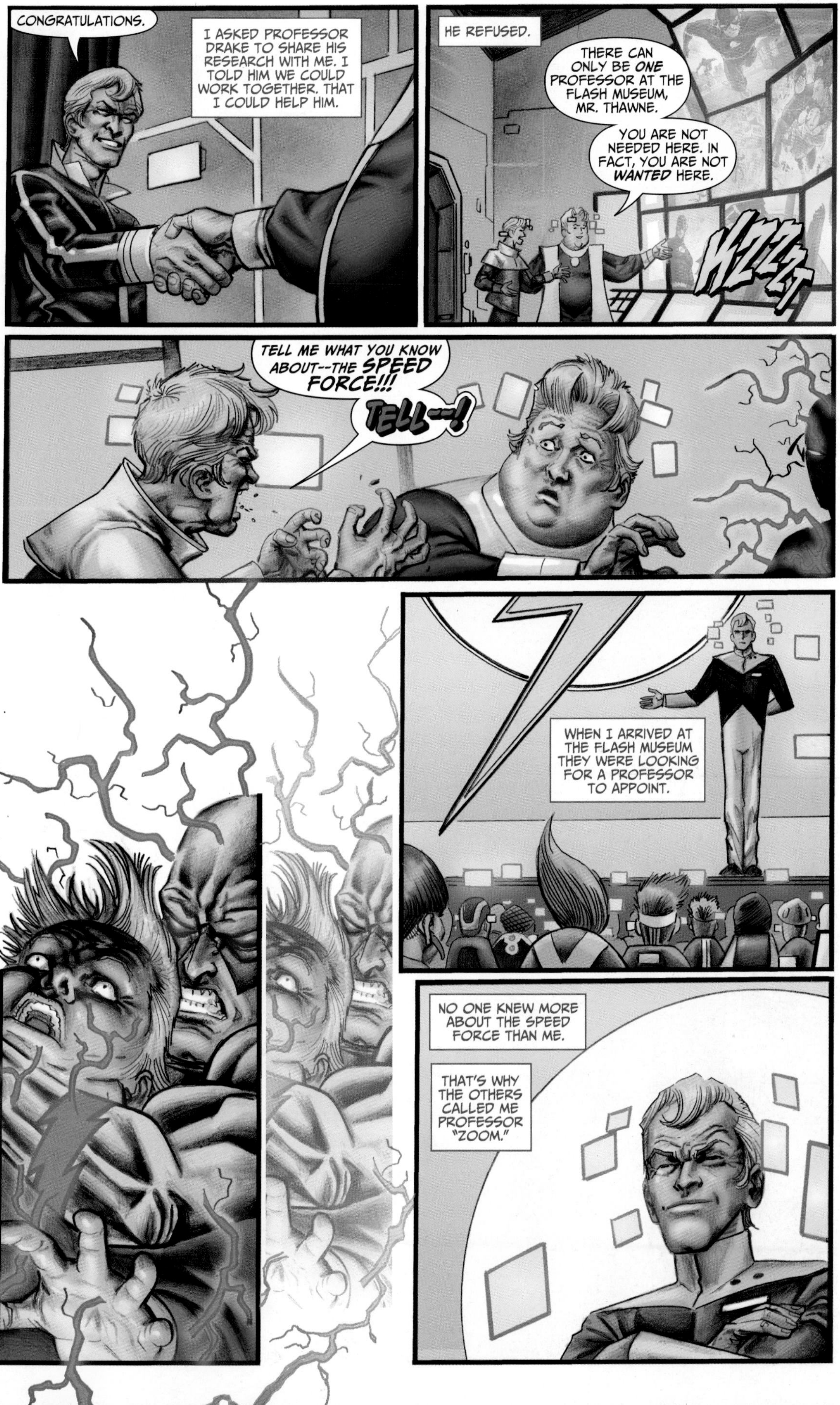
CONGRATULATIONS.
I ASKED PROFESSOR DRAKE TO SHARE HIS RESEARCH WITH ME. I TOLD HIM WE COULD WORK TOGETHER. THAT I COULD HELP HIM.
HE REFUSED.
THERE CAN ONLY BE ONE PROFESSOR AT THE FLASH MUSEUM, MR. THAWNE.
YOU ARE NOT NEEDED HERE. IN FACT, YOU ARE NOT WANTED HERE.
KZZZT
TELL ME WHAT YOU KNOW ABOUT--THE SPEED FORCE!!!
TELL--!
WHEN I ARRIVED AT THE FLASH MUSEUM THEY WERE LOOKING FOR A PROFESSOR TO APPOINT.
NO ONE KNEW MORE ABOUT THE SPEED FORCE THAN ME.
THAT'S WHY THE OTHERS CALLED ME PROFESSOR "ZOOM."

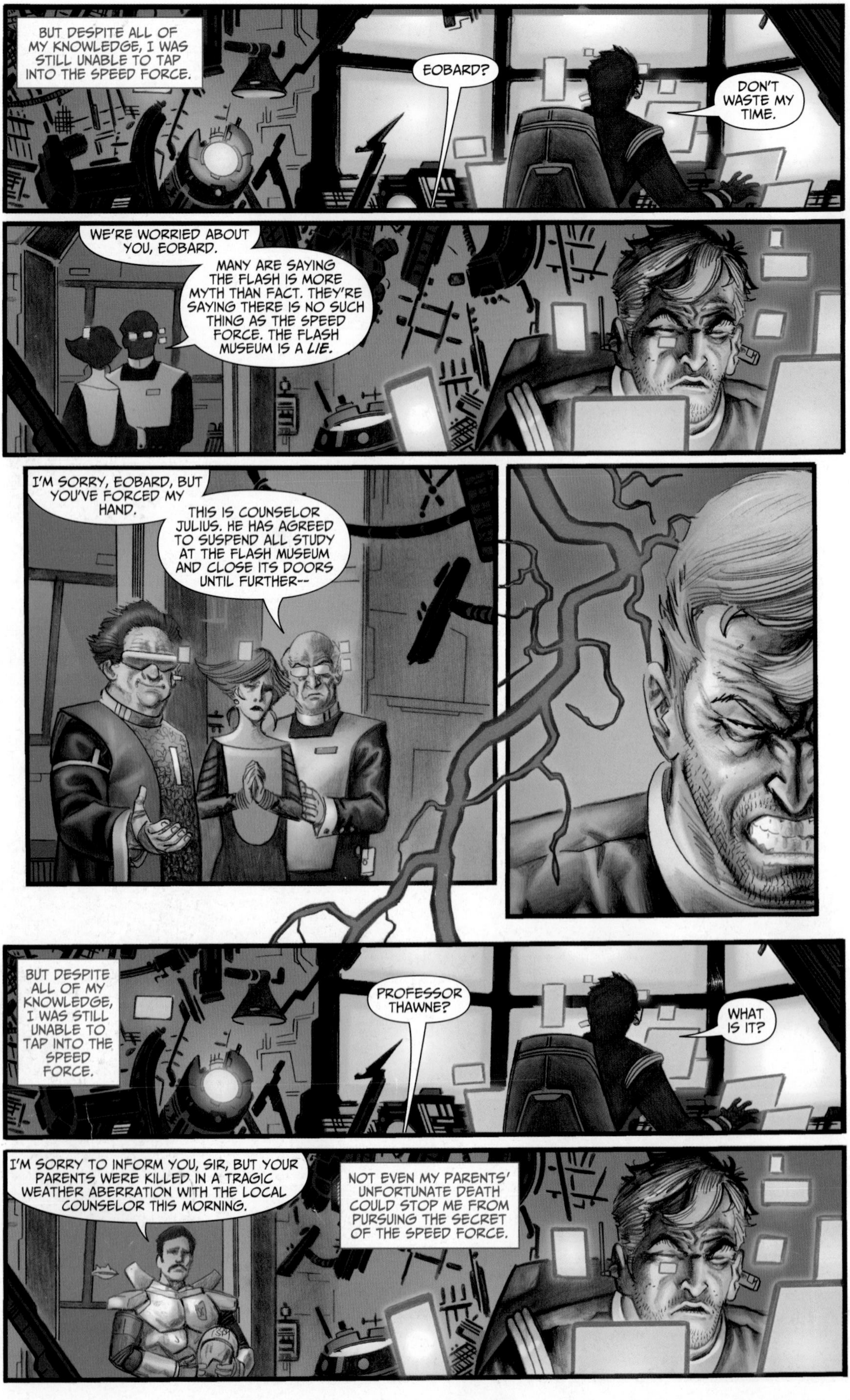

BUT DESPITE ALL OF MY KNOWLEDGE, I WAS STILL UNABLE TO TAP INTO THE SPEED FORCE.
EOBARD?
DON'T WASTE MY TIME.
WE'RE WORRIED ABOUT YOU, EOBARD.
MANY ARE SAYING THE FLASH IS MORE MYTH THAN FACT. THEY'RE SAYING THERE IS NO SUCH THING AS THE SPEED FORCE. THE FLASH MUSEUM IS A *LIE*.
I'M SORRY, EOBARD, BUT YOU'VE FORCED MY HAND.
THIS IS COUNSELOR JULIUS. HE HAS AGREED TO SUSPEND ALL STUDY AT THE FLASH MUSEUM AND CLOSE ITS DOORS UNTIL FURTHER--
BUT DESPITE ALL OF MY KNOWLEDGE, I WAS STILL UNABLE TO TAP INTO THE SPEED FORCE.
PROFESSOR THAWNE?
WHAT IS IT?
I'M SORRY TO INFORM YOU, SIR, BUT YOUR PARENTS WERE KILLED IN A TRAGIC WEATHER ABERRATION WITH THE LOCAL COUNSELOR THIS MORNING.
NOT EVEN MY PARENTS' UNFORTUNATE DEATH COULD STOP ME FROM PURSUING THE SECRET OF THE SPEED FORCE.

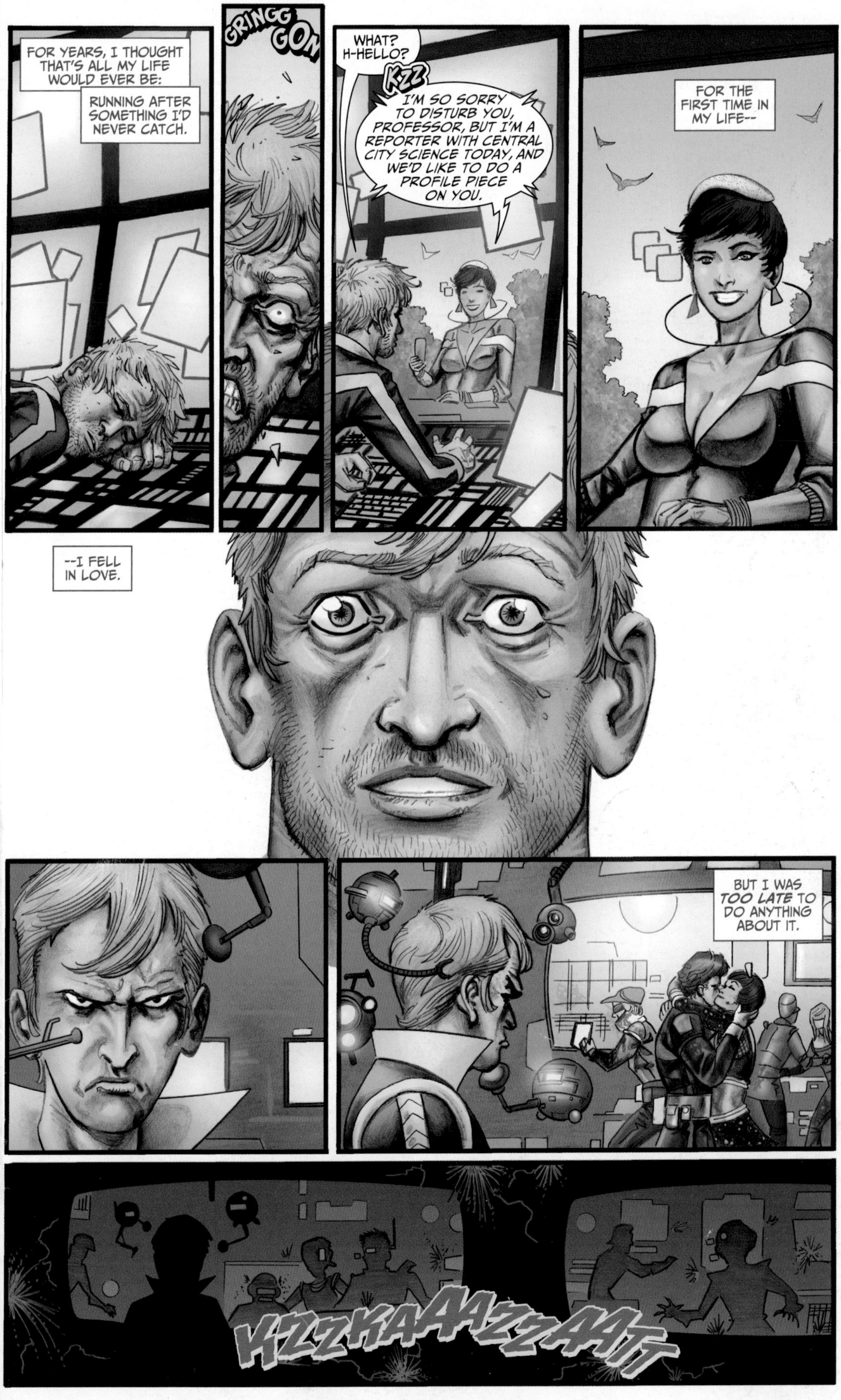
FOR YEARS, I THOUGHT THAT'S ALL MY LIFE WOULD EVER BE:
RUNNING AFTER SOMETHING I'D NEVER CATCH.
GRINGG
GON
WHAT? H-HELLO?
KZZ
I'M SO SORRY TO DISTURB YOU, PROFESSOR, BUT I'M A REPORTER WITH CENTRAL CITY SCIENCE TODAY, AND WE'D LIKE TO DO A PROFILE PIECE ON YOU.
FOR THE FIRST TIME IN MY LIFE--
--I FELL IN LOVE.
BUT I WAS *TOO LATE* TO DO ANYTHING ABOUT IT.
KZZKAAAAZZZAATT

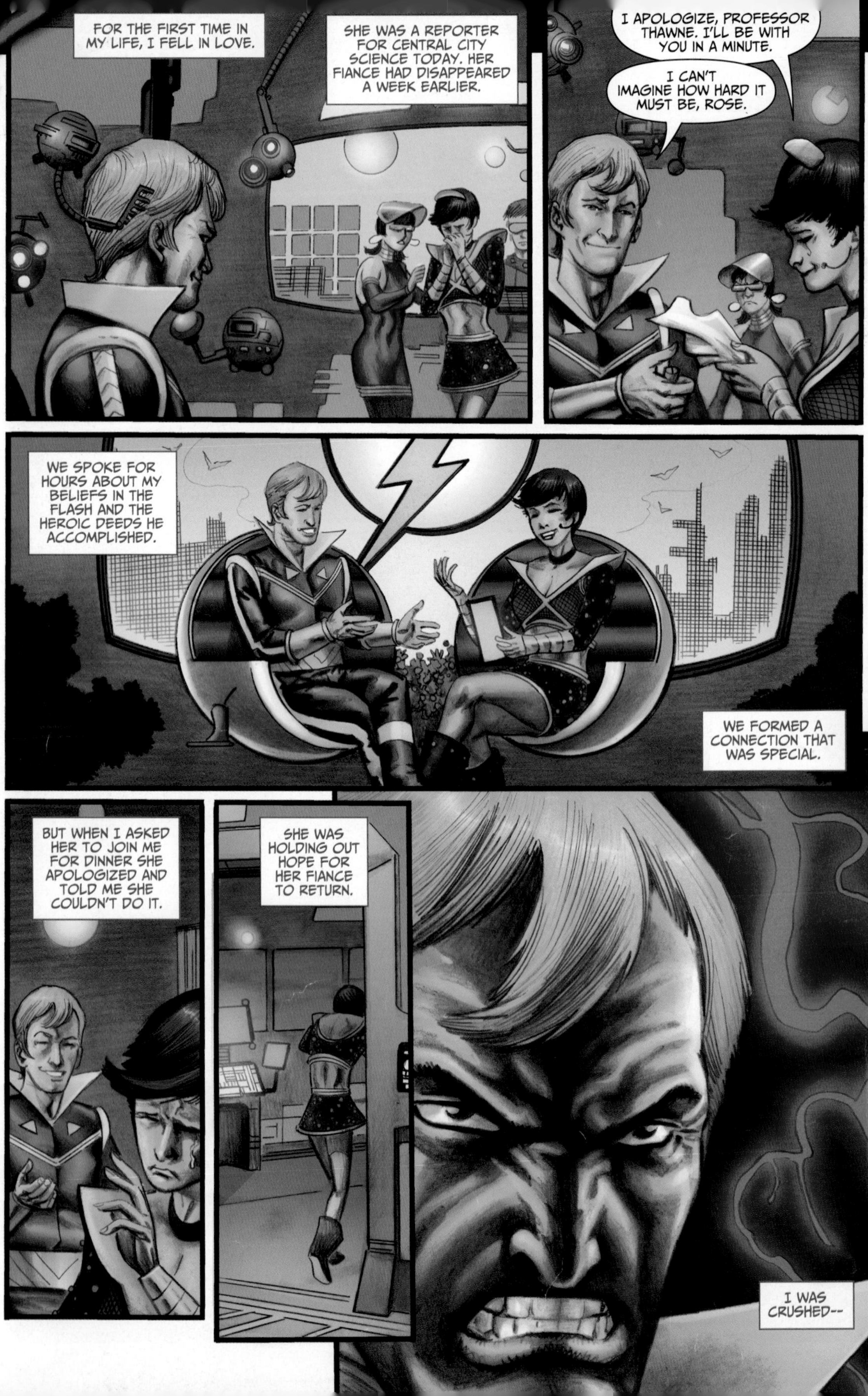
FOR THE FIRST TIME IN MY LIFE, I FELL IN LOVE.
SHE WAS A REPORTER FOR CENTRAL CITY SCIENCE TODAY. HER FIANCE HAD DISAPPEARED A WEEK EARLIER.
I APOLOGIZE, PROFESSOR THAWNE. I'LL BE WITH YOU IN A MINUTE.
I CAN'T IMAGINE HOW HARD IT MUST BE, ROSE.
WE SPOKE FOR HOURS ABOUT MY BELIEFS IN THE FLASH AND THE HEROIC DEEDS HE ACCOMPLISHED.
WE FORMED A CONNECTION THAT WAS SPECIAL.
BUT WHEN I ASKED HER TO JOIN ME FOR DINNER SHE APOLOGIZED AND TOLD ME SHE COULDN'T DO IT.
SHE WAS HOLDING OUT HOPE FOR HER FIANCE TO RETURN.
I WAS CRUSHED--

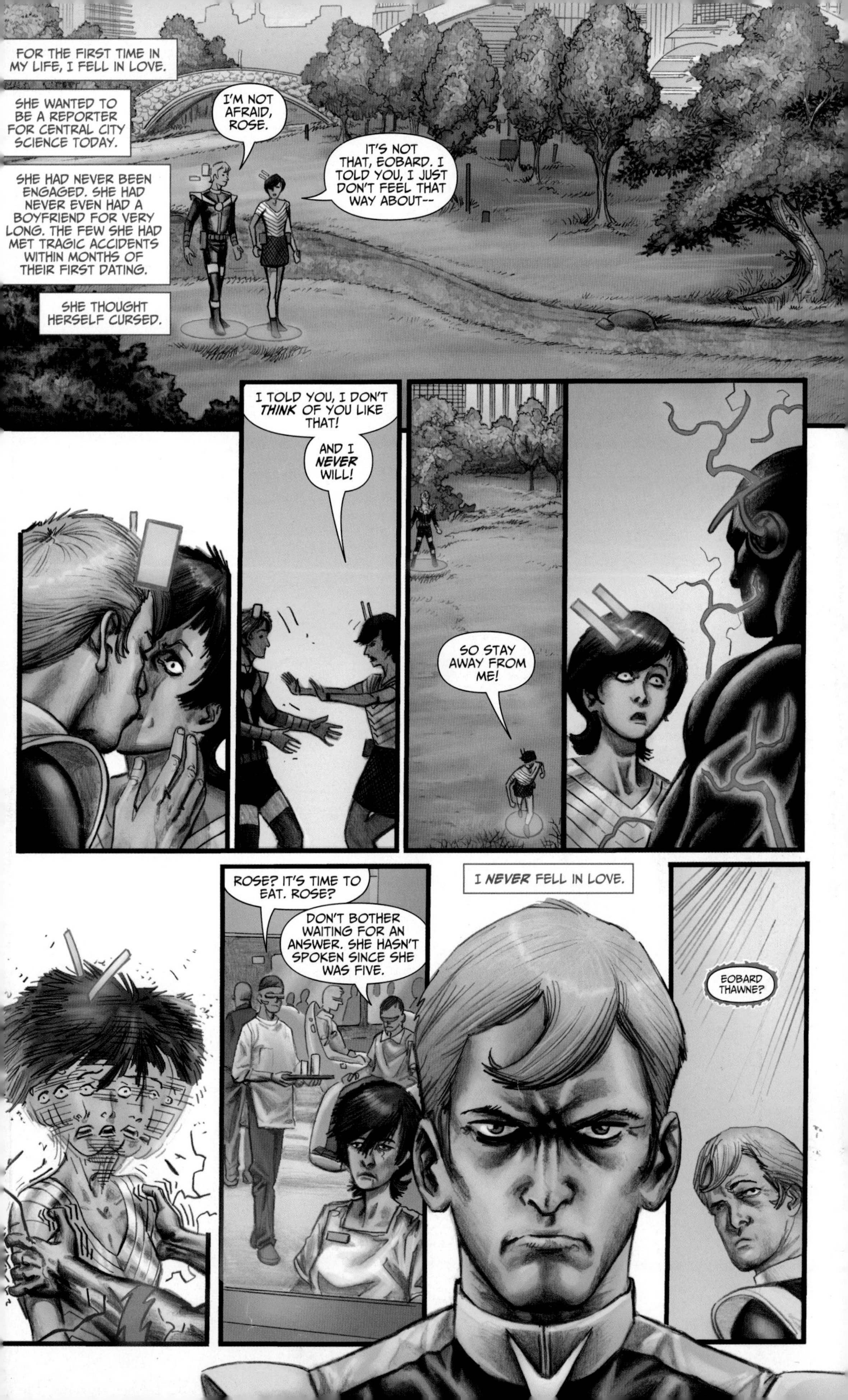

FOR THE FIRST TIME IN MY LIFE, I FELL IN LOVE.
SHE WANTED TO BE A REPORTER FOR CENTRAL CITY SCIENCE TODAY.
SHE HAD NEVER BEEN ENGAGED. SHE HAD NEVER EVEN HAD A BOYFRIEND FOR VERY LONG. THE FEW SHE HAD MET TRAGIC ACCIDENTS WITHIN MONTHS OF THEIR FIRST DATING.
SHE THOUGHT HERSELF CURSED.
I'M NOT AFRAID, ROSE.
IT'S NOT THAT, EOBARD. I TOLD YOU, I JUST DON'T FEEL THAT WAY ABOUT--
I TOLD YOU, I DON'T THINK OF YOU LIKE THAT!
AND I NEVER WILL!
SO STAY AWAY FROM ME!
ROSE? IT'S TIME TO EAT. ROSE?
DON'T BOTHER WAITING FOR AN ANSWER. SHE HASN'T SPOKEN SINCE SHE WAS FIVE.
I NEVER FELL IN LOVE.
EOBARD THAWNE?

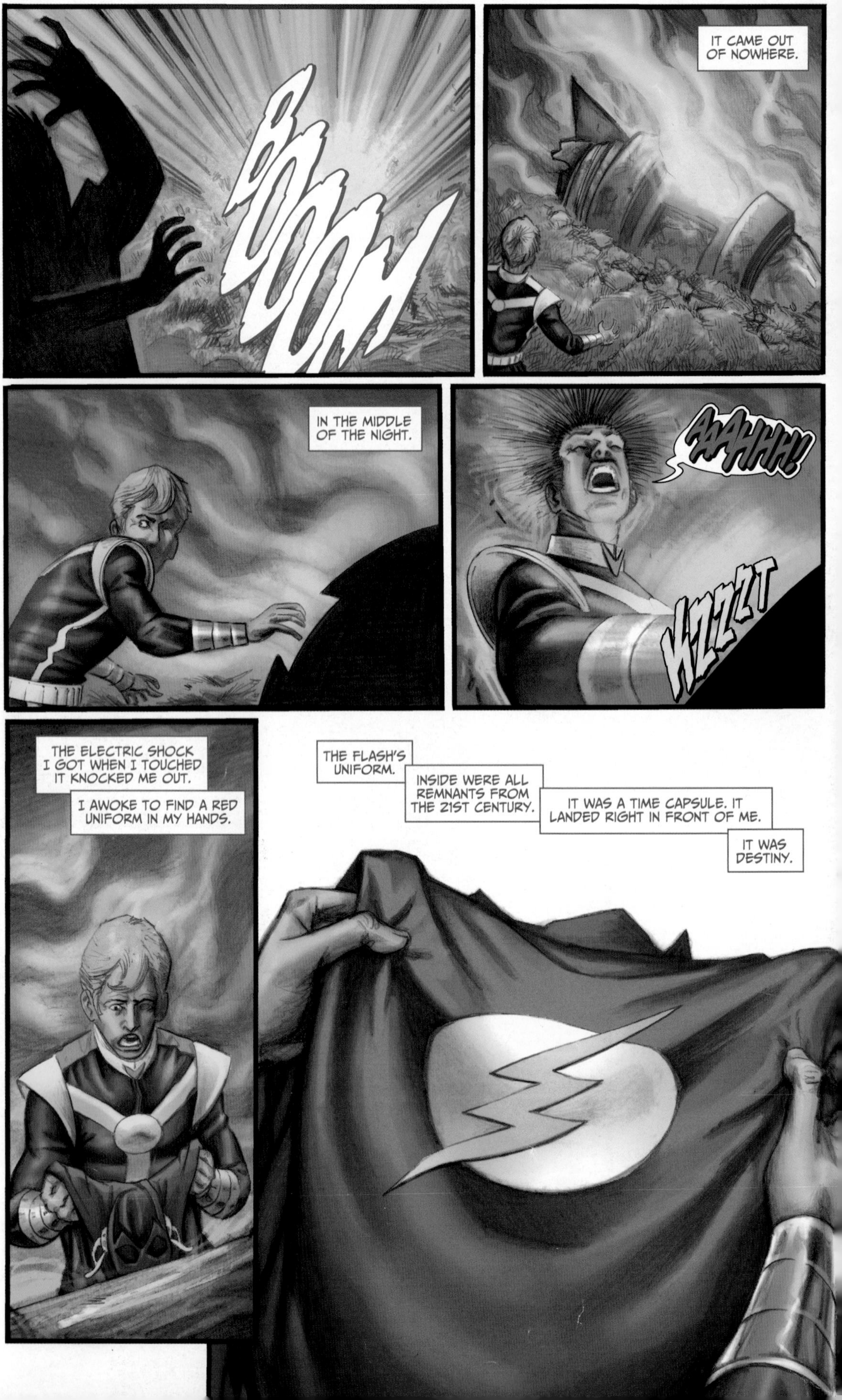
BOOOM
IT CAME OUT OF NOWHERE.
IN THE MIDDLE OF THE NIGHT.
AAAHHH!
KZZZT
THE ELECTRIC SHOCK I GOT WHEN I TOUCHED IT KNOCKED ME OUT.
I AWOKE TO FIND A RED UNIFORM IN MY HANDS.
THE FLASH'S UNIFORM.
INSIDE WERE ALL REMNANTS FROM THE 21ST CENTURY.
IT WAS A TIME CAPSULE. IT LANDED RIGHT IN FRONT OF ME.
IT WAS DESTINY.

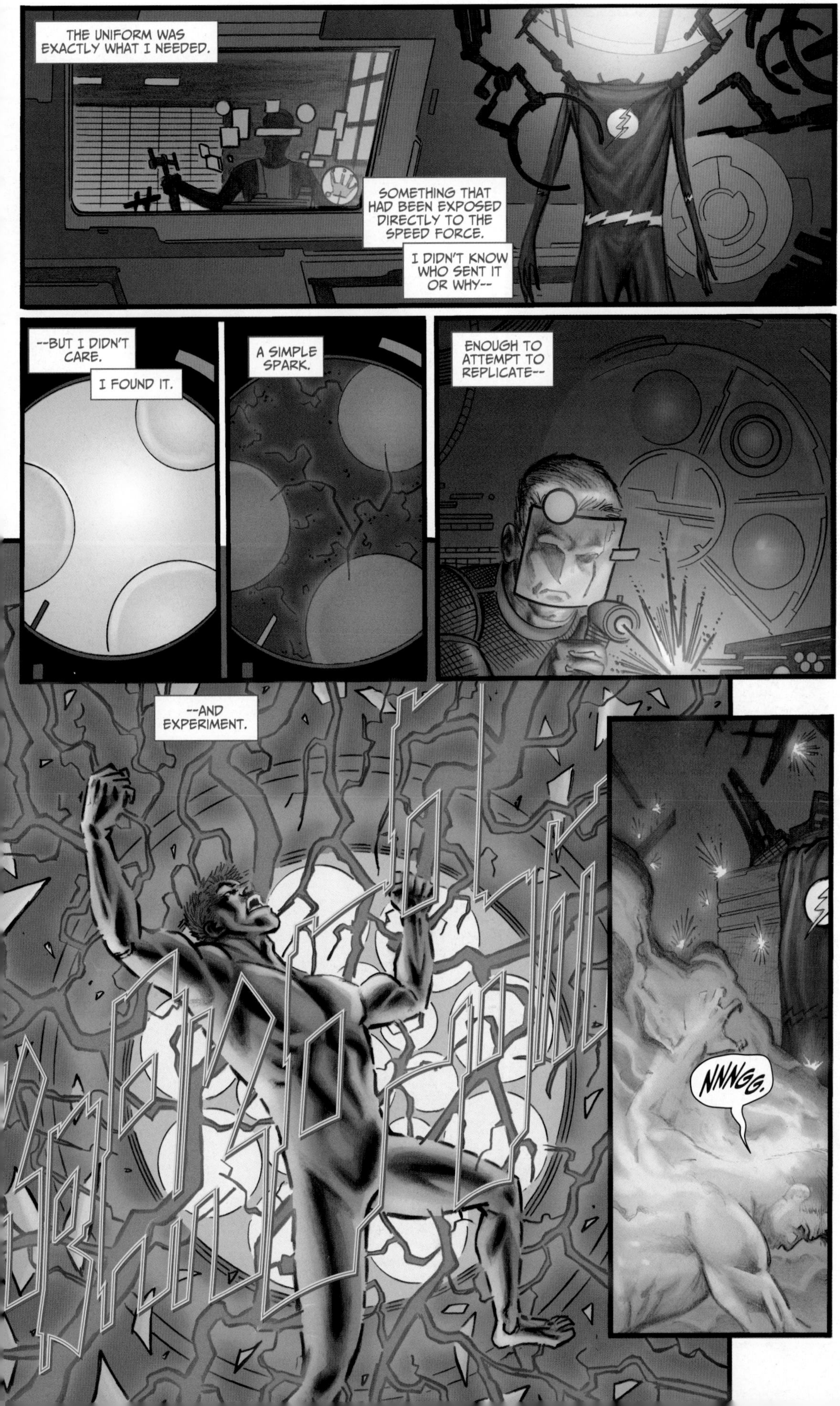
THE UNIFORM WAS EXACTLY WHAT I NEEDED.
SOMETHING THAT HAD BEEN EXPOSED DIRECTLY TO THE SPEED FORCE.
I DIDN'T KNOW WHO SENT IT OR WHY--
--BUT I DIDN'T CARE.
I FOUND IT.
A SIMPLE SPARK.
ENOUGH TO ATTEMPT TO REPLICATE--
--AND EXPERIMENT.
NNNGG.

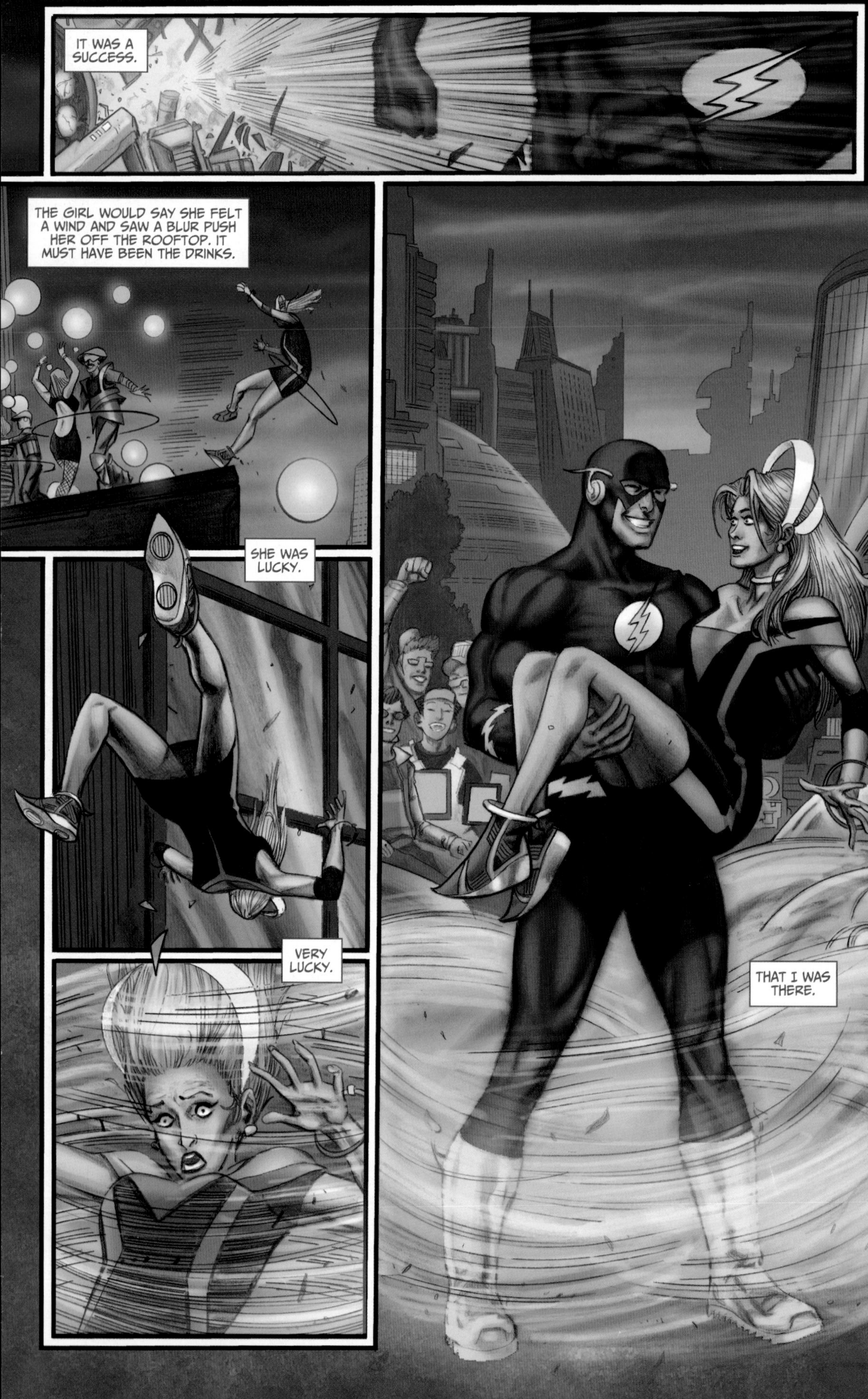
IT WAS A SUCCESS.
THE GIRL WOULD SAY SHE FELT A WIND AND SAW A BLUR PUSH HER OFF THE ROOFTOP. IT MUST HAVE BEEN THE DRINKS.
SHE WAS LUCKY.
VERY LUCKY.
THAT I WAS THERE.

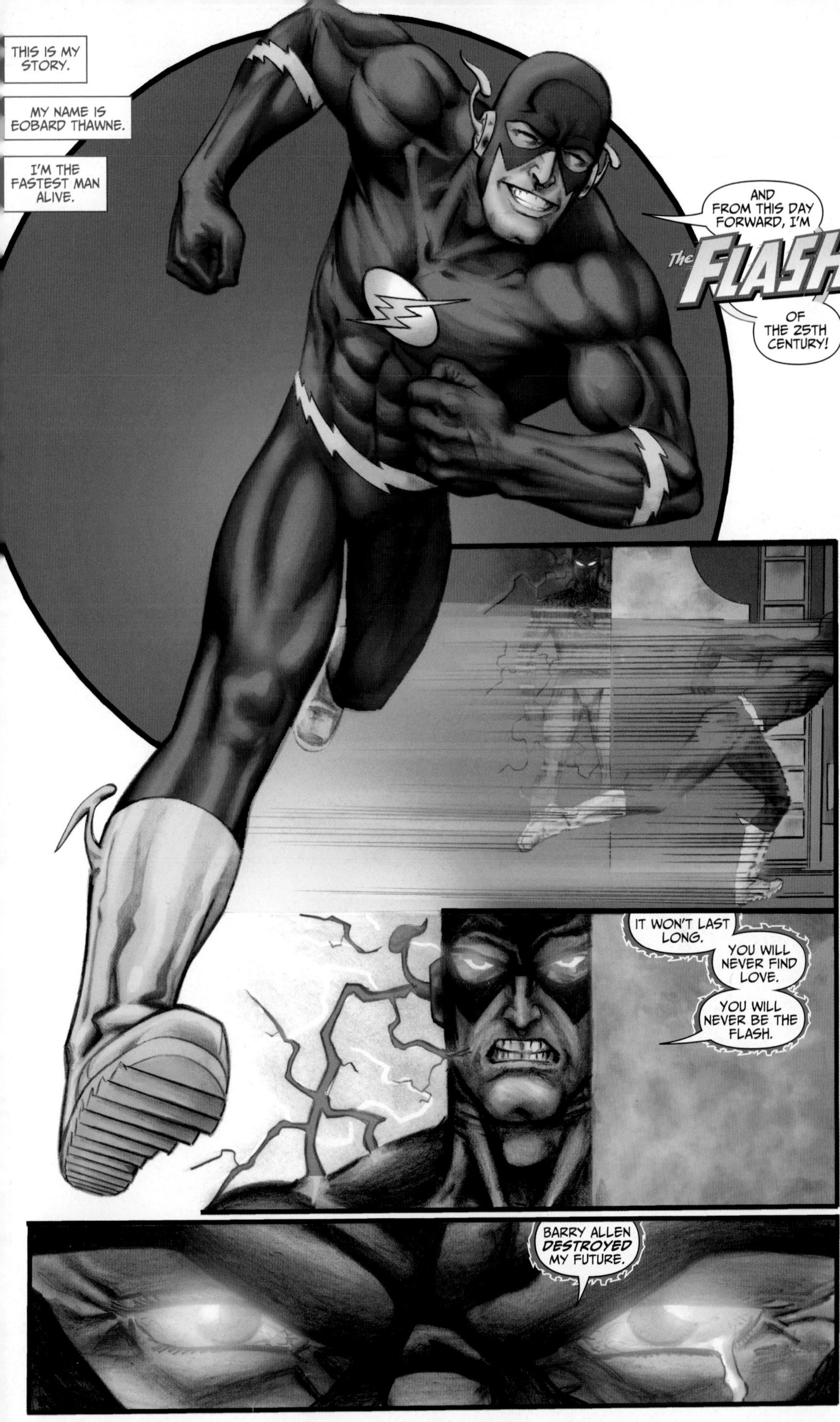
THIS IS MY STORY.
MY NAME IS EOBARD THAWNE.
I'M THE FASTEST MAN ALIVE.
AND FROM THIS DAY FORWARD, I'M
The FLASH
OF THE 25TH CENTURY!
IT WON'T LAST LONG.
YOU WILL NEVER FIND LOVE.
YOU WILL NEVER BE THE FLASH.
BARRY ALLEN DESTROYED MY FUTURE.

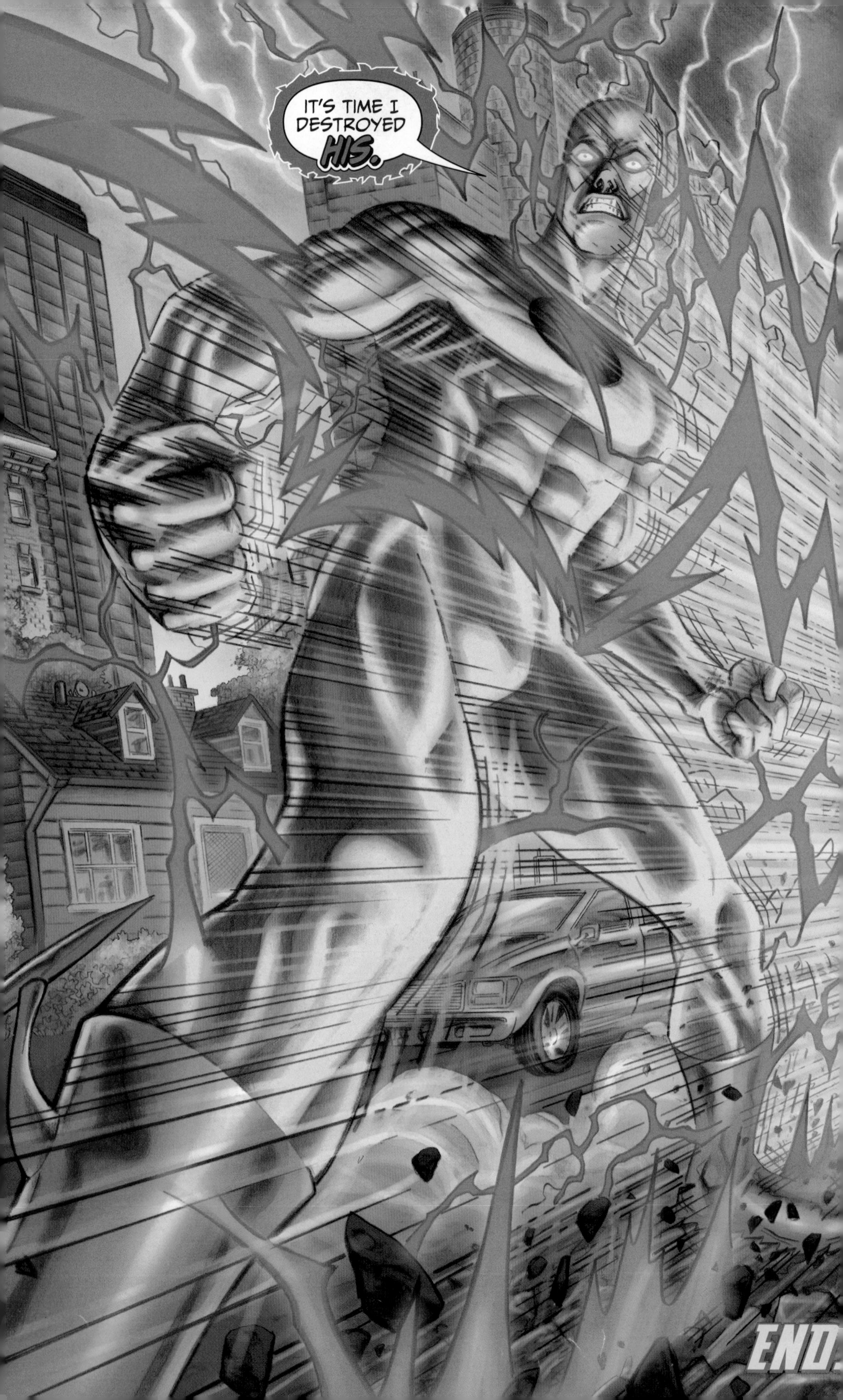
IT'S TIME I DESTROYED HIS.
END

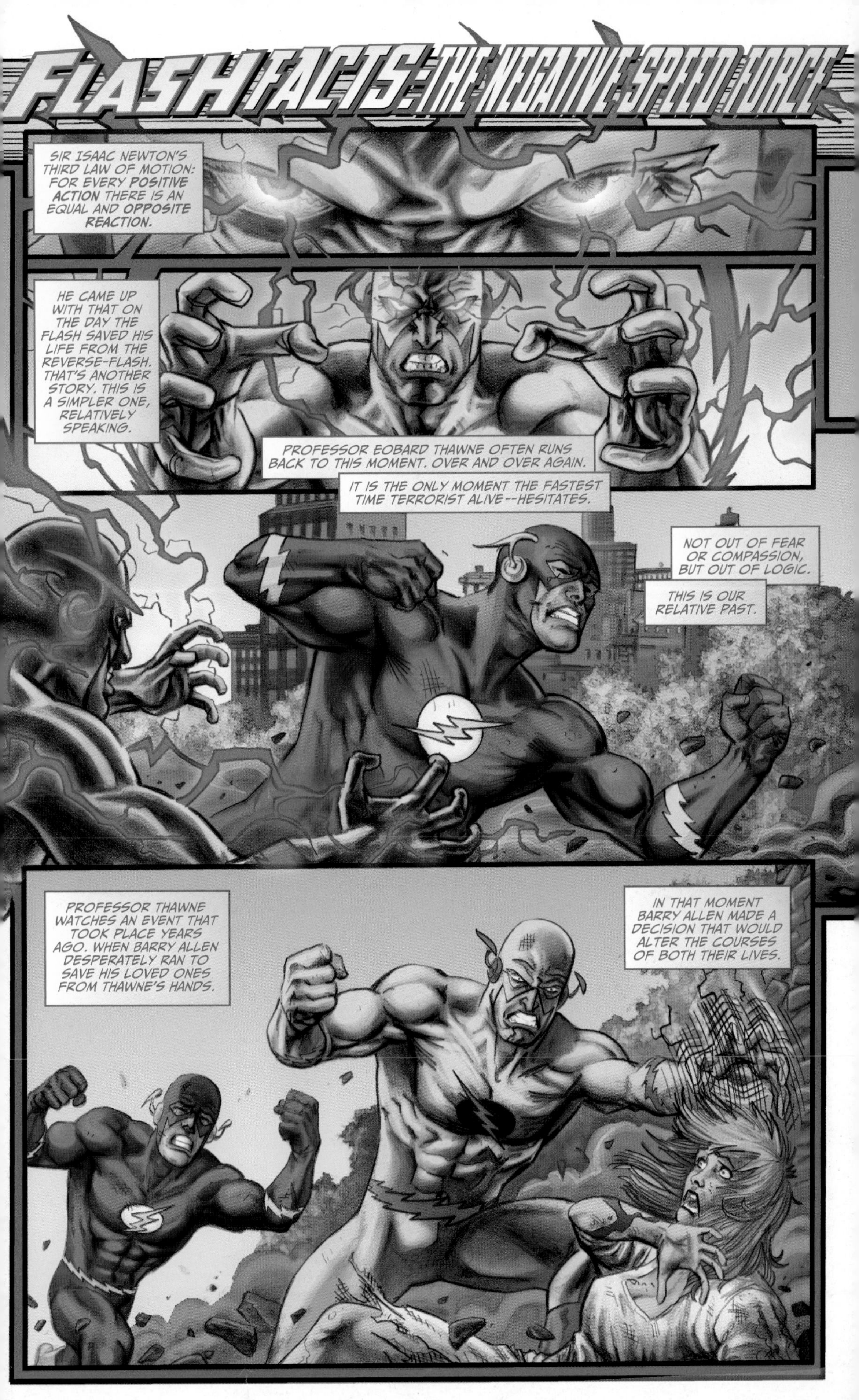
FLASH FACTS: THE NEGATIVE SPEED FORCE
SIR ISAAC NEWTON'S THIRD LAW OF MOTION: FOR EVERY POSITIVE ACTION THERE IS AN EQUAL AND OPPOSITE REACTION.
HE CAME UP WITH THAT ON THE DAY THE FLASH SAVED HIS LIFE FROM THE REVERSE-FLASH. THAT'S ANOTHER STORY. THIS IS A SIMPLER ONE, RELATIVELY SPEAKING.
PROFESSOR EOBARD THAWNE OFTEN RUNS BACK TO THIS MOMENT. OVER AND OVER AGAIN.
IT IS THE ONLY MOMENT THE FASTEST TIME TERRORIST ALIVE--HESITATES.
NOT OUT OF FEAR OR COMPASSION, BUT OUT OF LOGIC.
THIS IS OUR RELATIVE PAST.
PROFESSOR THAWNE WATCHES AN EVENT THAT TOOK PLACE YEARS AGO. WHEN BARRY ALLEN DESPERATELY RAN TO SAVE HIS LOVED ONES FROM THAWNE'S HANDS.
IN THAT MOMENT BARRY ALLEN MADE A DECISION THAT WOULD ALTER THE COURSES OF BOTH THEIR LIVES.

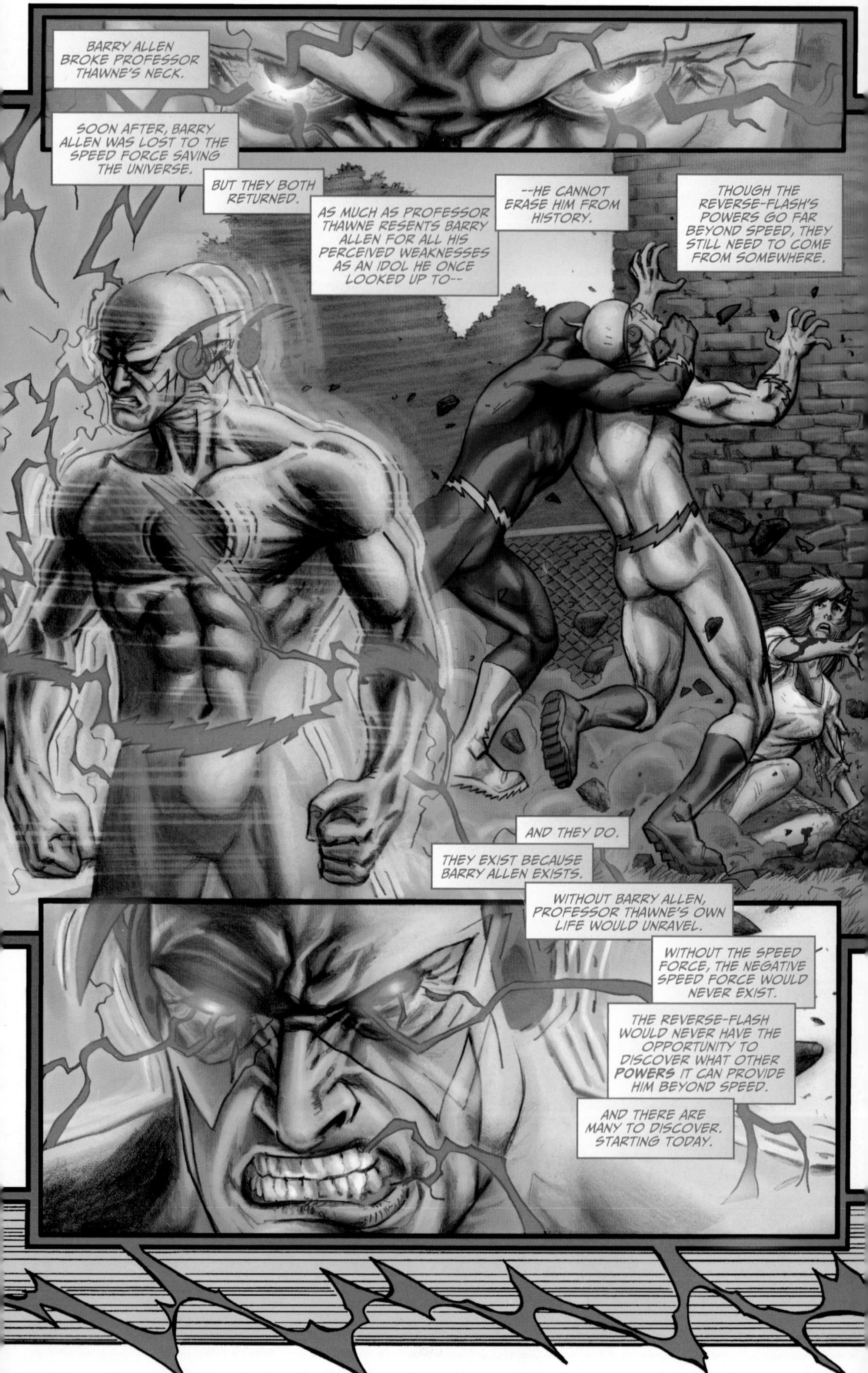
BARRY ALLEN BROKE PROFESSOR THAWNE'S NECK.
SOON AFTER, BARRY ALLEN WAS LOST TO THE SPEED FORCE SAVING THE UNIVERSE.
BUT THEY BOTH RETURNED.
AS MUCH AS PROFESSOR THAWNE RESENTS BARRY ALLEN FOR ALL HIS PERCEIVED WEAKNESSES AS AN IDOL HE ONCE LOOKED UP TO--
--HE CANNOT ERASE HIM FROM HISTORY.
THOUGH THE REVERSE-FLASH'S POWERS GO FAR BEYOND SPEED, THEY STILL NEED TO COME FROM SOMEWHERE.
AND THEY DO.
THEY EXIST BECAUSE BARRY ALLEN EXISTS.
WITHOUT BARRY ALLEN, PROFESSOR THAWNE'S OWN LIFE WOULD UNRAVEL.
WITHOUT THE SPEED FORCE, THE NEGATIVE SPEED FORCE WOULD NEVER EXIST.
THE REVERSE-FLASH WOULD NEVER HAVE THE OPPORTUNITY TO DISCOVER WHAT OTHER POWERS IT CAN PROVIDE HIM BEYOND SPEED.
AND THERE ARE MANY TO DISCOVER. STARTING TODAY.

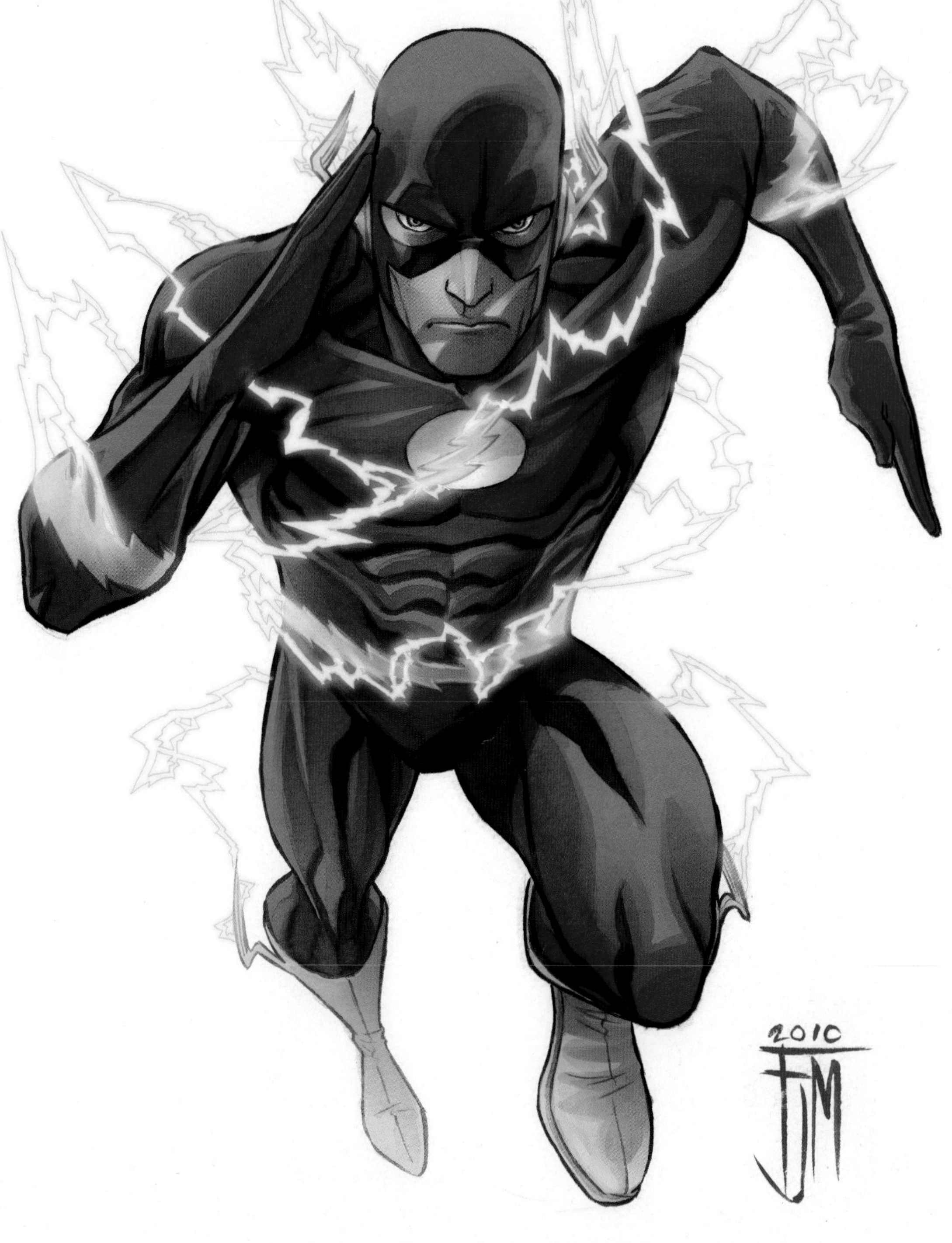

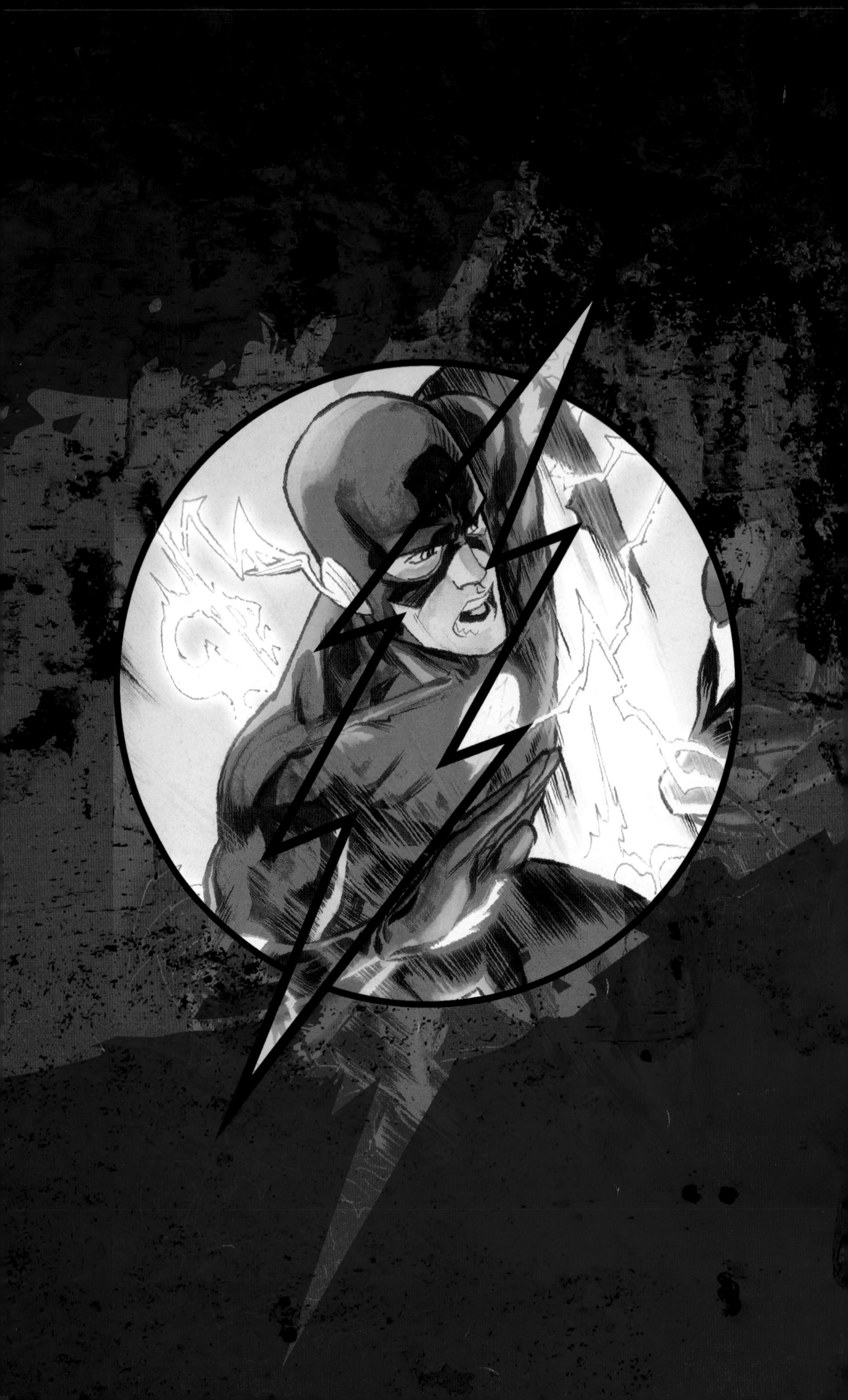

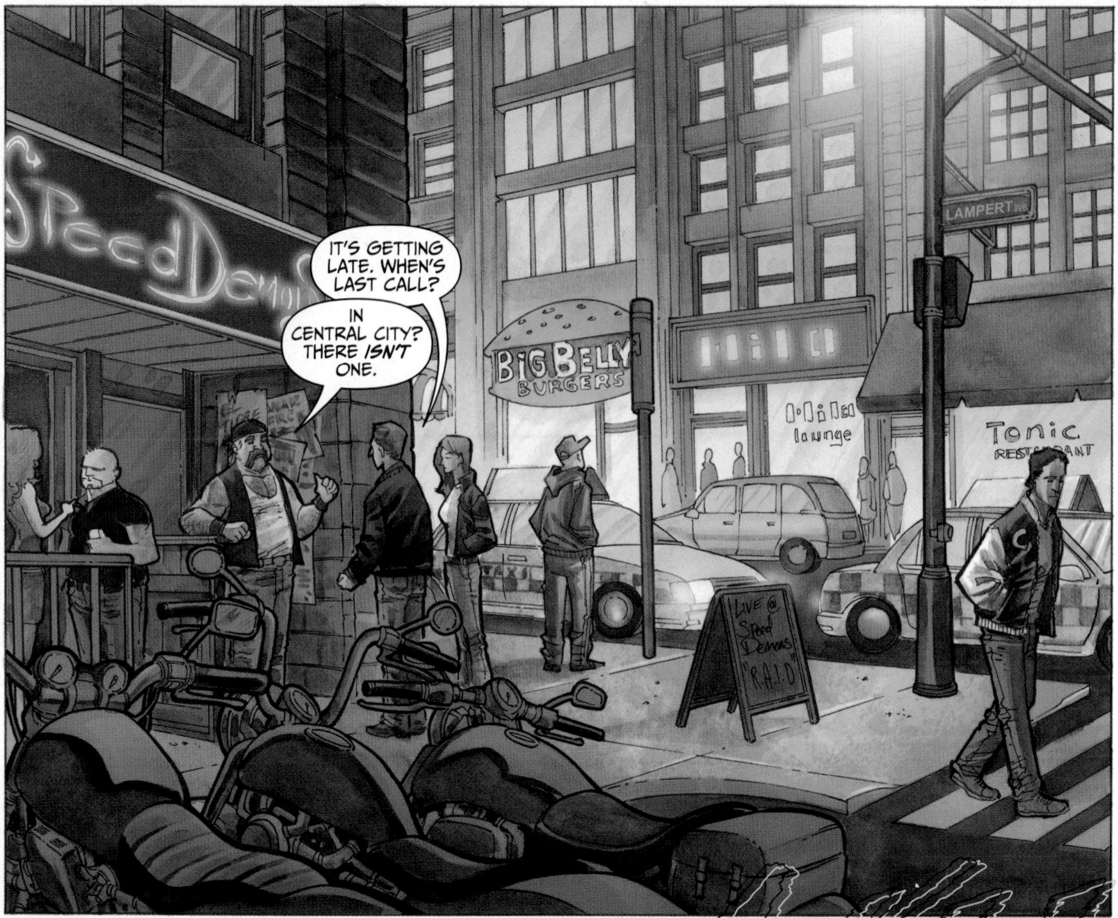
Speed Demons
IT'S GETTING LATE. WHEN'S LAST CALL?
IN CENTRAL CITY? THERE *ISN'T* ONE.
BIG BELLY BURGERS
LAMPERT
lounge
Tonic RESTAURANT
LIVE @ Speed Demons "R.A.I.D"

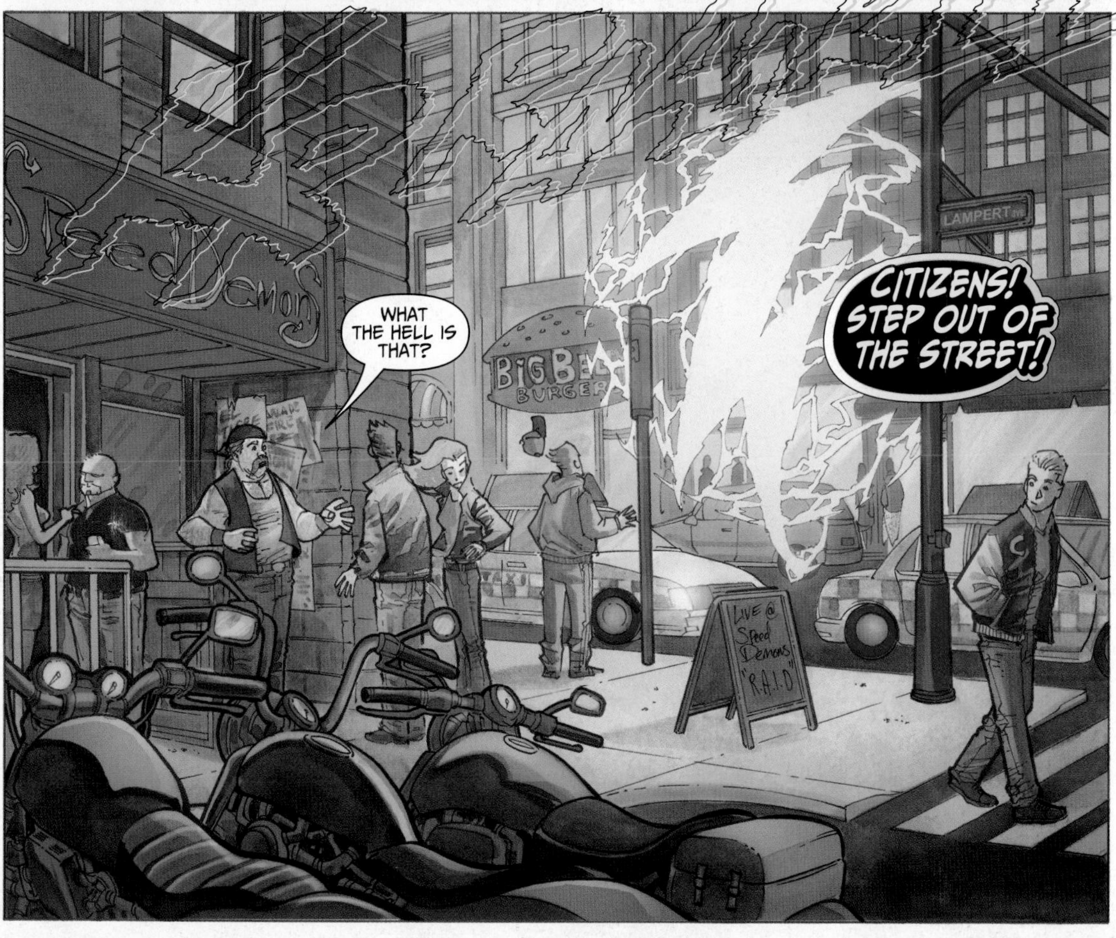
Speed Demons
WHAT THE HELL IS THAT?
CITIZENS! STEP OUT OF THE STREET!
LAMPERT
LIVE @ Speed Demons "R.A.I.D"

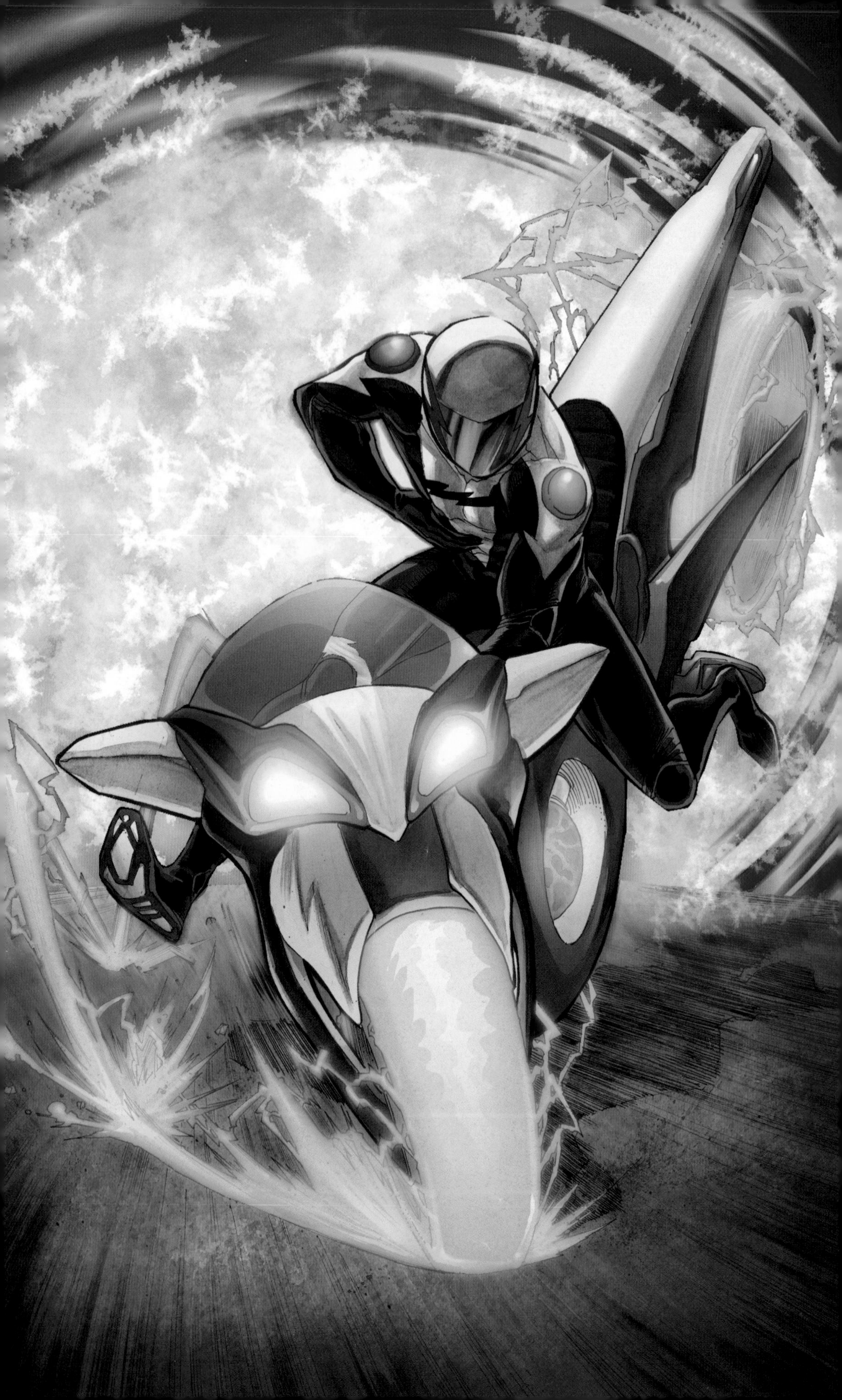

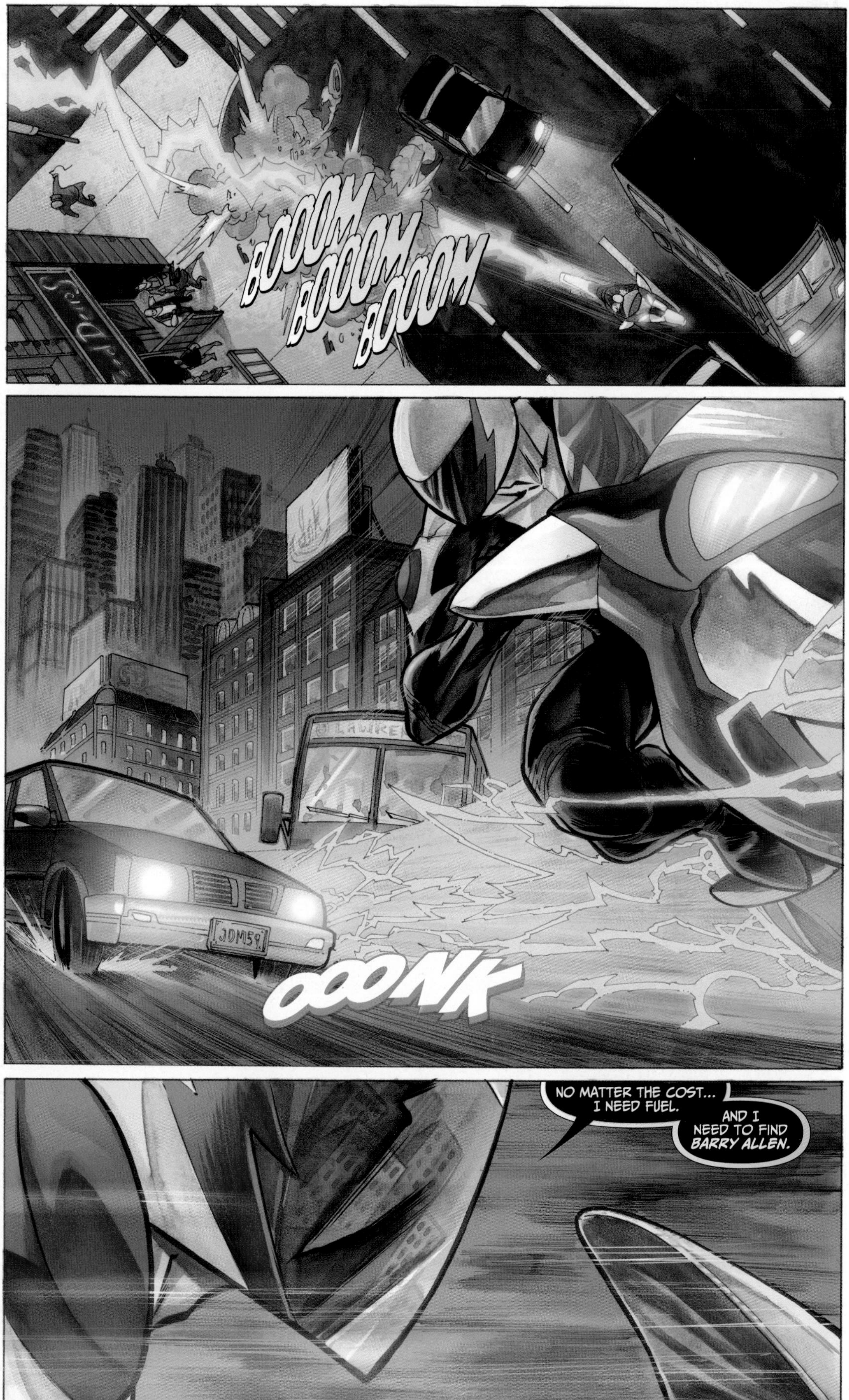
BOOOM
BOOOM
BOOOM
OOONK
NO MATTER THE COST... I NEED FUEL.
AND I NEED TO FIND BARRY ALLEN.

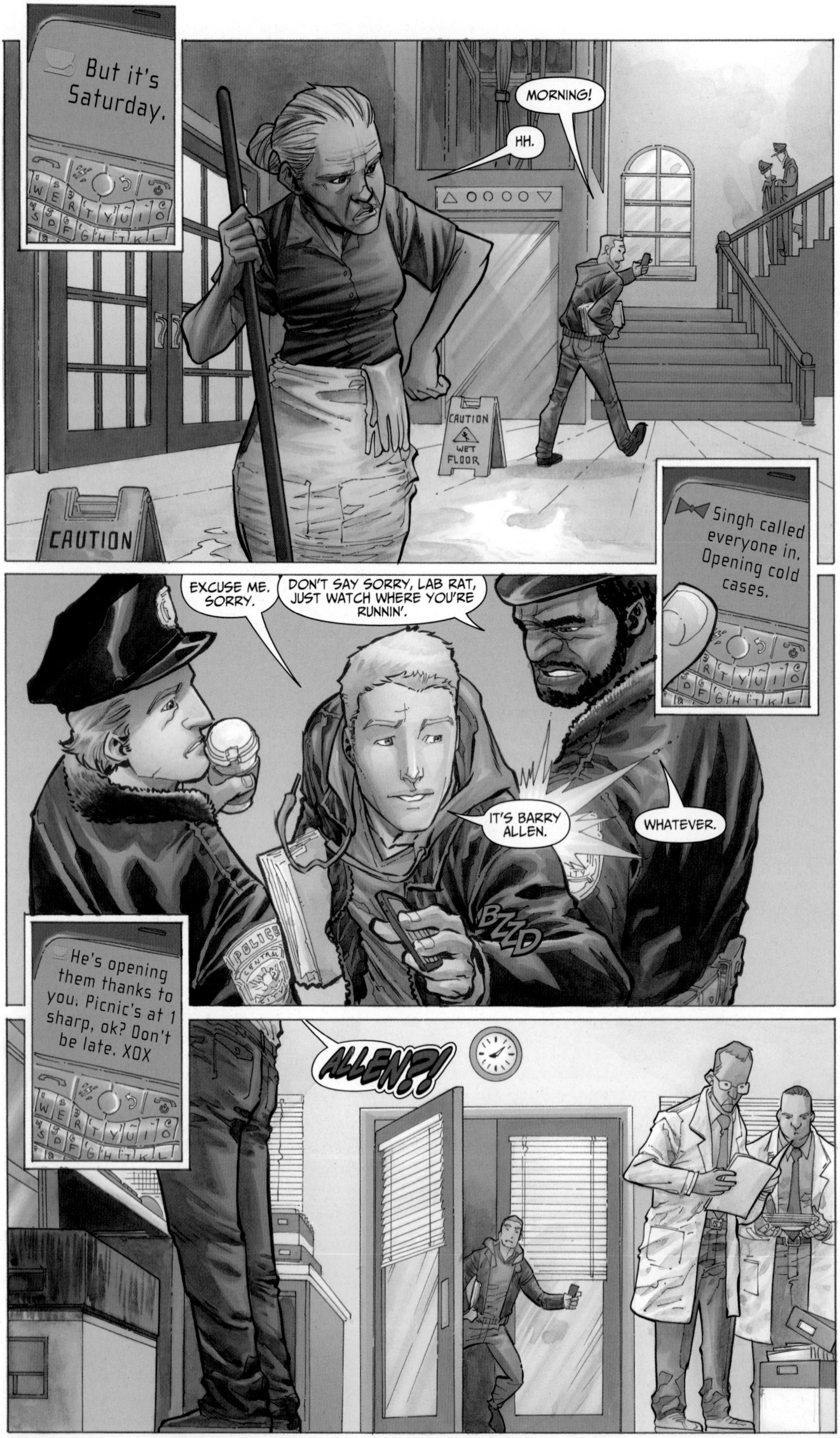
But it's Saturday.
MORNING!
HH.
CAUTION
CAUTION WET FLOOR
Singh called everyone in. Opening cold cases.
EXCUSE ME. SORRY.
DON'T SAY SORRY, LAB RAT, JUST WATCH WHERE YOU'RE RUNNIN'.
IT'S BARRY ALLEN.
WHATEVER.
BZZD
POLICE CENTRAL CITY
He's opening them thanks to you. Picnic's at 1 sharp, ok? Don't be late. XOX
ALLEN?!

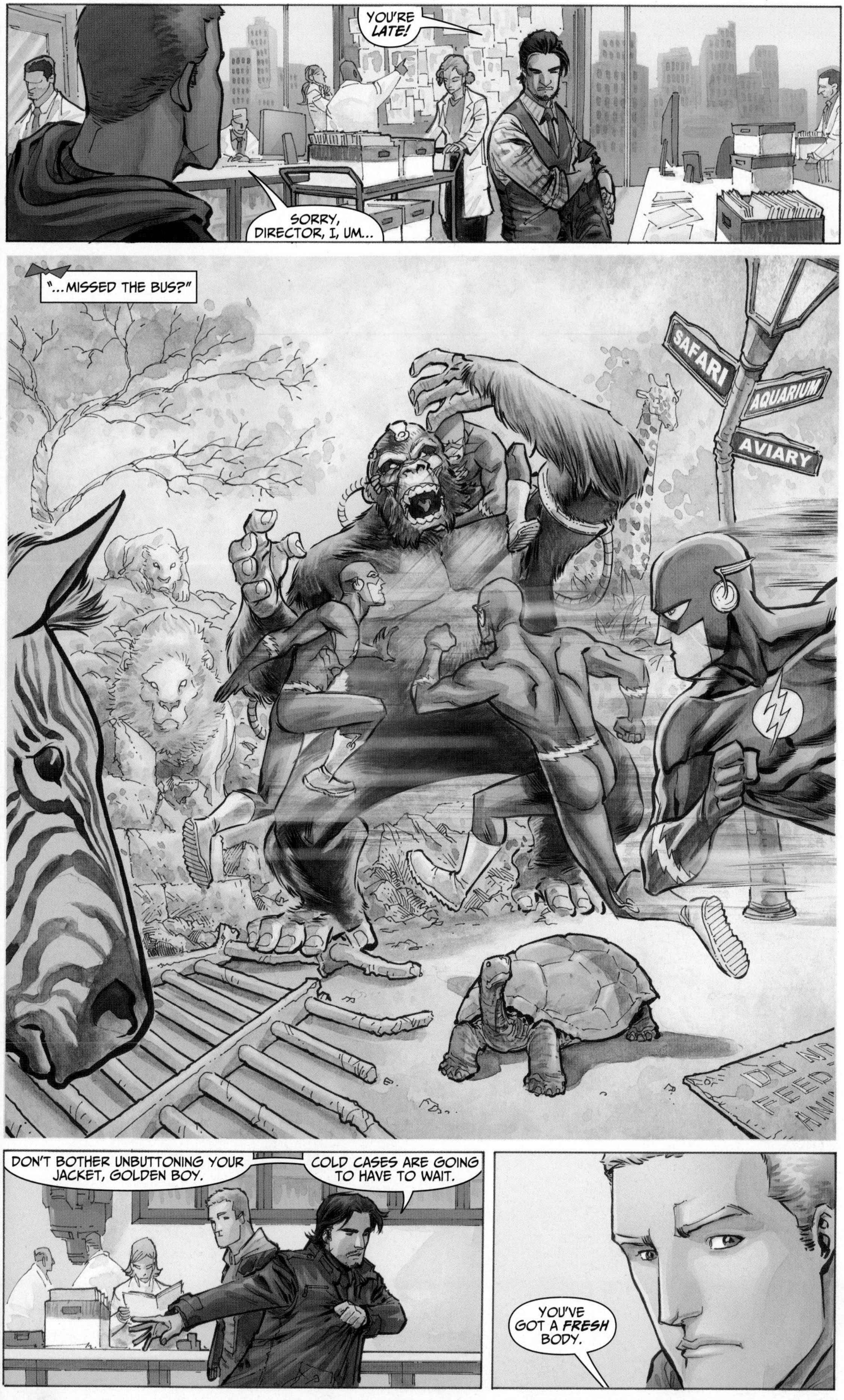
YOU'RE LATE!
SORRY, DIRECTOR, I, UM...
"...MISSED THE BUS?"
SAFARI
AQUARIUM
AVIARY
DON'T BOTHER UNBUTTONING YOUR JACKET, GOLDEN BOY.
COLD CASES ARE GOING TO HAVE TO WAIT.
YOU'VE GOT A FRESH BODY.

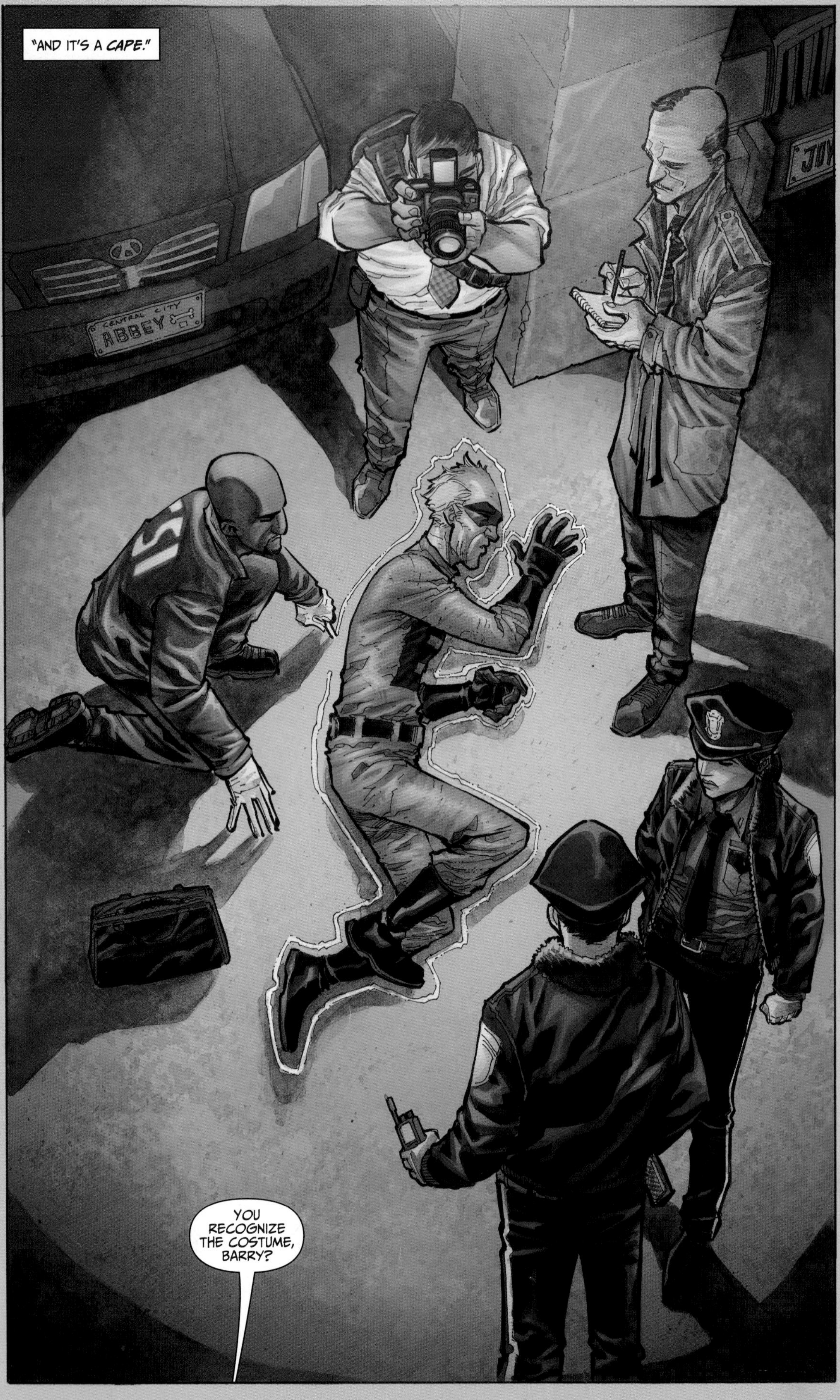
"AND IT'S A *CAPE*."
CENTRAL CITY
ABBEY
YOU RECOGNIZE THE COSTUME, BARRY?

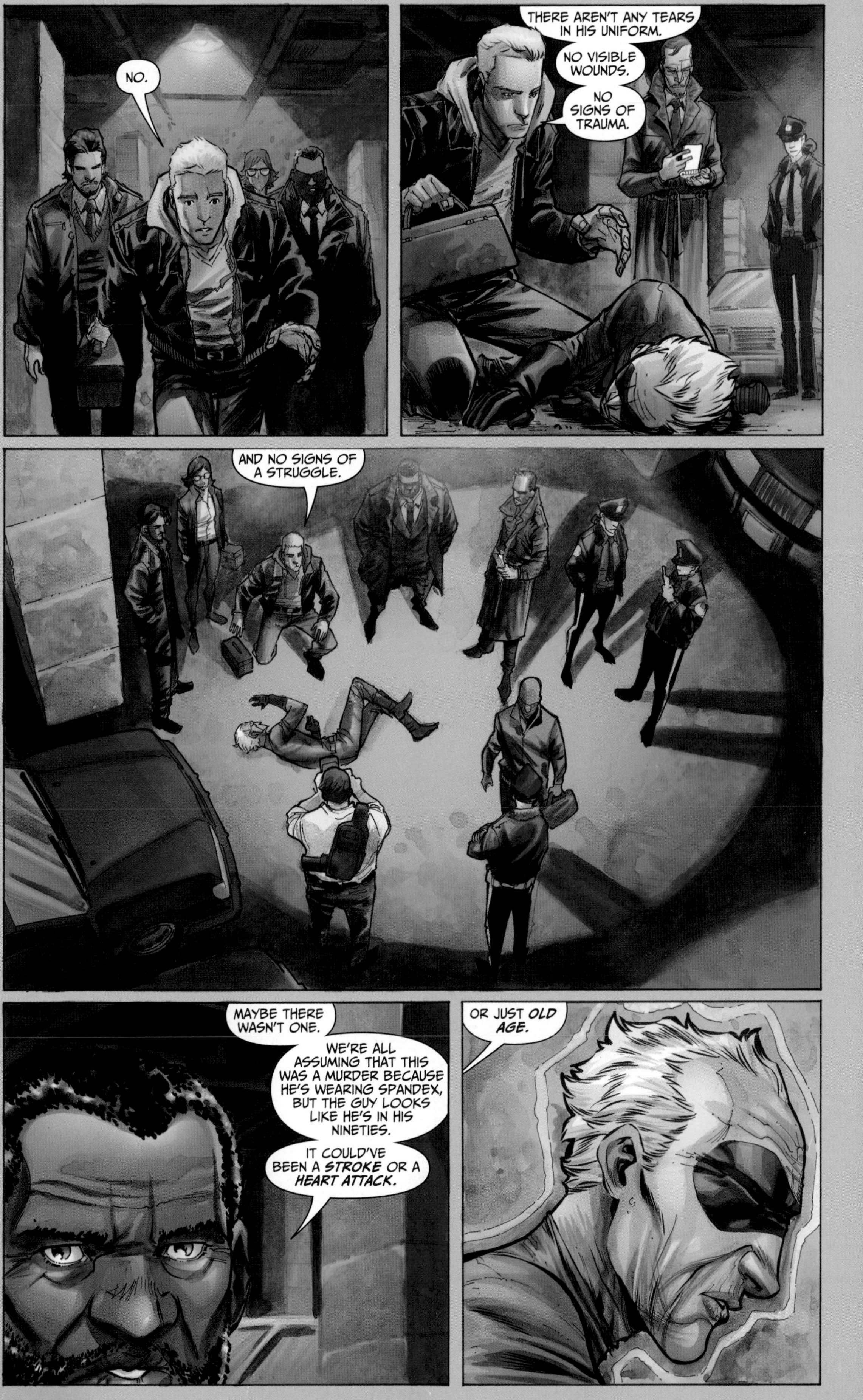
NO.
THERE AREN'T ANY TEARS IN HIS UNIFORM.
NO VISIBLE WOUNDS.
NO SIGNS OF TRAUMA.
AND NO SIGNS OF A STRUGGLE.
MAYBE THERE WASN'T ONE.
WE'RE ALL ASSUMING THAT THIS WAS A MURDER BECAUSE HE'S WEARING SPANDEX, BUT THE GUY LOOKS LIKE HE'S IN HIS NINETIES.
IT COULD'VE BEEN A *STROKE* OR A *HEART ATTACK.*
OR JUST *OLD AGE.*

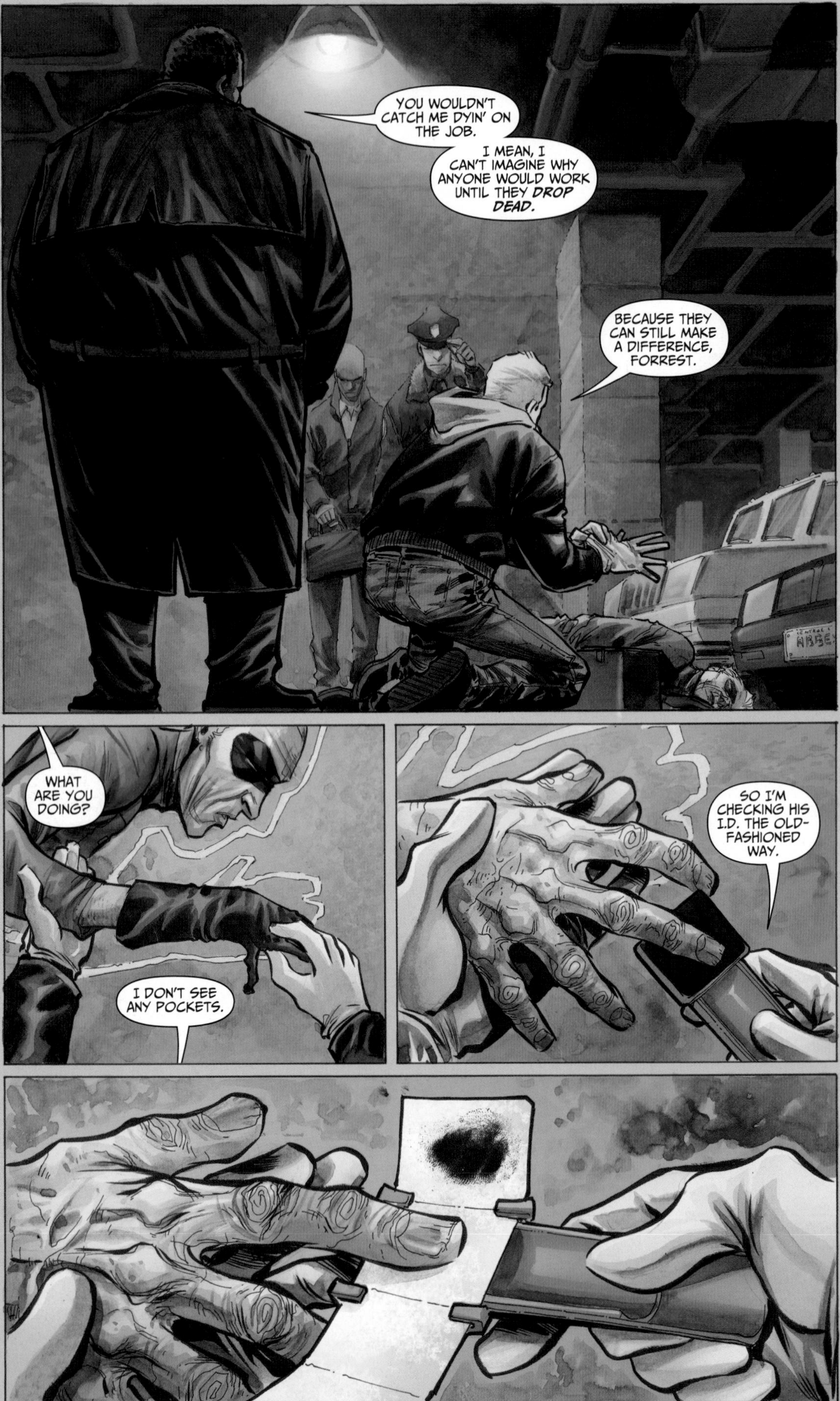
YOU WOULDN'T CATCH ME DYIN' ON THE JOB.
I MEAN, I CAN'T IMAGINE WHY ANYONE WOULD WORK UNTIL THEY *DROP DEAD.*
BECAUSE THEY CAN STILL MAKE A DIFFERENCE, FORREST.
WHAT ARE YOU DOING?
I DON'T SEE ANY POCKETS.
SO I'M CHECKING HIS I.D. THE OLD-FASHIONED WAY.

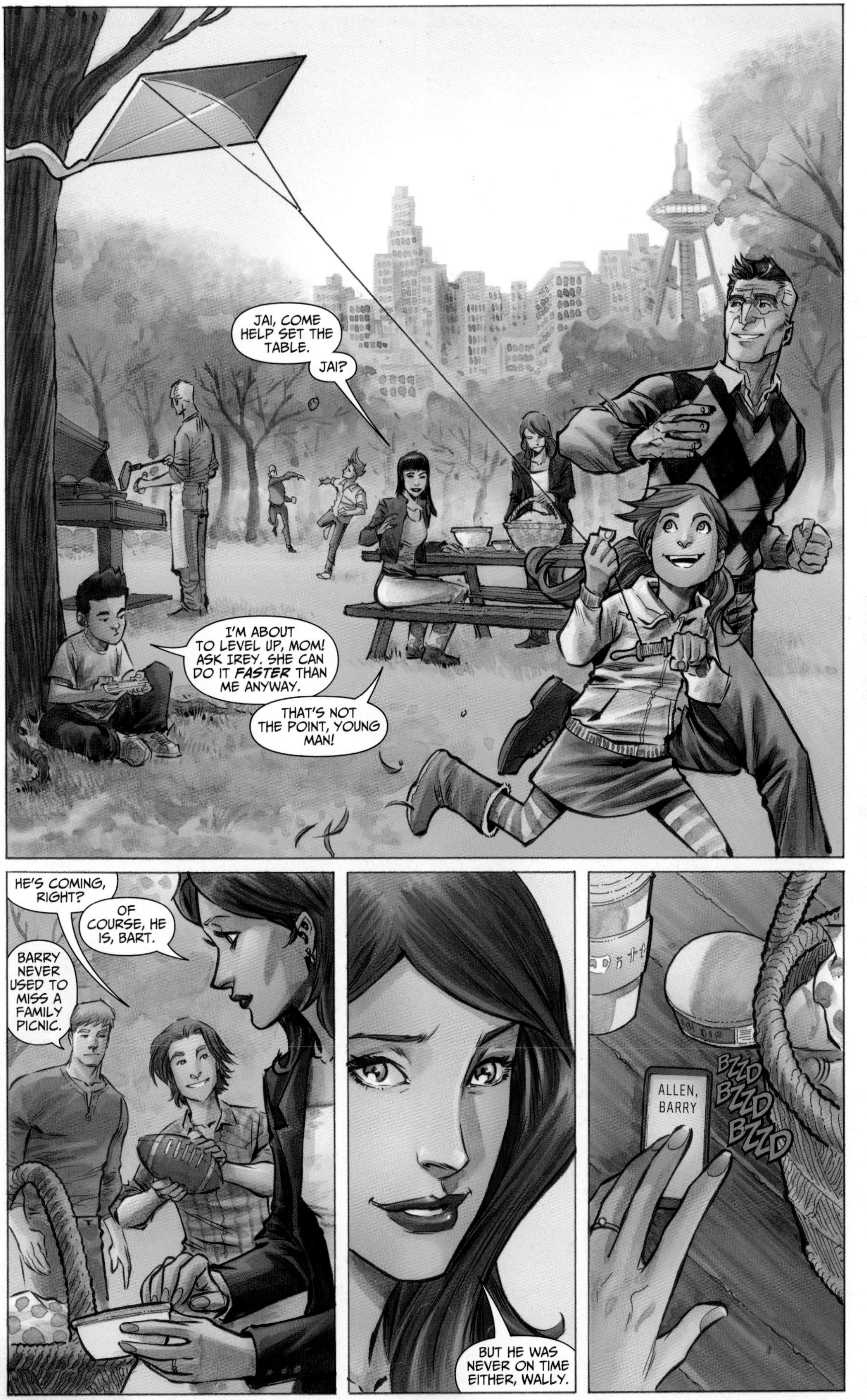
JAI, COME HELP SET THE TABLE.
JAI?
I'M ABOUT TO LEVEL UP, MOM! ASK IREY. SHE CAN DO IT FASTER THAN ME ANYWAY.
THAT'S NOT THE POINT, YOUNG MAN!
HE'S COMING, RIGHT?
OF COURSE, HE IS, BART.
BARRY NEVER USED TO MISS A FAMILY PICNIC.
BUT HE WAS NEVER ON TIME EITHER, WALLY.
ALLEN, BARRY
BZZZD BZZZD BZZZD

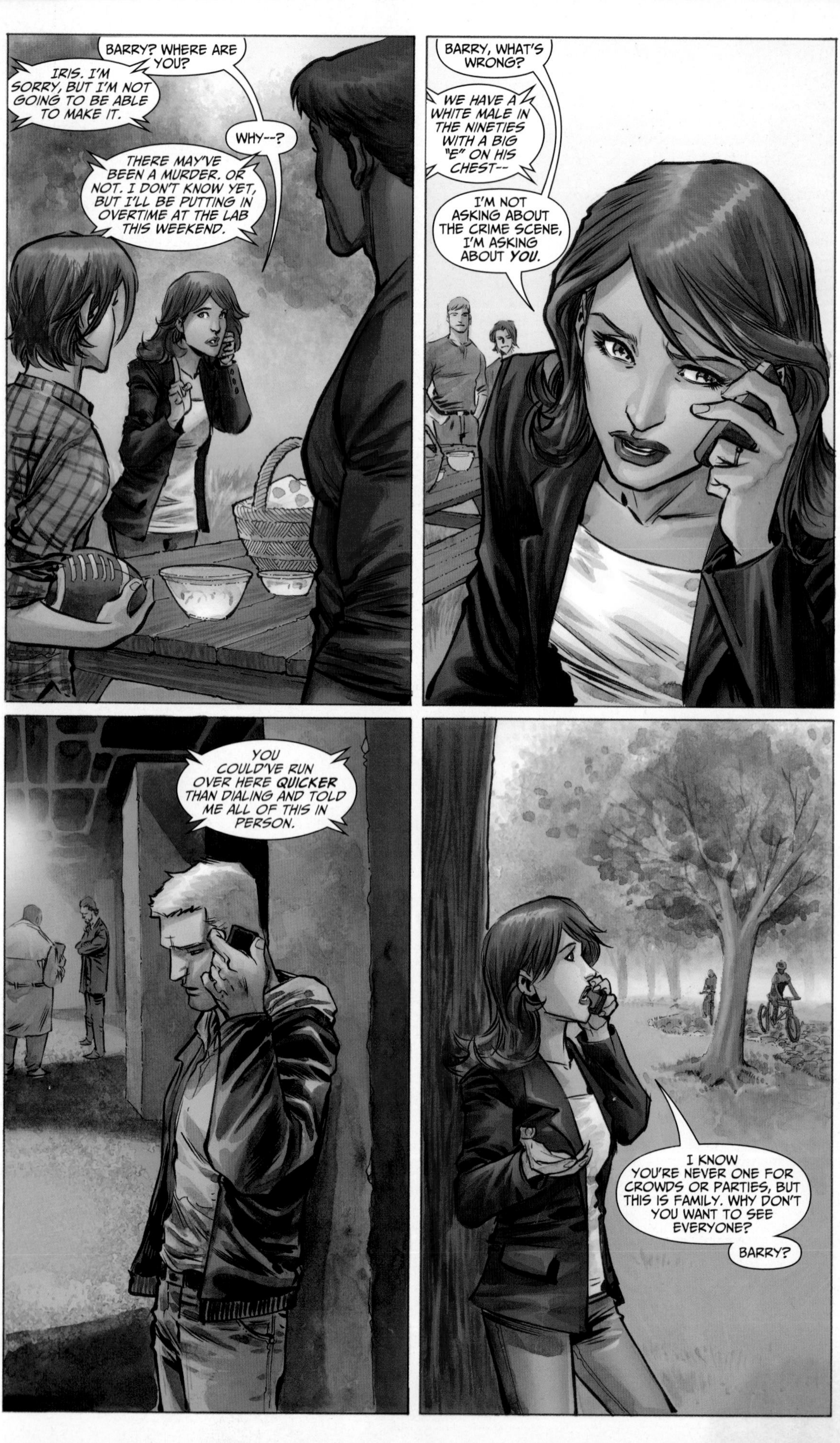
BARRY? WHERE ARE YOU?
IRIS. I'M SORRY, BUT I'M NOT GOING TO BE ABLE TO MAKE IT.
WHY--?
THERE MAY'VE BEEN A MURDER. OR NOT. I DON'T KNOW YET, BUT I'LL BE PUTTING IN OVERTIME AT THE LAB THIS WEEKEND.
BARRY, WHAT'S WRONG?
WE HAVE A WHITE MALE IN THE NINETIES WITH A BIG "E" ON HIS CHEST--
I'M NOT ASKING ABOUT THE CRIME SCENE, I'M ASKING ABOUT YOU.
YOU COULD'VE RUN OVER HERE QUICKER THAN DIALING AND TOLD ME ALL OF THIS IN PERSON.
I KNOW YOU'RE NEVER ONE FOR CROWDS OR PARTIES, BUT THIS IS FAMILY. WHY DON'T YOU WANT TO SEE EVERYONE?
BARRY?

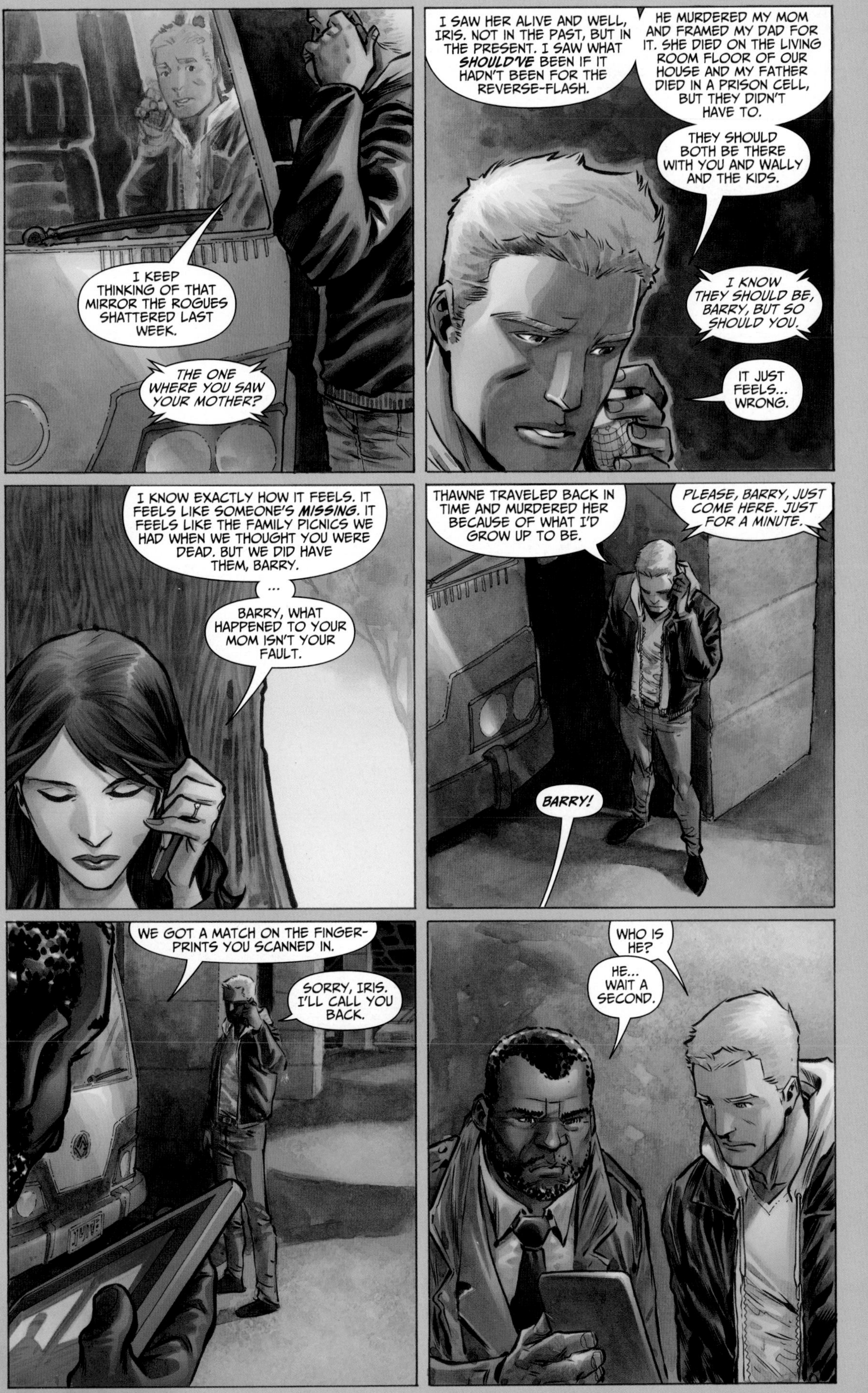
I KEEP THINKING OF THAT MIRROR THE ROGUES SHATTERED LAST WEEK.
THE ONE WHERE YOU SAW YOUR MOTHER?
I SAW HER ALIVE AND WELL, IRIS. NOT IN THE PAST, BUT IN THE PRESENT. I SAW WHAT SHOULD'VE BEEN IF IT HADN'T BEEN FOR THE REVERSE-FLASH.
HE MURDERED MY MOM AND FRAMED MY DAD FOR IT. SHE DIED ON THE LIVING ROOM FLOOR OF OUR HOUSE AND MY FATHER DIED IN A PRISON CELL, BUT THEY DIDN'T HAVE TO.
THEY SHOULD BOTH BE THERE WITH YOU AND WALLY AND THE KIDS.
I KNOW THEY SHOULD BE, BARRY, BUT SO SHOULD YOU.
IT JUST FEELS... WRONG.
I KNOW EXACTLY HOW IT FEELS. IT FEELS LIKE SOMEONE'S MISSING. IT FEELS LIKE THE FAMILY PICNICS WE HAD WHEN WE THOUGHT YOU WERE DEAD. BUT WE DID HAVE THEM, BARRY.
...
BARRY, WHAT HAPPENED TO YOUR MOM ISN'T YOUR FAULT.
THAWNE TRAVELED BACK IN TIME AND MURDERED HER BECAUSE OF WHAT I'D GROW UP TO BE.
PLEASE, BARRY, JUST COME HERE. JUST FOR A MINUTE.
BARRY!
WE GOT A MATCH ON THE FINGER-PRINTS YOU SCANNED IN.
SORRY, IRIS. I'LL CALL YOU BACK.
WHO IS HE?
HE... WAIT A SECOND.

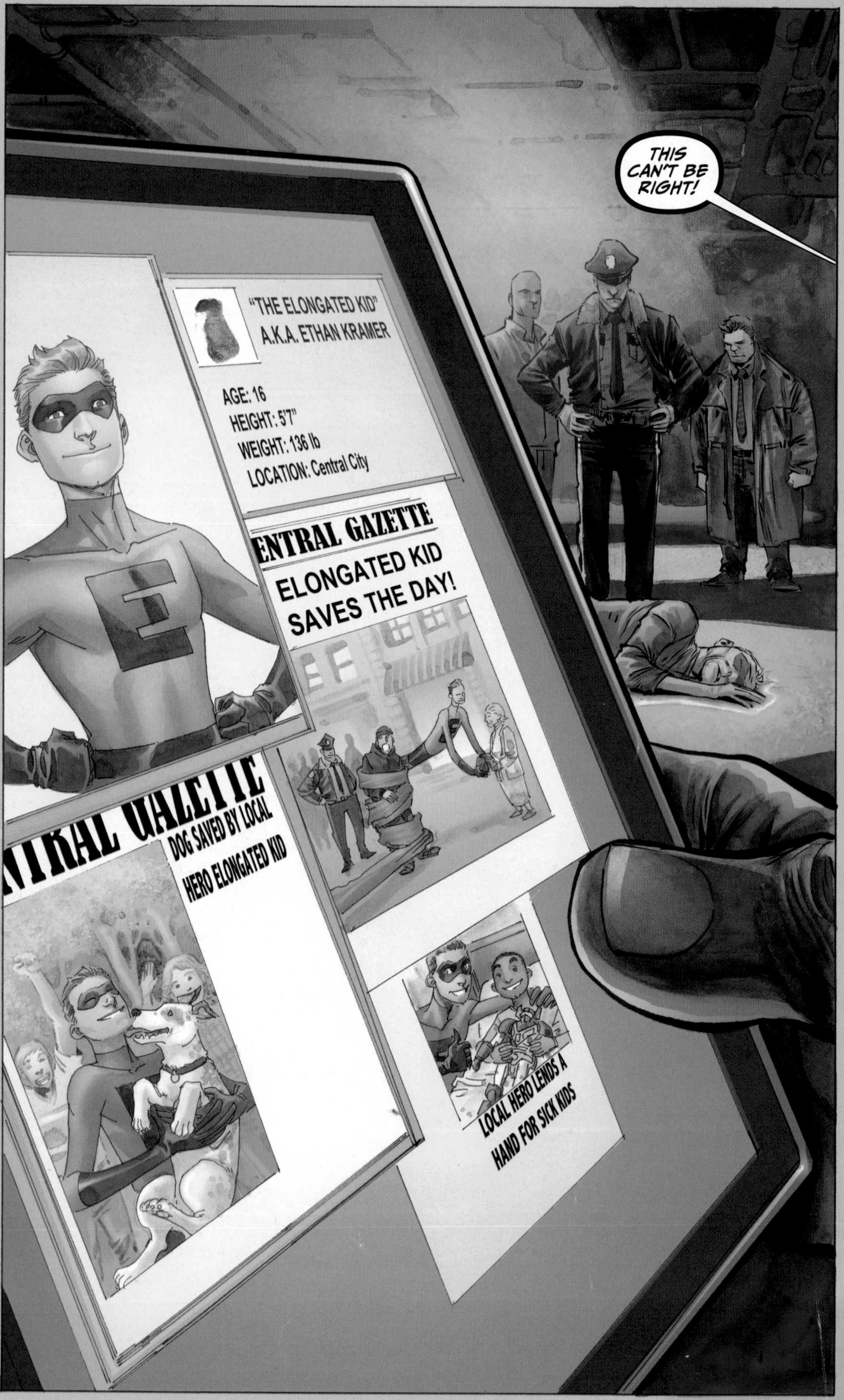
THIS CAN'T BE RIGHT!
"THE ELONGATED KID"
A.K.A. ETHAN KRAMER
AGE: 16
HEIGHT: 5'7"
WEIGHT: 136 lb
LOCATION: Central City
ENTRAL GAZETTE
ELONGATED KID SAVES THE DAY!
NTRAL GAZETTE
DOG SAVED BY LOCAL HERO ELONGATED KID
LOCAL HERO LENDS A HAND FOR SICK KIDS

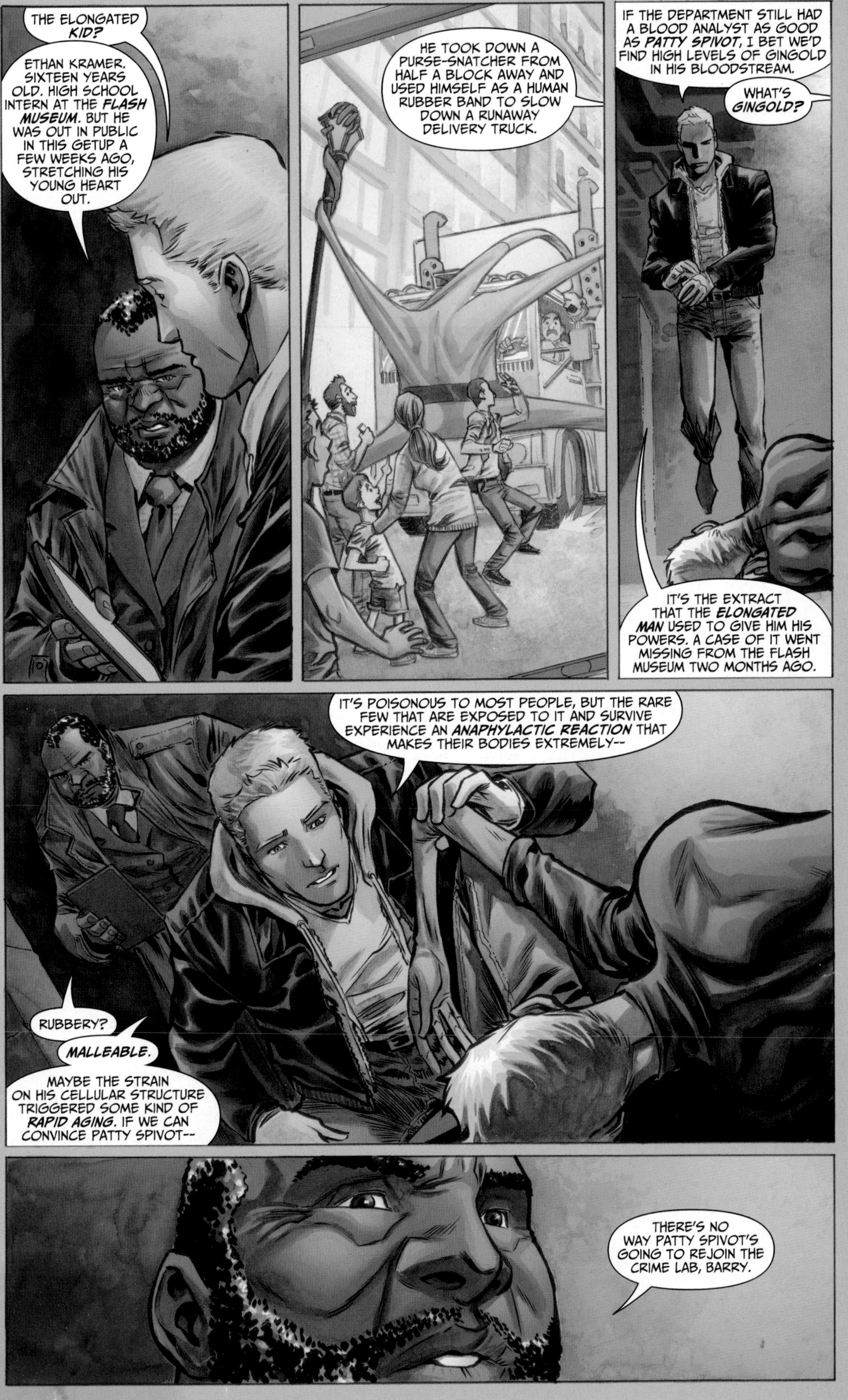
THE ELONGATED KID?
ETHAN KRAMER. SIXTEEN YEARS OLD. HIGH SCHOOL INTERN AT THE FLASH MUSEUM. BUT HE WAS OUT IN PUBLIC IN THIS GETUP A FEW WEEKS AGO, STRETCHING HIS YOUNG HEART OUT.
HE TOOK DOWN A PURSE-SNATCHER FROM HALF A BLOCK AWAY AND USED HIMSELF AS A HUMAN RUBBER BAND TO SLOW DOWN A RUNAWAY DELIVERY TRUCK.
IF THE DEPARTMENT STILL HAD A BLOOD ANALYST AS GOOD AS PATTY SPIVOT, I BET WE'D FIND HIGH LEVELS OF GINGOLD IN HIS BLOODSTREAM.
WHAT'S GINGOLD?
IT'S THE EXTRACT THAT THE ELONGATED MAN USED TO GIVE HIM HIS POWERS. A CASE OF IT WENT MISSING FROM THE FLASH MUSEUM TWO MONTHS AGO.
IT'S POISONOUS TO MOST PEOPLE, BUT THE RARE FEW THAT ARE EXPOSED TO IT AND SURVIVE EXPERIENCE AN ANAPHYLACTIC REACTION THAT MAKES THEIR BODIES EXTREMELY--
RUBBERY?
MALLEABLE.
MAYBE THE STRAIN ON HIS CELLULAR STRUCTURE TRIGGERED SOME KIND OF RAPID AGING. IF WE CAN CONVINCE PATTY SPIVOT--
THERE'S NO WAY PATTY SPIVOT'S GOING TO REJOIN THE CRIME LAB, BARRY.

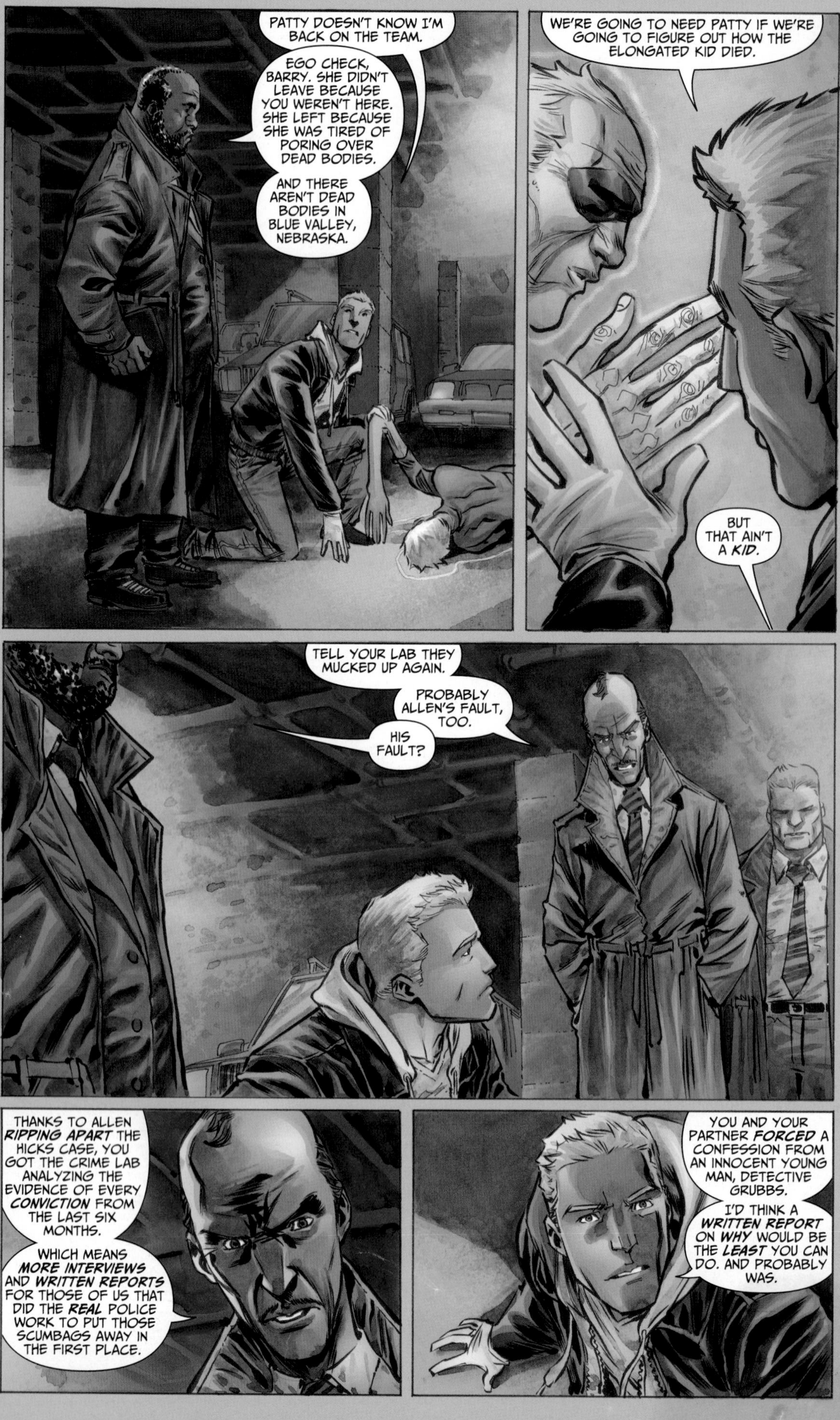
PATTY DOESN'T KNOW I'M BACK ON THE TEAM.
EGO CHECK, BARRY. SHE DIDN'T LEAVE BECAUSE YOU WEREN'T HERE. SHE LEFT BECAUSE SHE WAS TIRED OF PORING OVER DEAD BODIES.
AND THERE AREN'T DEAD BODIES IN BLUE VALLEY, NEBRASKA.
WE'RE GOING TO NEED PATTY IF WE'RE GOING TO FIGURE OUT HOW THE ELONGATED KID DIED.
BUT THAT AIN'T A *KID*.
TELL YOUR LAB THEY MUCKED UP AGAIN.
PROBABLY ALLEN'S FAULT, TOO.
HIS FAULT?
THANKS TO ALLEN *RIPPING APART* THE HICKS CASE, YOU GOT THE CRIME LAB ANALYZING THE EVIDENCE OF EVERY *CONVICTION* FROM THE LAST SIX MONTHS.
WHICH MEANS *MORE INTERVIEWS* AND *WRITTEN REPORTS* FOR THOSE OF US THAT DID THE *REAL* POLICE WORK TO PUT THOSE SCUMBAGS AWAY IN THE FIRST PLACE.
YOU AND YOUR PARTNER *FORCED* A CONFESSION FROM AN INNOCENT YOUNG MAN, DETECTIVE GRUBBS.
I'D THINK A *WRITTEN REPORT* ON *WHY* WOULD BE THE *LEAST* YOU CAN DO. AND PROBABLY WAS.

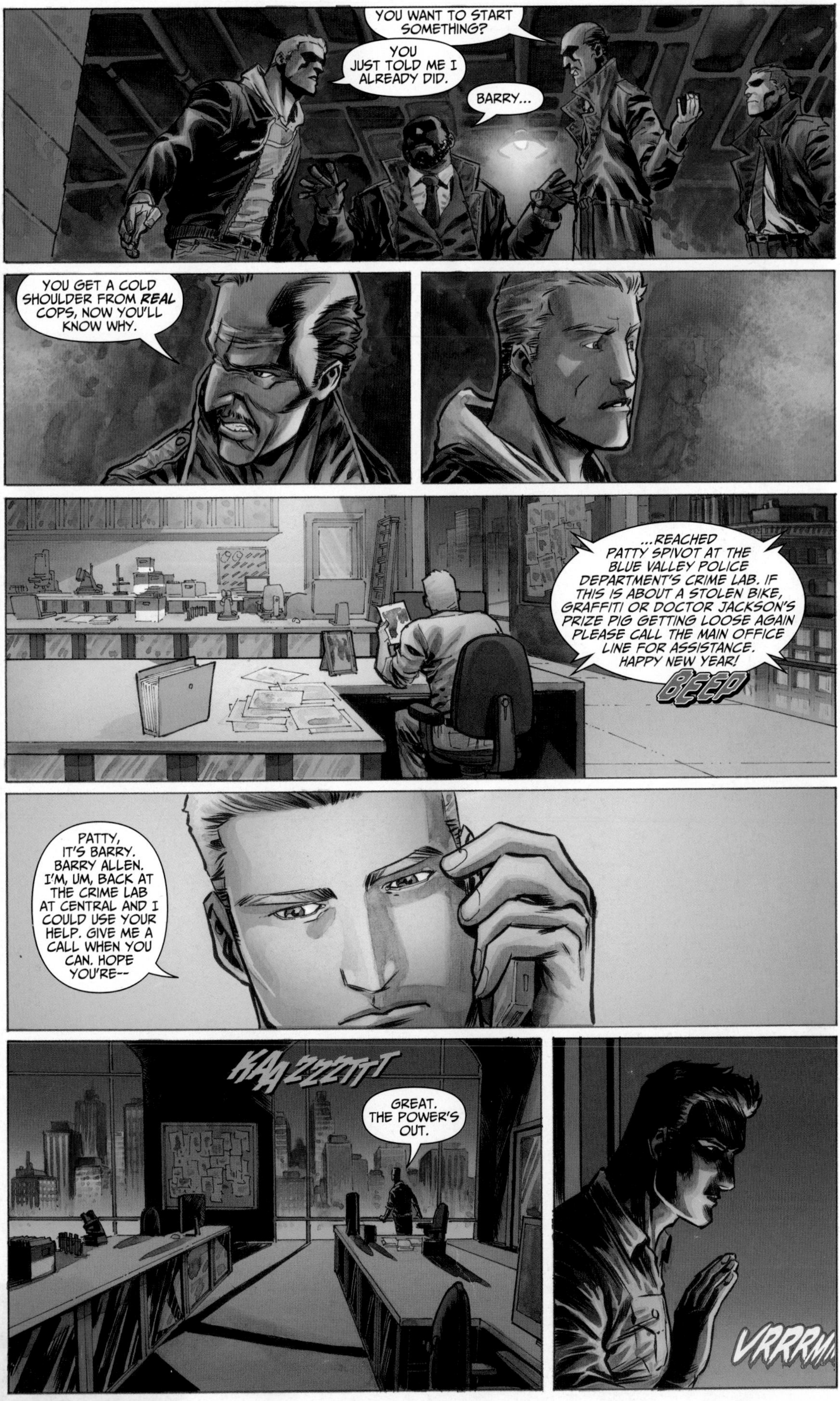
YOU WANT TO START SOMETHING?
YOU JUST TOLD ME I ALREADY DID.
BARRY...
YOU GET A COLD SHOULDER FROM REAL COPS, NOW YOU'LL KNOW WHY.
...REACHED PATTY SPIVOT AT THE BLUE VALLEY POLICE DEPARTMENT'S CRIME LAB. IF THIS IS ABOUT A STOLEN BIKE, GRAFFITI OR DOCTOR JACKSON'S PRIZE PIG GETTING LOOSE AGAIN PLEASE CALL THE MAIN OFFICE LINE FOR ASSISTANCE. HAPPY NEW YEAR!
BEEP
PATTY, IT'S BARRY. BARRY ALLEN. I'M, UM, BACK AT THE CRIME LAB AT CENTRAL AND I COULD USE YOUR HELP. GIVE ME A CALL WHEN YOU CAN. HOPE YOU'RE--
KAAZZZTTT
GREAT. THE POWER'S OUT.
VRRRM

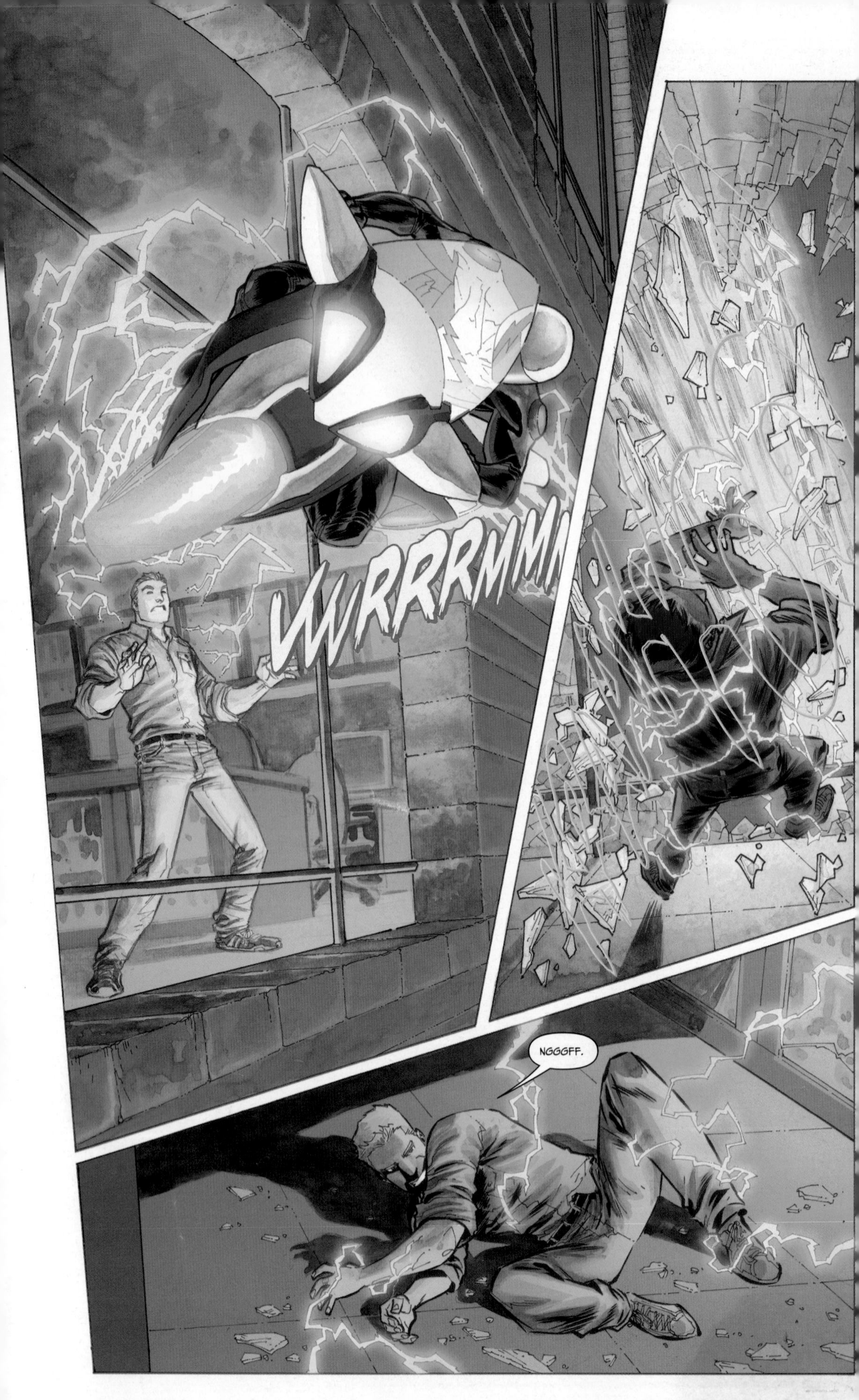

VVRRRMMM
NGGGFF.

WWRRRMMM

FLSSH

STOP.

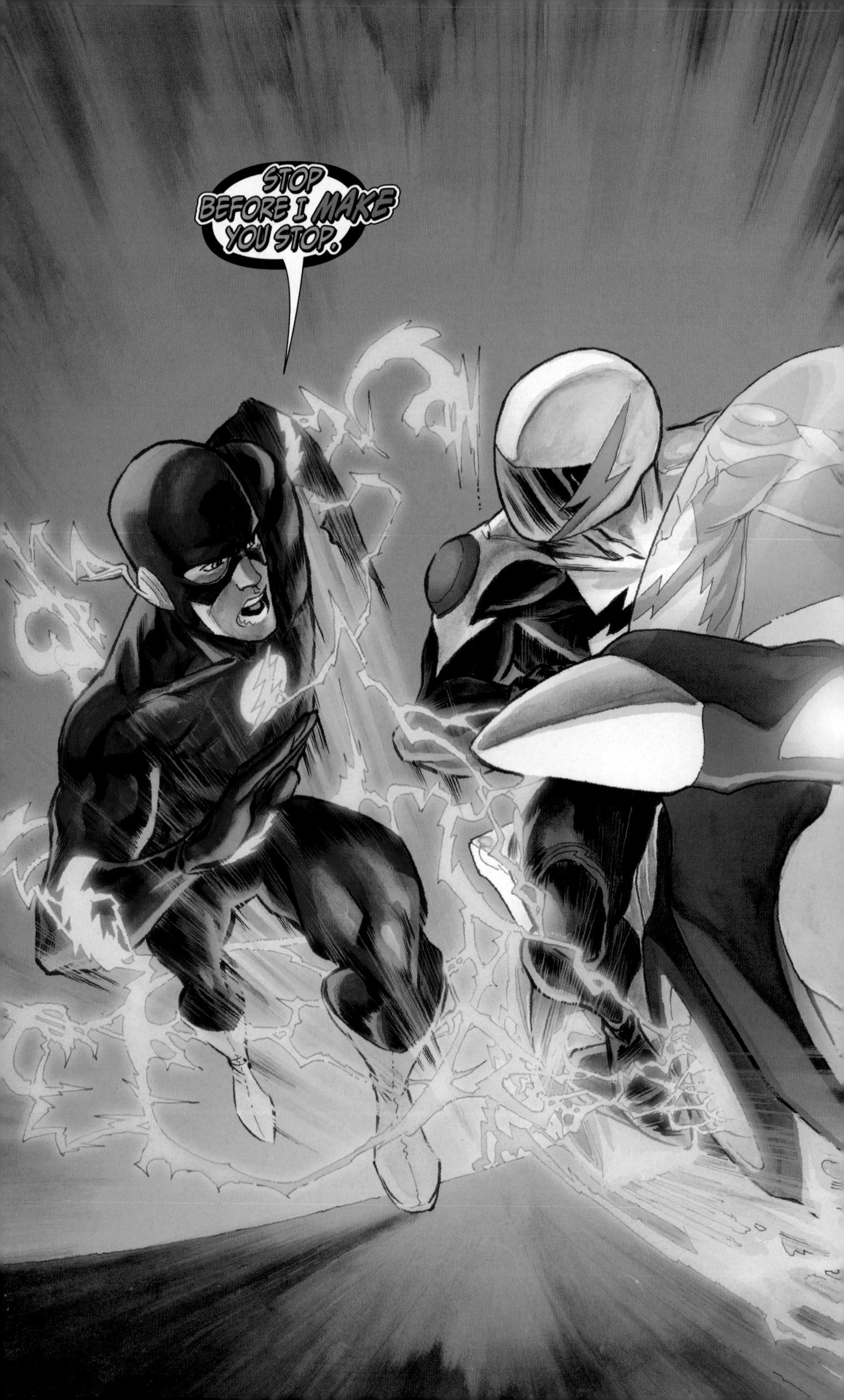
STOP BEFORE I MAKE YOU STOP.

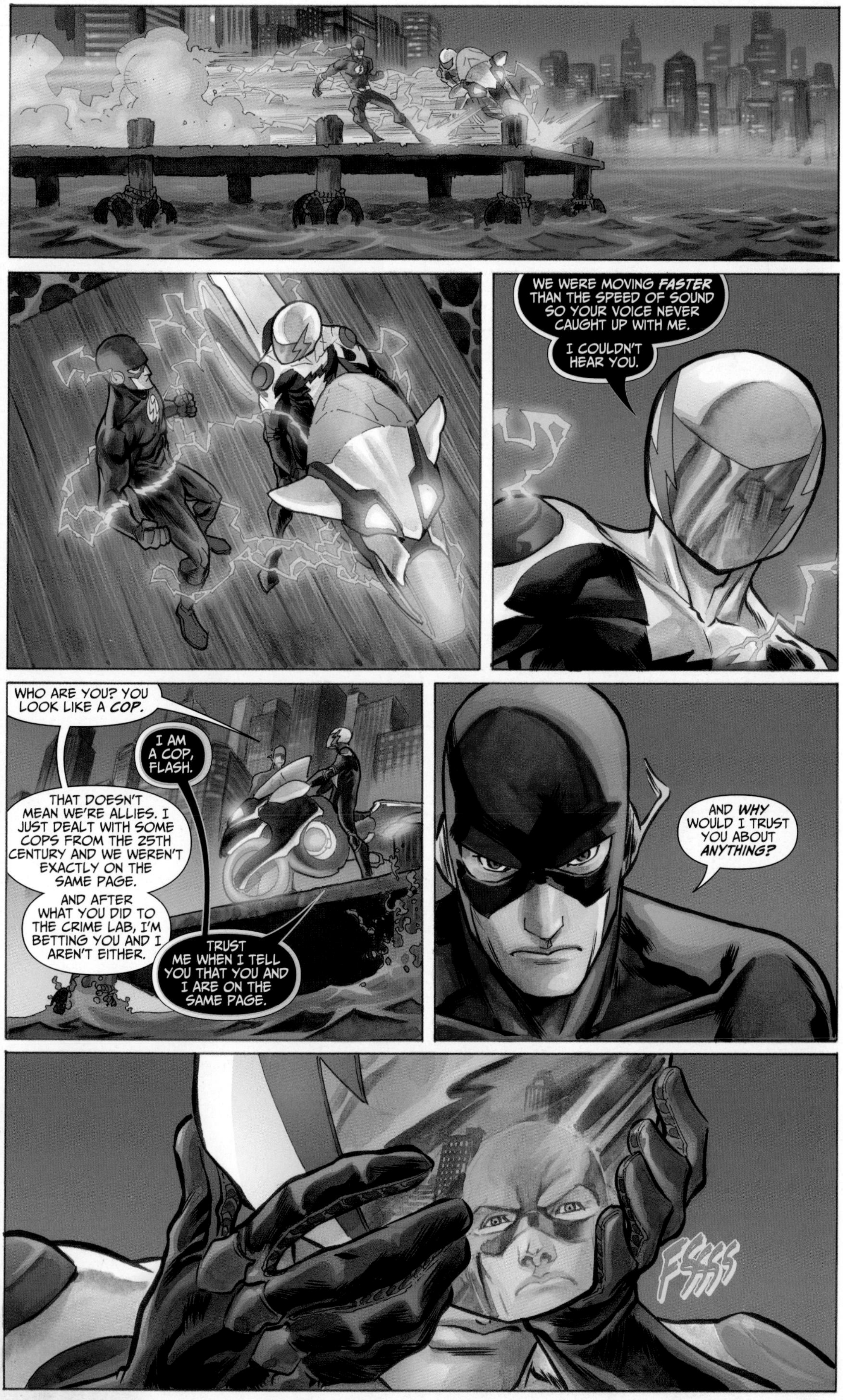
WE WERE MOVING FASTER THAN THE SPEED OF SOUND SO YOUR VOICE NEVER CAUGHT UP WITH ME.
I COULDN'T HEAR YOU.
WHO ARE YOU? YOU LOOK LIKE A COP.
I AM A COP, FLASH.
THAT DOESN'T MEAN WE'RE ALLIES. I JUST DEALT WITH SOME COPS FROM THE 25TH CENTURY AND WE WEREN'T EXACTLY ON THE SAME PAGE.
AND AFTER WHAT YOU DID TO THE CRIME LAB, I'M BETTING YOU AND I AREN'T EITHER.
TRUST ME WHEN I TELL YOU THAT YOU AND I ARE ON THE SAME PAGE.
AND WHY WOULD I TRUST YOU ABOUT ANYTHING?
FSSSS

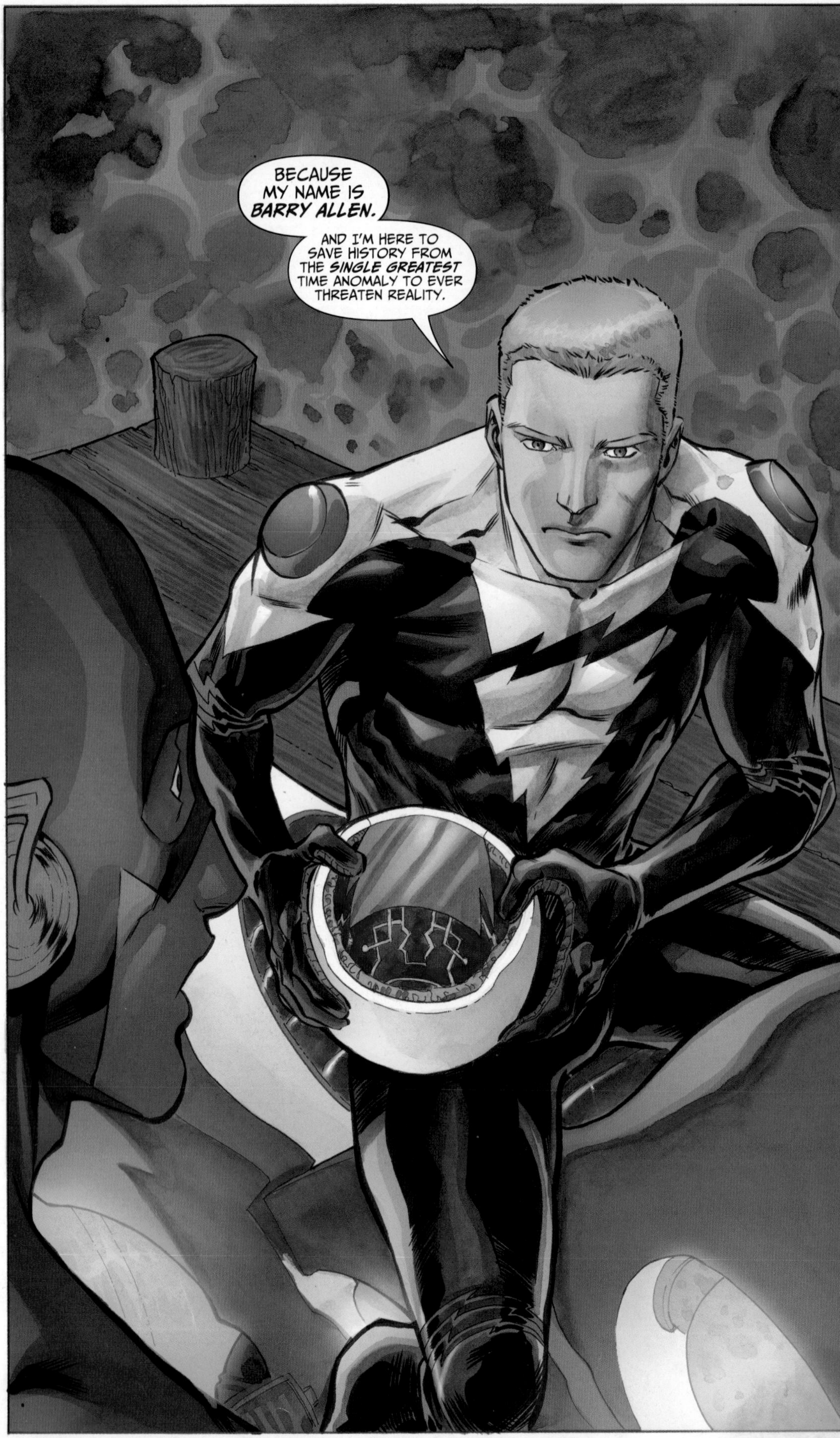
BECAUSE MY NAME IS *BARRY ALLEN.*
AND I'M HERE TO SAVE HISTORY FROM THE *SINGLE GREATEST* TIME ANOMALY TO EVER THREATEN REALITY.

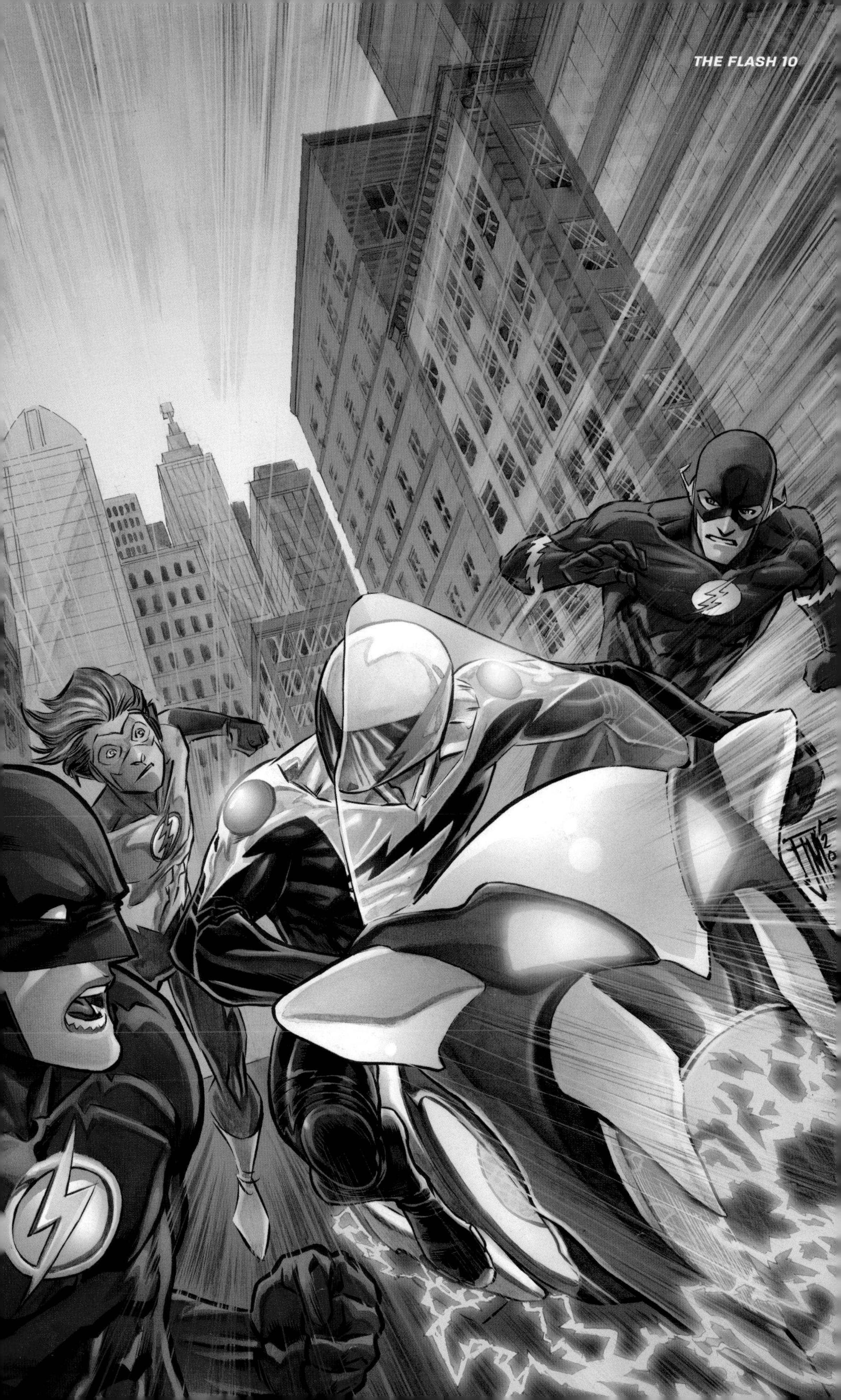

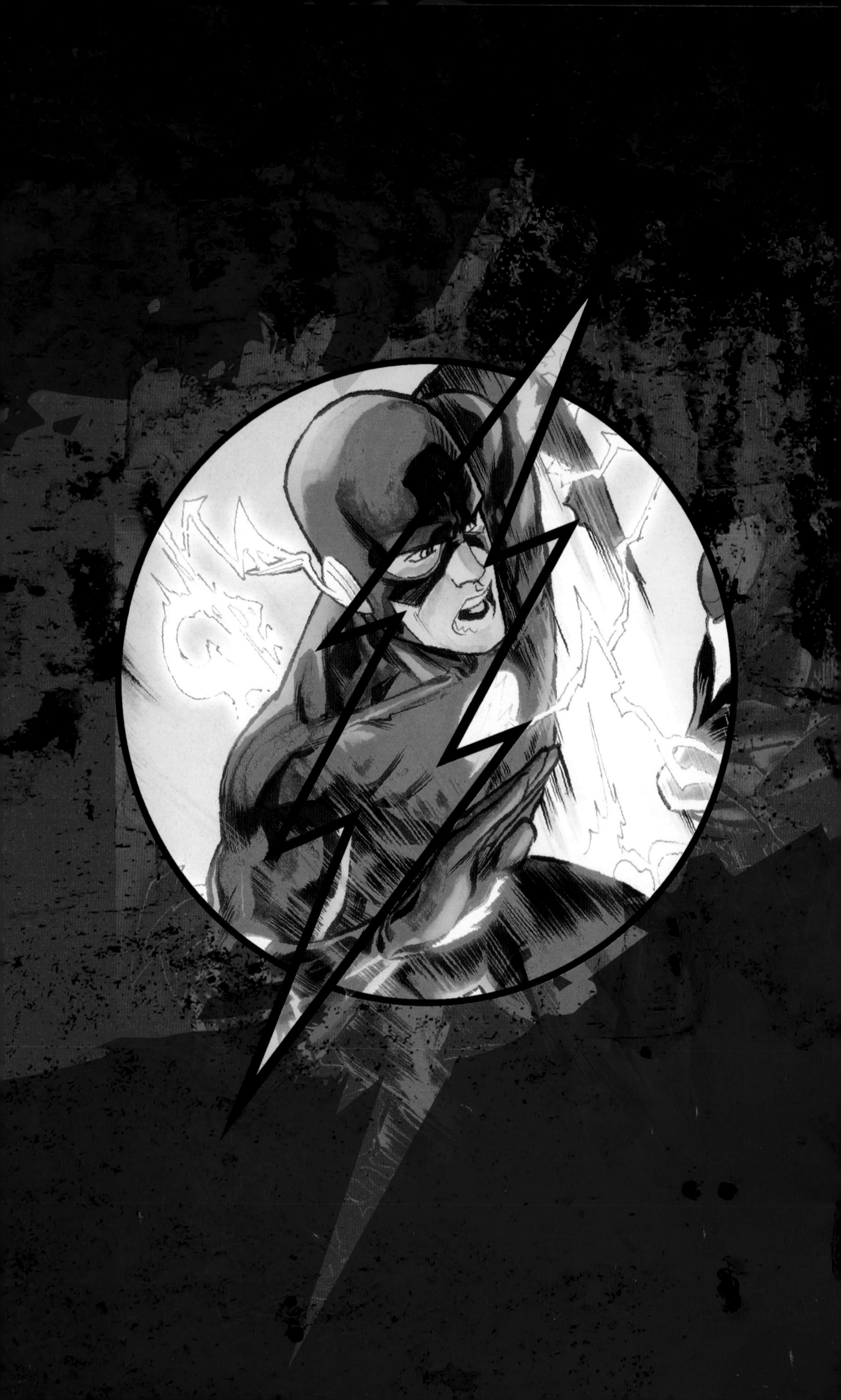

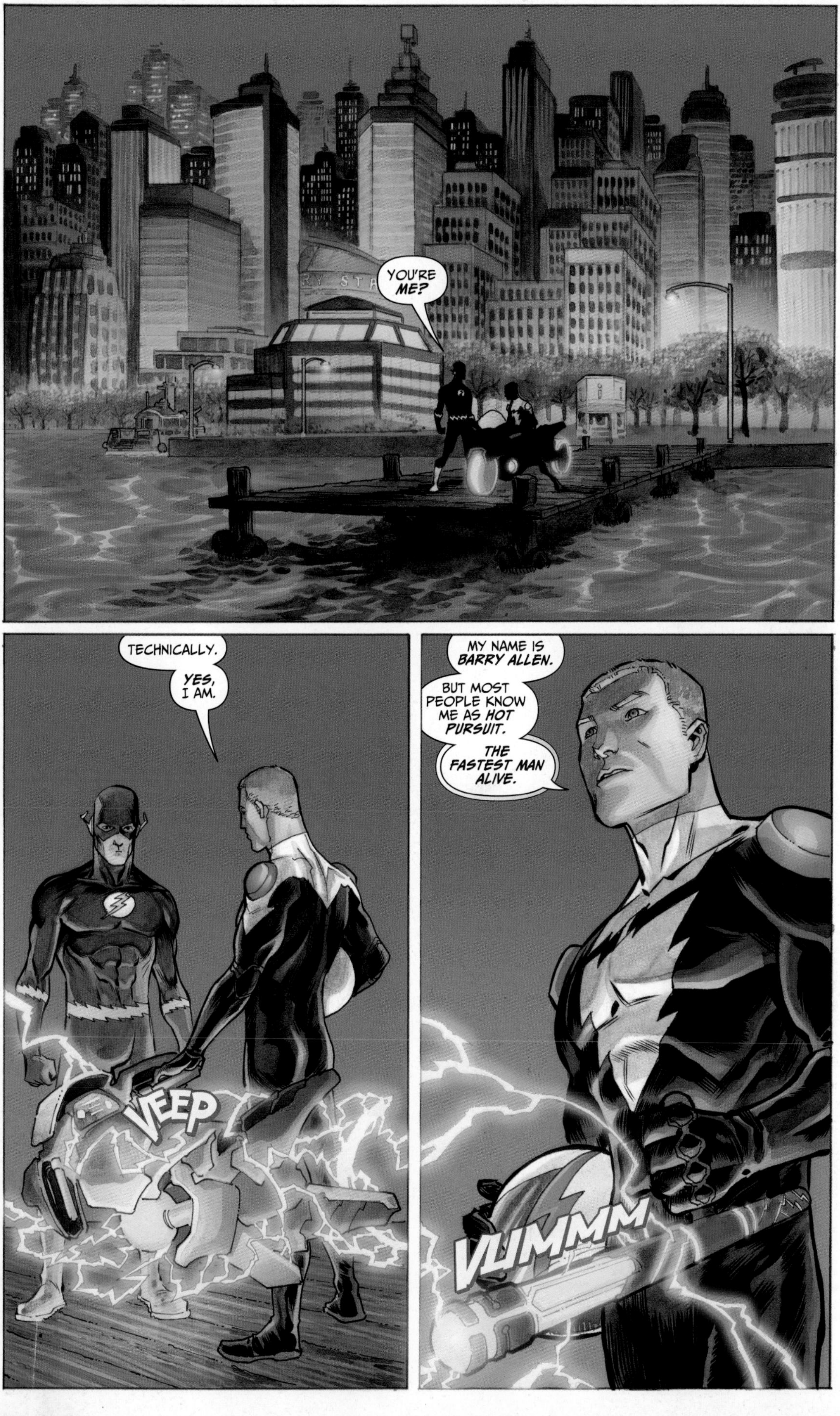
YOU'RE ME?
TECHNICALLY.
YES, I AM.
VEEP
MY NAME IS BARRY ALLEN.
BUT MOST PEOPLE KNOW ME AS HOT PURSUIT.
THE FASTEST MAN ALIVE.
VUMMM

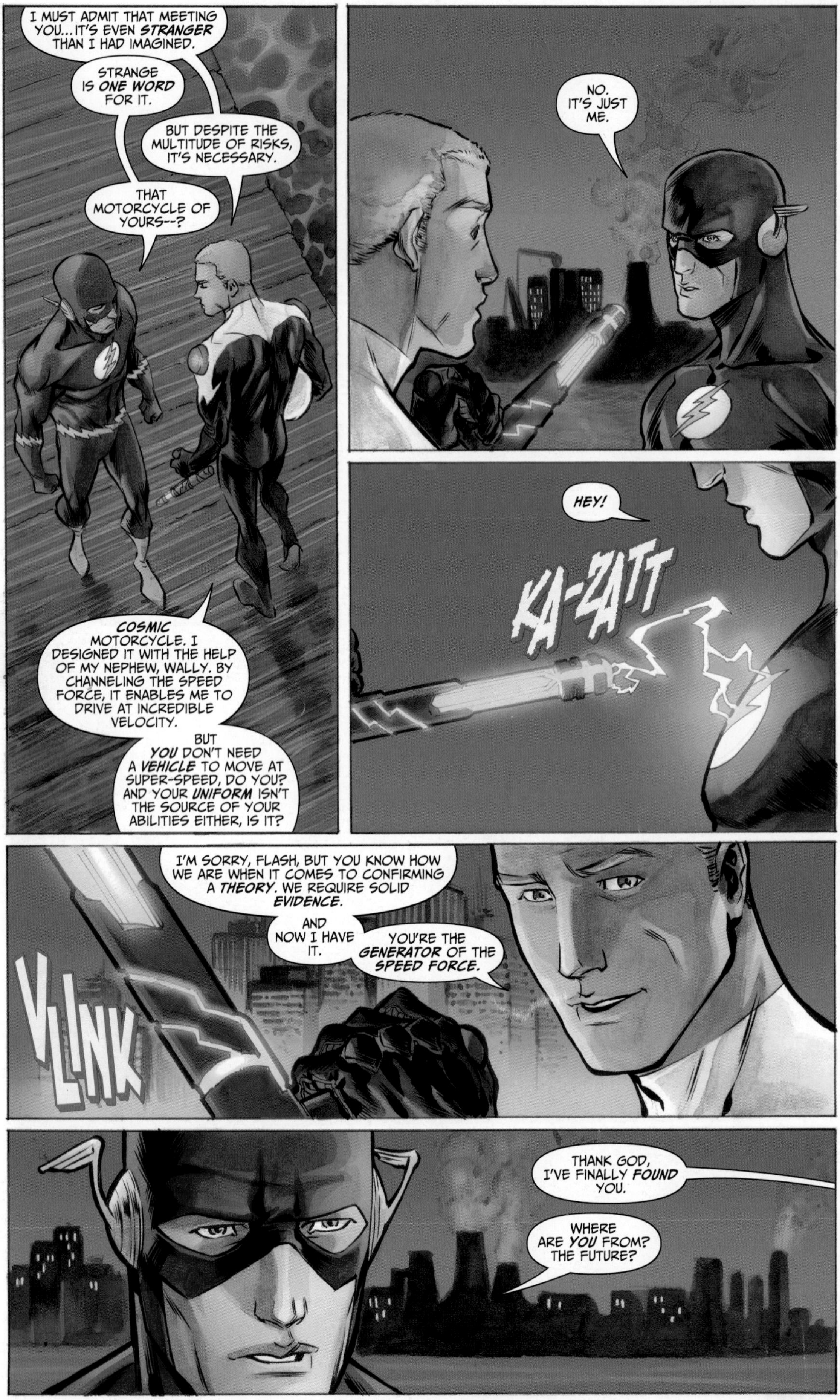

I MUST ADMIT THAT MEETING YOU...IT'S EVEN STRANGER THAN I HAD IMAGINED.
STRANGE IS ONE WORD FOR IT.
BUT DESPITE THE MULTITUDE OF RISKS, IT'S NECESSARY.
THAT MOTORCYCLE OF YOURS--?
COSMIC MOTORCYCLE. I DESIGNED IT WITH THE HELP OF MY NEPHEW, WALLY. BY CHANNELING THE SPEED FORCE, IT ENABLES ME TO DRIVE AT INCREDIBLE VELOCITY.
BUT YOU DON'T NEED A VEHICLE TO MOVE AT SUPER-SPEED, DO YOU? AND YOUR UNIFORM ISN'T THE SOURCE OF YOUR ABILITIES EITHER, IS IT?
NO. IT'S JUST ME.
HEY!
KA-ZATT
I'M SORRY, FLASH, BUT YOU KNOW HOW WE ARE WHEN IT COMES TO CONFIRMING A THEORY. WE REQUIRE SOLID EVIDENCE.
AND NOW I HAVE IT.
YOU'RE THE GENERATOR OF THE SPEED FORCE.
VLINK
THANK GOD, I'VE FINALLY FOUND YOU.
WHERE ARE YOU FROM? THE FUTURE?

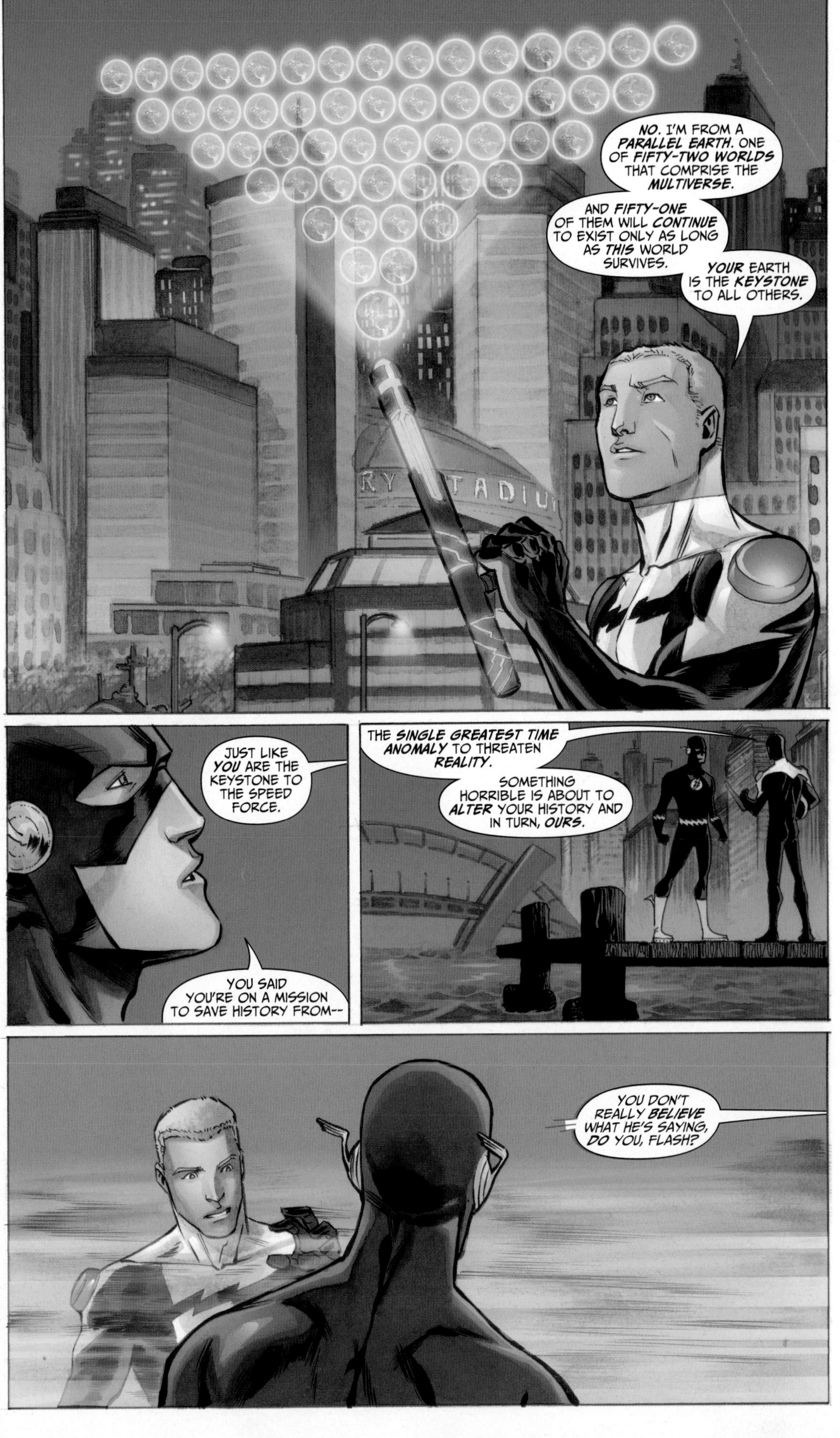
NO. I'M FROM A PARALLEL EARTH. ONE OF FIFTY-TWO WORLDS THAT COMPRISE THE MULTIVERSE.
AND FIFTY-ONE OF THEM WILL CONTINUE TO EXIST ONLY AS LONG AS THIS WORLD SURVIVES.
YOUR EARTH IS THE KEYSTONE TO ALL OTHERS.
JUST LIKE YOU ARE THE KEYSTONE TO THE SPEED FORCE.
YOU SAID YOU'RE ON A MISSION TO SAVE HISTORY FROM--
THE SINGLE GREATEST TIME ANOMALY TO THREATEN REALITY.
SOMETHING HORRIBLE IS ABOUT TO ALTER YOUR HISTORY AND IN TURN, OURS.
YOU DON'T REALLY BELIEVE WHAT HE'S SAYING, DO YOU, FLASH?

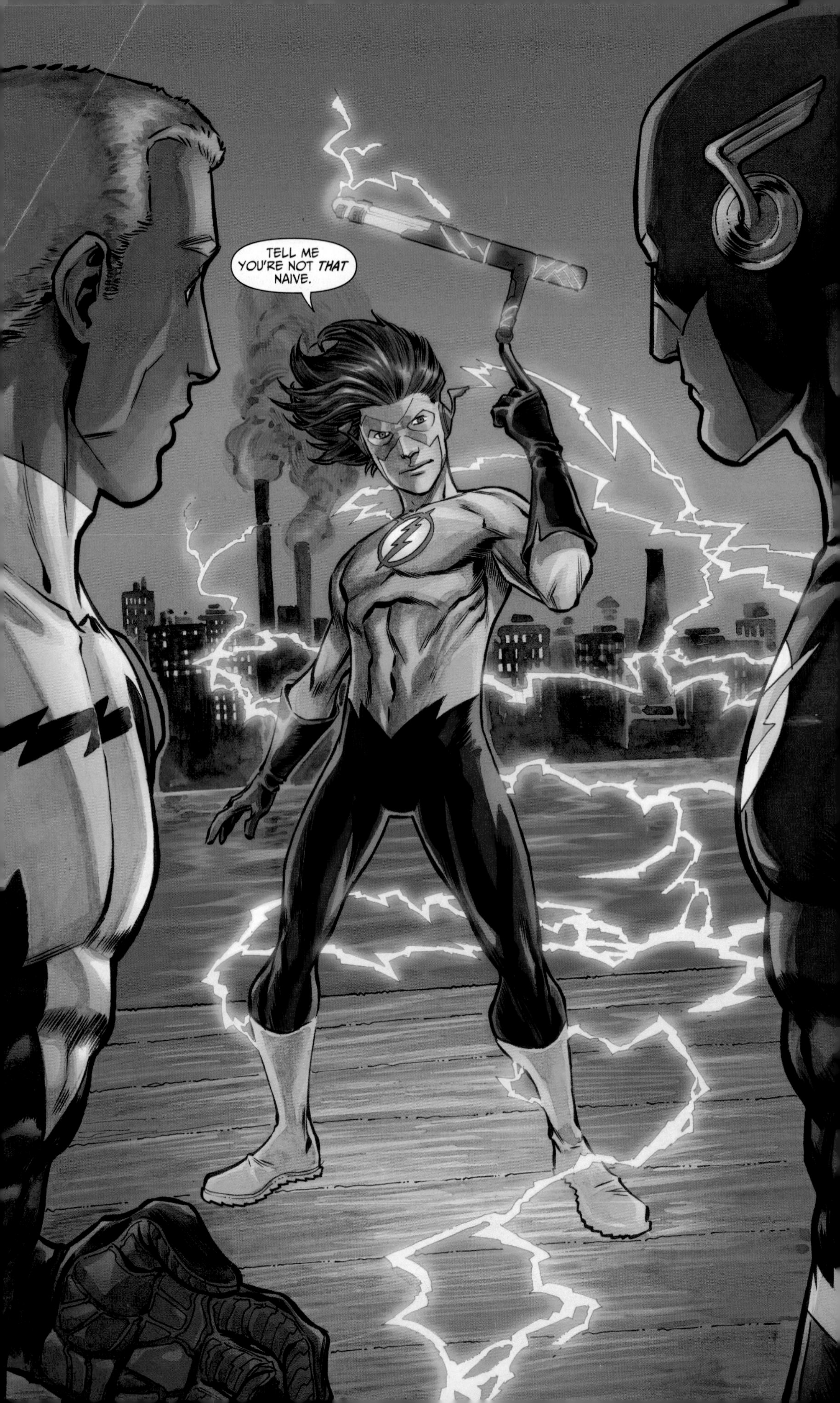
TELL ME YOU'RE NOT *THAT* NAIVE.

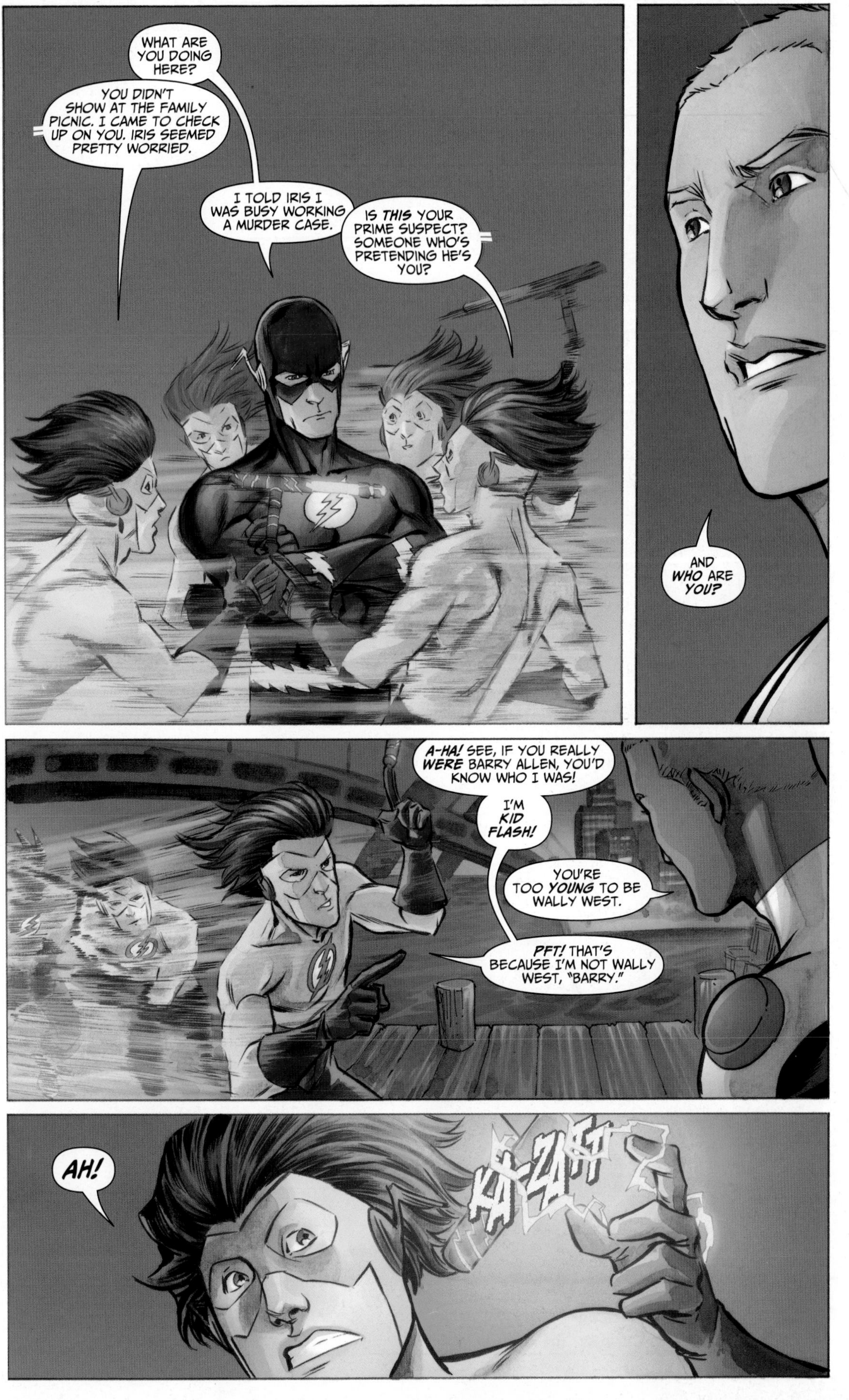

WHAT ARE YOU DOING HERE?
YOU DIDN'T SHOW AT THE FAMILY PICNIC. I CAME TO CHECK UP ON YOU. IRIS SEEMED PRETTY WORRIED.
I TOLD IRIS I WAS BUSY WORKING A MURDER CASE.
IS *THIS* YOUR PRIME SUSPECT? SOMEONE WHO'S PRETENDING HE'S YOU?
AND *WHO* ARE *YOU?*
A-HA! SEE, IF YOU REALLY *WERE* BARRY ALLEN, YOU'D KNOW WHO I WAS!
I'M *KID FLASH!*
YOU'RE TOO *YOUNG* TO BE WALLY WEST.
PFT! THAT'S BECAUSE I'M NOT WALLY WEST, "BARRY."
AH!
KA-ZAPT

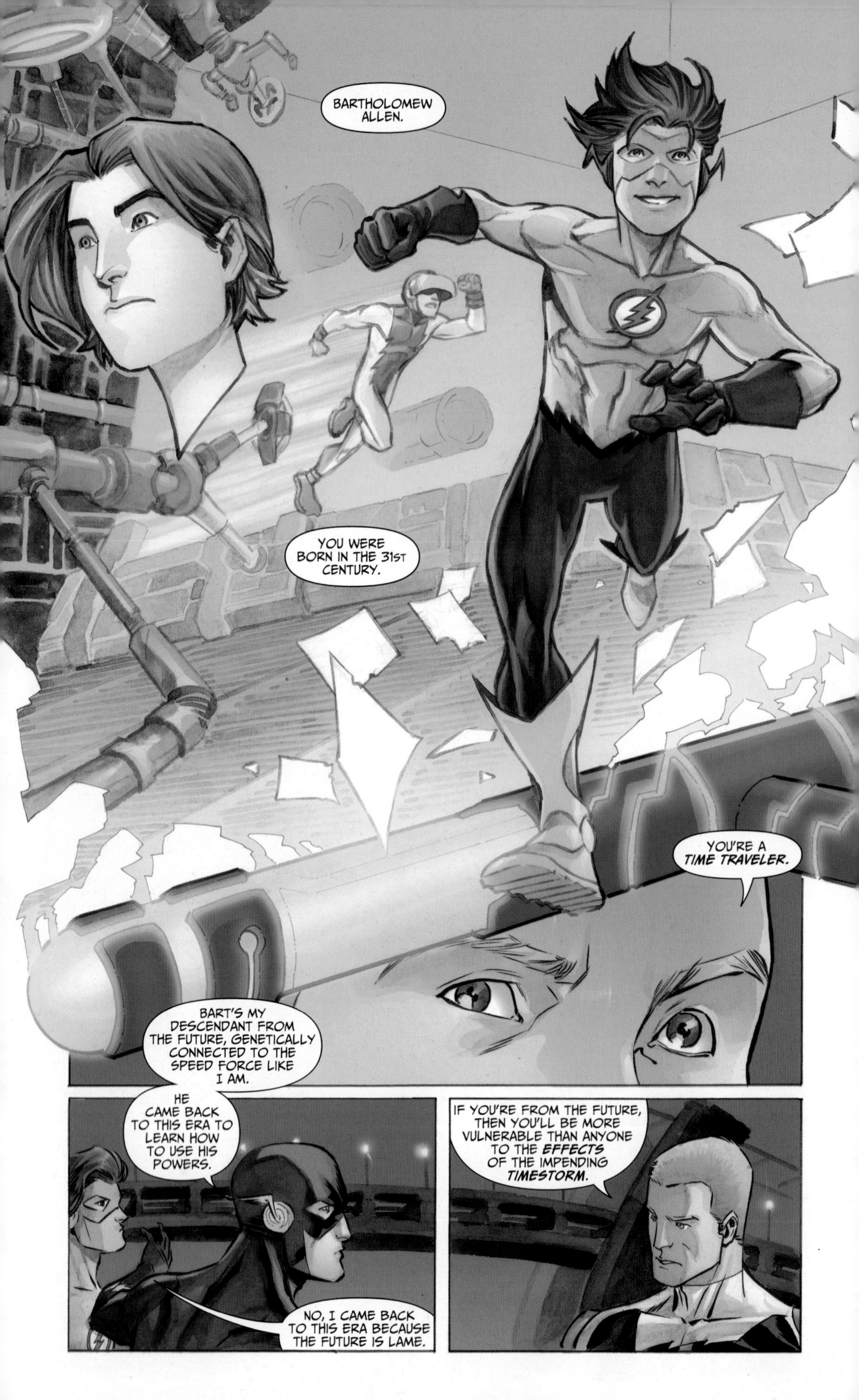
BARTHOLOMEW ALLEN.
YOU WERE BORN IN THE 31ST CENTURY.
YOU'RE A *TIME TRAVELER.*
BART'S MY DESCENDANT FROM THE FUTURE, GENETICALLY CONNECTED TO THE SPEED FORCE LIKE I AM.
HE CAME BACK TO THIS ERA TO LEARN HOW TO USE HIS POWERS.
NO, I CAME BACK TO THIS ERA BECAUSE THE FUTURE IS LAME.
IF YOU'RE FROM THE FUTURE, THEN YOU'LL BE MORE VULNERABLE THAN ANYONE TO THE ***EFFECTS*** OF THE IMPENDING ***TIMESTORM***.

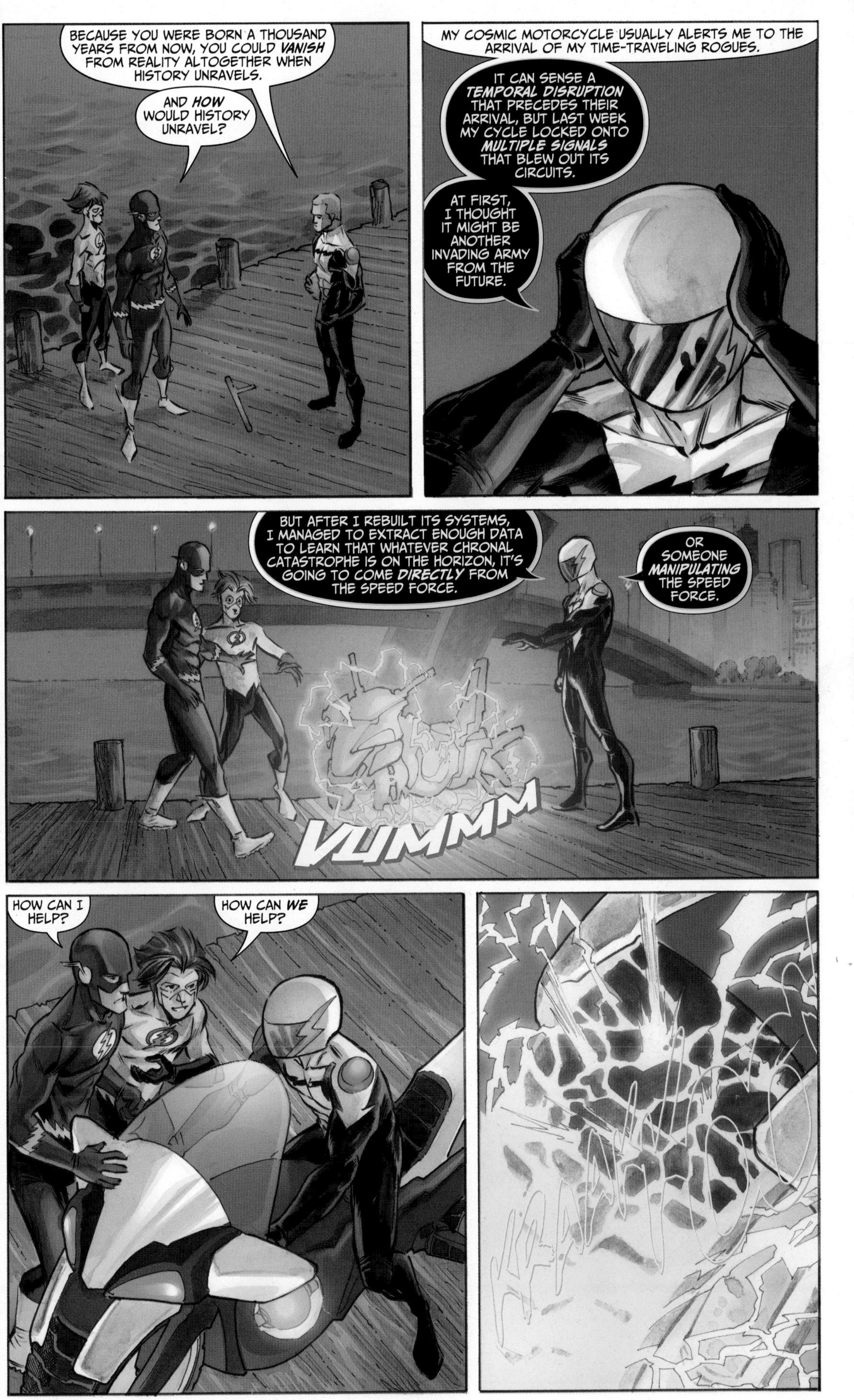
BECAUSE YOU WERE BORN A THOUSAND YEARS FROM NOW, YOU COULD VANISH FROM REALITY ALTOGETHER WHEN HISTORY UNRAVELS.
AND HOW WOULD HISTORY UNRAVEL?
MY COSMIC MOTORCYCLE USUALLY ALERTS ME TO THE ARRIVAL OF MY TIME-TRAVELING ROGUES.
IT CAN SENSE A TEMPORAL DISRUPTION THAT PRECEDES THEIR ARRIVAL, BUT LAST WEEK MY CYCLE LOCKED ONTO MULTIPLE SIGNALS THAT BLEW OUT ITS CIRCUITS.
AT FIRST, I THOUGHT IT MIGHT BE ANOTHER INVADING ARMY FROM THE FUTURE.
BUT AFTER I REBUILT ITS SYSTEMS, I MANAGED TO EXTRACT ENOUGH DATA TO LEARN THAT WHATEVER CHRONAL CATASTROPHE IS ON THE HORIZON, IT'S GOING TO COME DIRECTLY FROM THE SPEED FORCE.
OR SOMEONE MANIPULATING THE SPEED FORCE.
VUMMM
HOW CAN I HELP?
HOW CAN WE HELP?

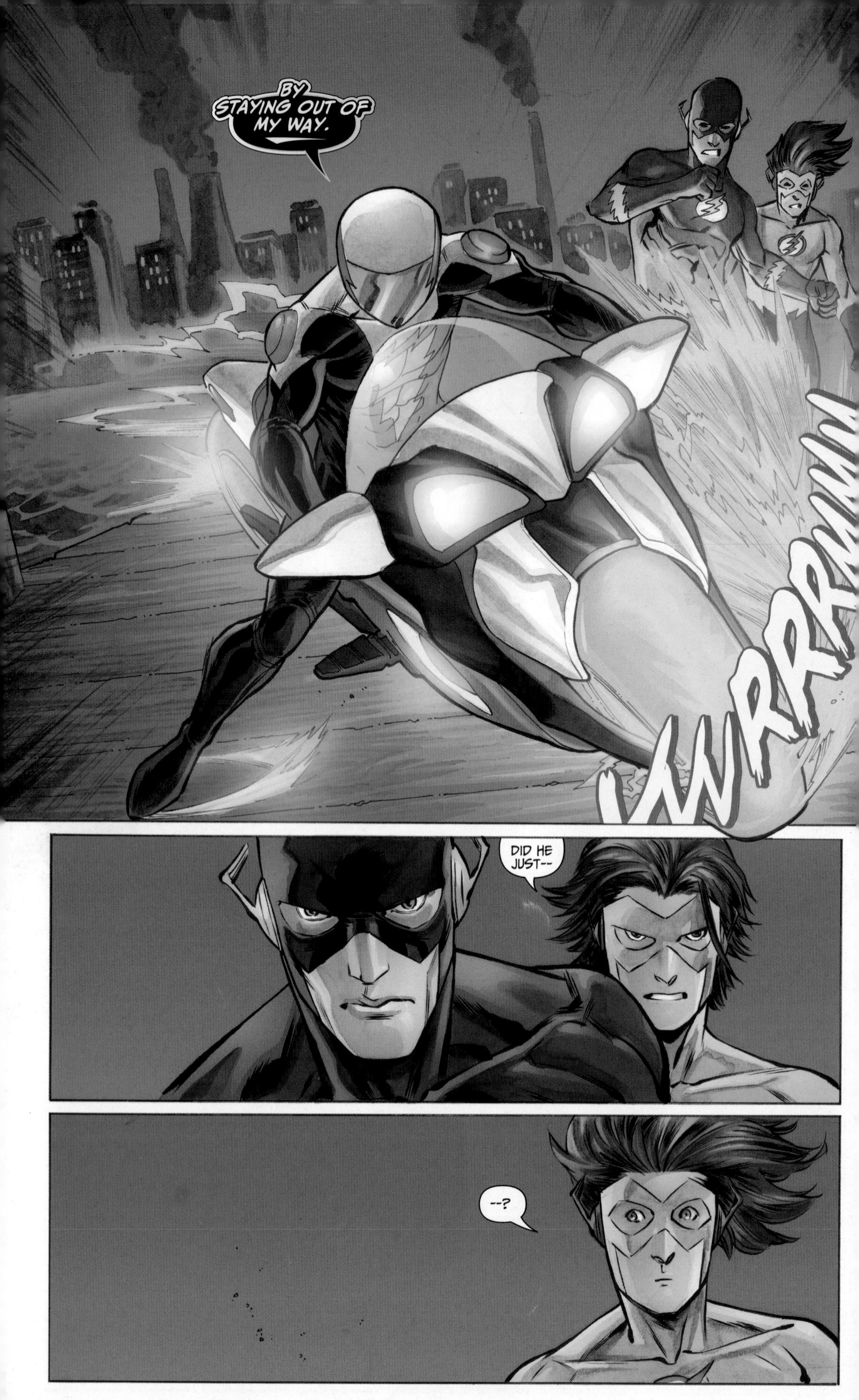

BY STAYING OUT OF MY WAY.
WRRRMMM
DID HE JUST--
--?

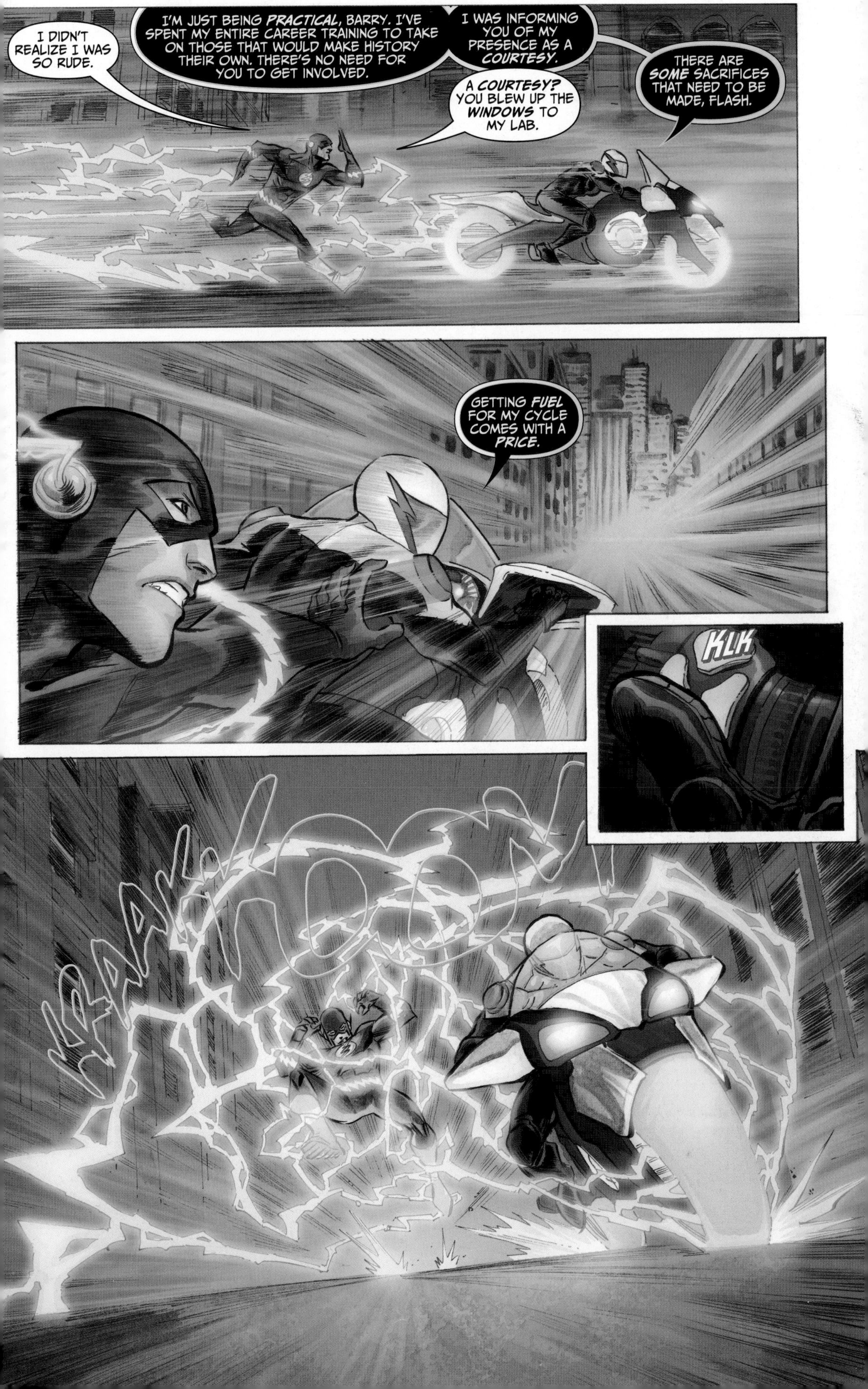

I DIDN'T REALIZE I WAS SO RUDE.
I'M JUST BEING PRACTICAL, BARRY. I'VE SPENT MY ENTIRE CAREER TRAINING TO TAKE ON THOSE THAT WOULD MAKE HISTORY THEIR OWN. THERE'S NO NEED FOR YOU TO GET INVOLVED.
I WAS INFORMING YOU OF MY PRESENCE AS A COURTESY.
A COURTESY? YOU BLEW UP THE WINDOWS TO MY LAB.
THERE ARE SOME SACRIFICES THAT NEED TO BE MADE, FLASH.
GETTING FUEL FOR MY CYCLE COMES WITH A PRICE.
KLK

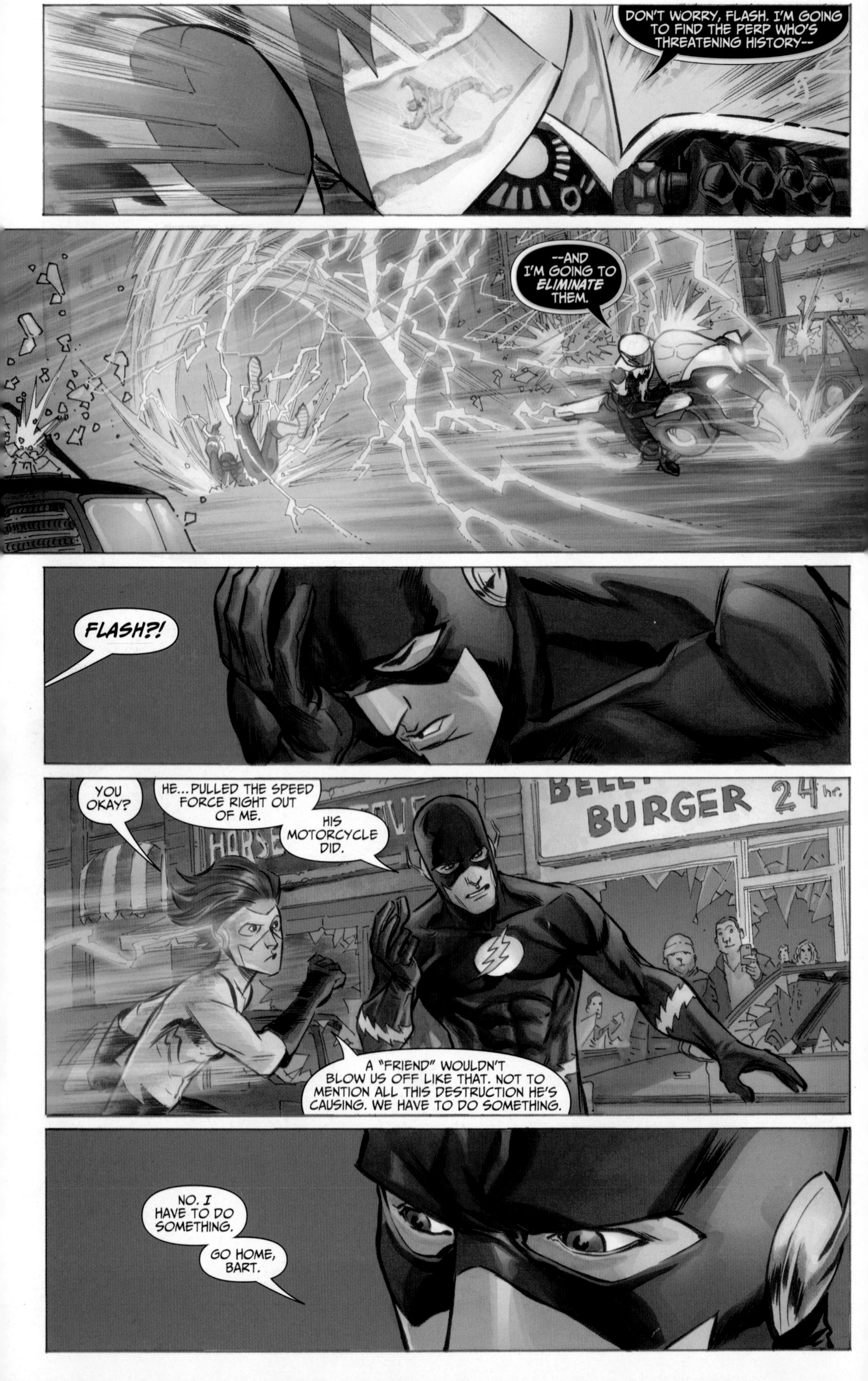
DON'T WORRY, FLASH. I'M GOING TO FIND THE PERP WHO'S THREATENING HISTORY--
--AND I'M GOING TO *ELIMINATE* THEM.
FLASH?!
YOU OKAY?
HE...PULLED THE SPEED FORCE RIGHT OUT OF ME.
HIS MOTORCYCLE DID.
BURGER 24 hr.
A "FRIEND" WOULDN'T BLOW US OFF LIKE THAT. NOT TO MENTION ALL THIS DESTRUCTION HE'S CAUSING. WE HAVE TO DO SOMETHING.
NO. *I* HAVE TO DO SOMETHING.
GO HOME, BART.

GO HOME?

I'VE HAD PLENTY OF EXPERIENCE WITH THE MULTIVERSE.

YOU NEED A *REALITY CHECK*, FLASH. HOW COME YOU'RE SO READY TO BELIEVE THAT THIS GUY IS REALLY FROM A PARALLEL...

UH... WHAT'S *THAT*?

IT'S A *HAIR FOLLICLE* FROM HOT PURSUIT. I GOT IT WHEN HE TOOK OFF HIS HELMET.

AND YOU MOVED SO FAST HE COULDN'T SEE YOU? *COOL.*

I'M AS SKEPTICAL AS YOU ARE, BART, BUT NOT AS IMPATIENT.

I'M GOING TO THE LAB TO DO A *DNA* TEST TO SEE IF AT LEAST THE *DOPPEL-GANGER* PART OF HOT PURSUIT'S STORY IS *TRUE.*

I'LL COME WITH YOU.

NO, YOU WON'T.

WELL, WHAT CAN I DO THEN?

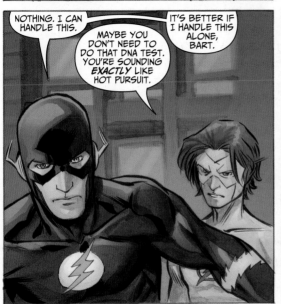

NOTHING. I CAN HANDLE THIS.

MAYBE YOU DON'T NEED TO DO THAT DNA TEST. YOU'RE SOUNDING *EXACTLY* LIKE HOT PURSUIT.

IT'S BETTER IF I HANDLE THIS ALONE, BART.

WAIT A SECOND. DID YOU NOT COME TO THE PICNIC BECAUSE OF ME?

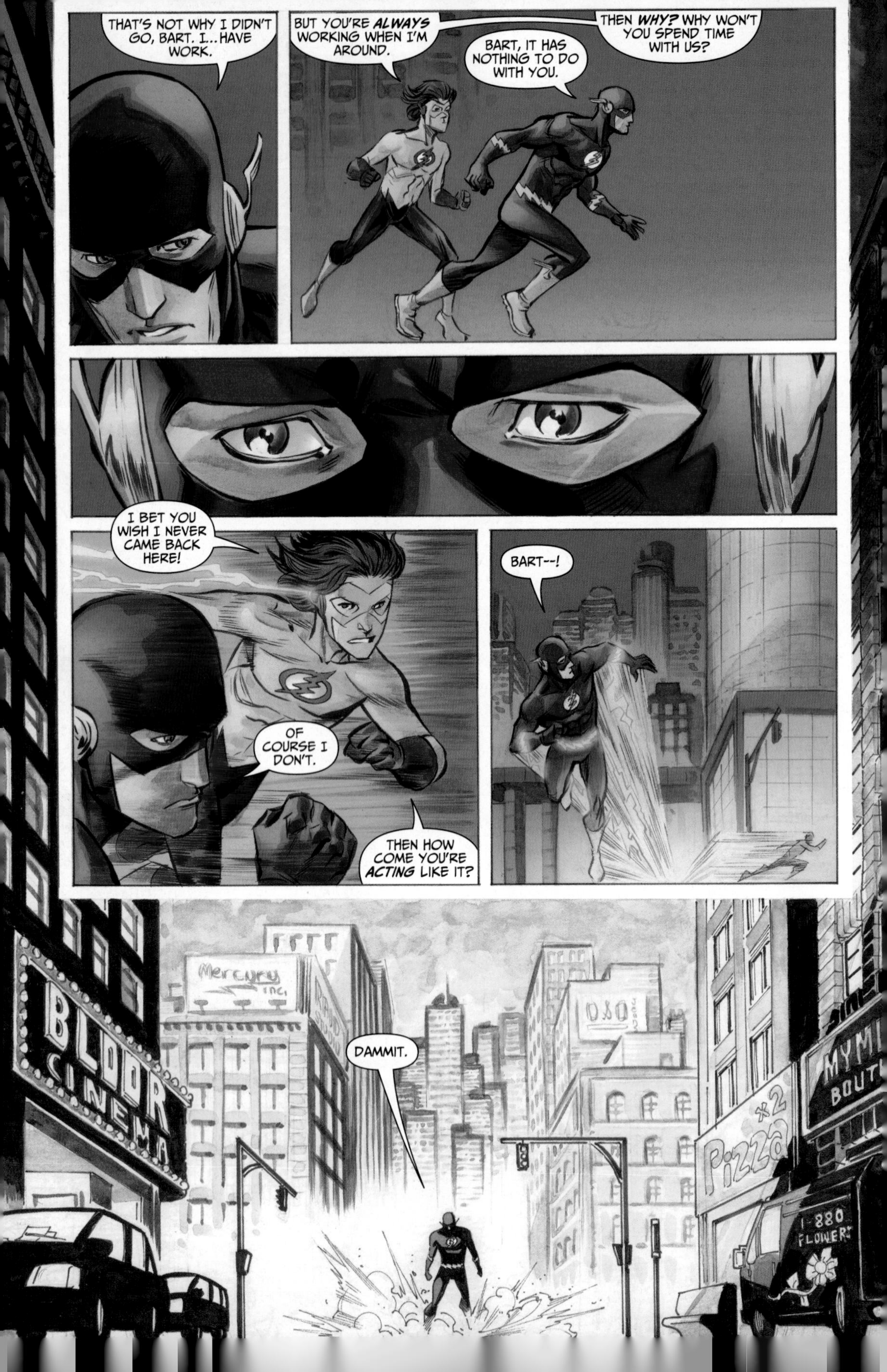

THAT'S NOT WHY I DIDN'T GO, BART. I... HAVE WORK.
BUT YOU'RE *ALWAYS* WORKING WHEN I'M AROUND.
THEN *WHY?* WHY WON'T YOU SPEND TIME WITH US?
BART, IT HAS NOTHING TO DO WITH YOU.
I BET YOU WISH I NEVER CAME BACK HERE!
OF COURSE I DON'T.
THEN HOW COME YOU'RE *ACTING* LIKE IT?
BART--!
Mercury Inc.
BLOOR CINEMA
Pizza
1-880 FLOWERS
DAMMIT.

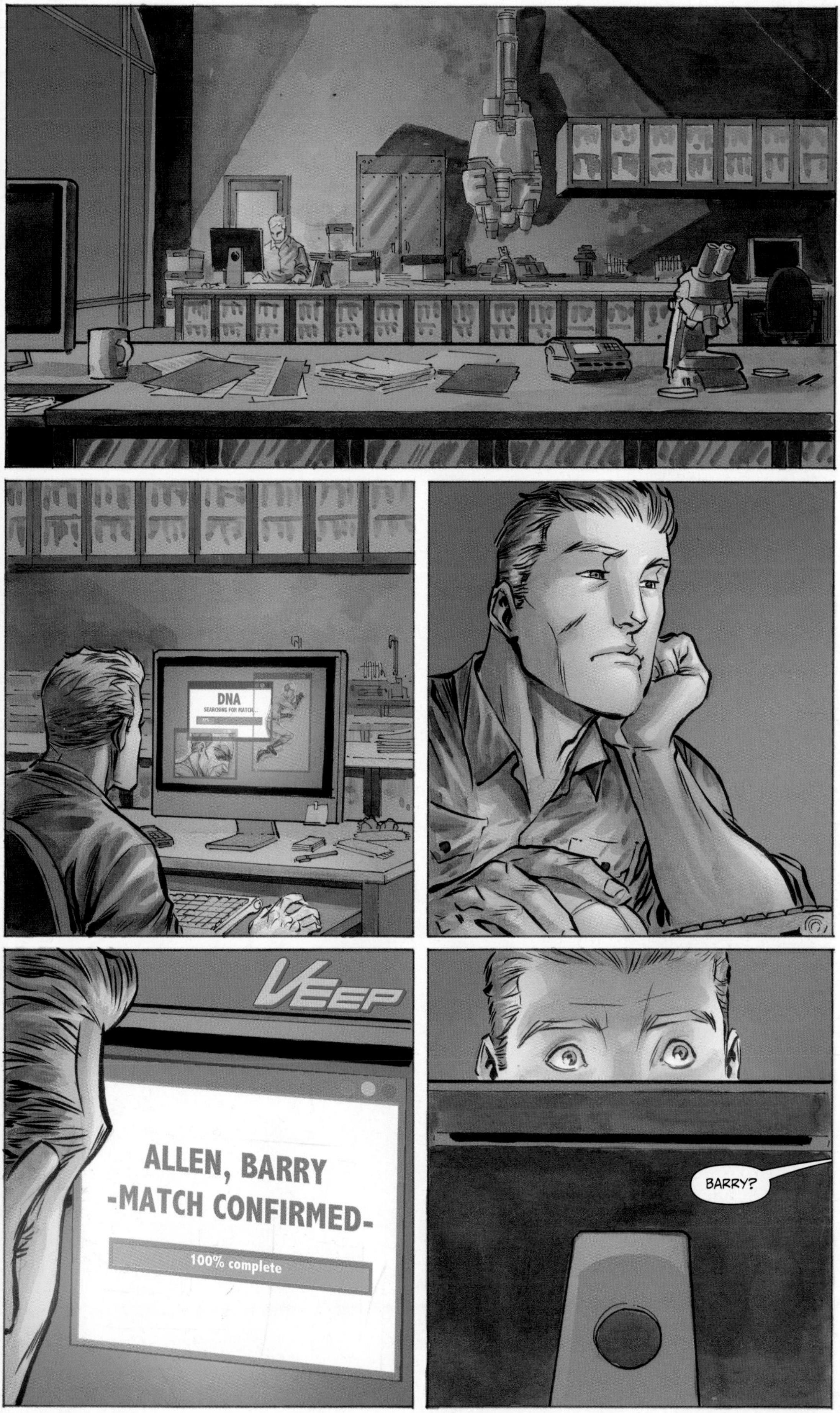
DNA
SEARCHING FOR MATCH...
VEEP
ALLEN, BARRY
-MATCH CONFIRMED-
100% complete
BARRY?

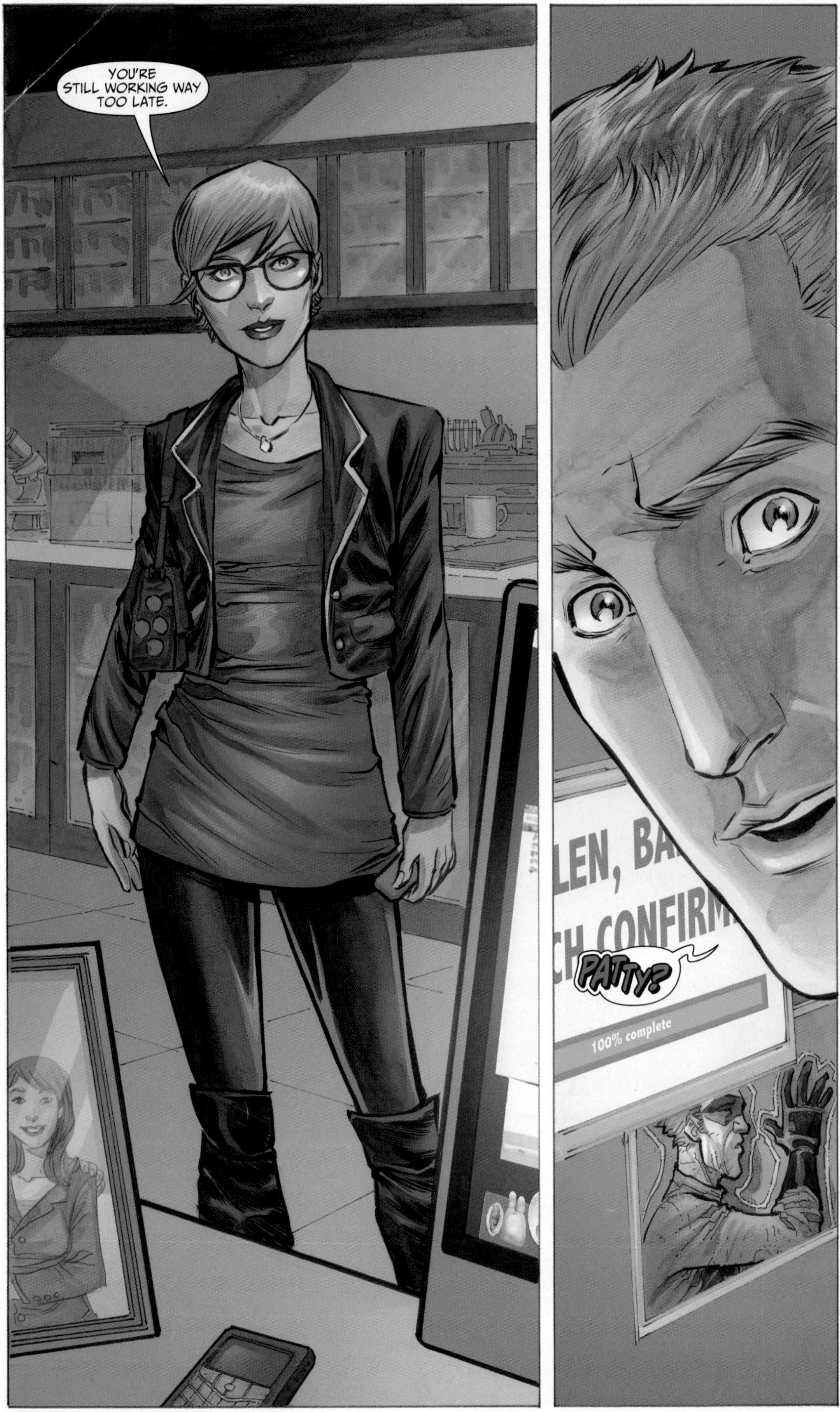
YOU'RE STILL WORKING WAY TOO LATE.
LEN, BA
CH CONFIRM
PATTY?
100% complete

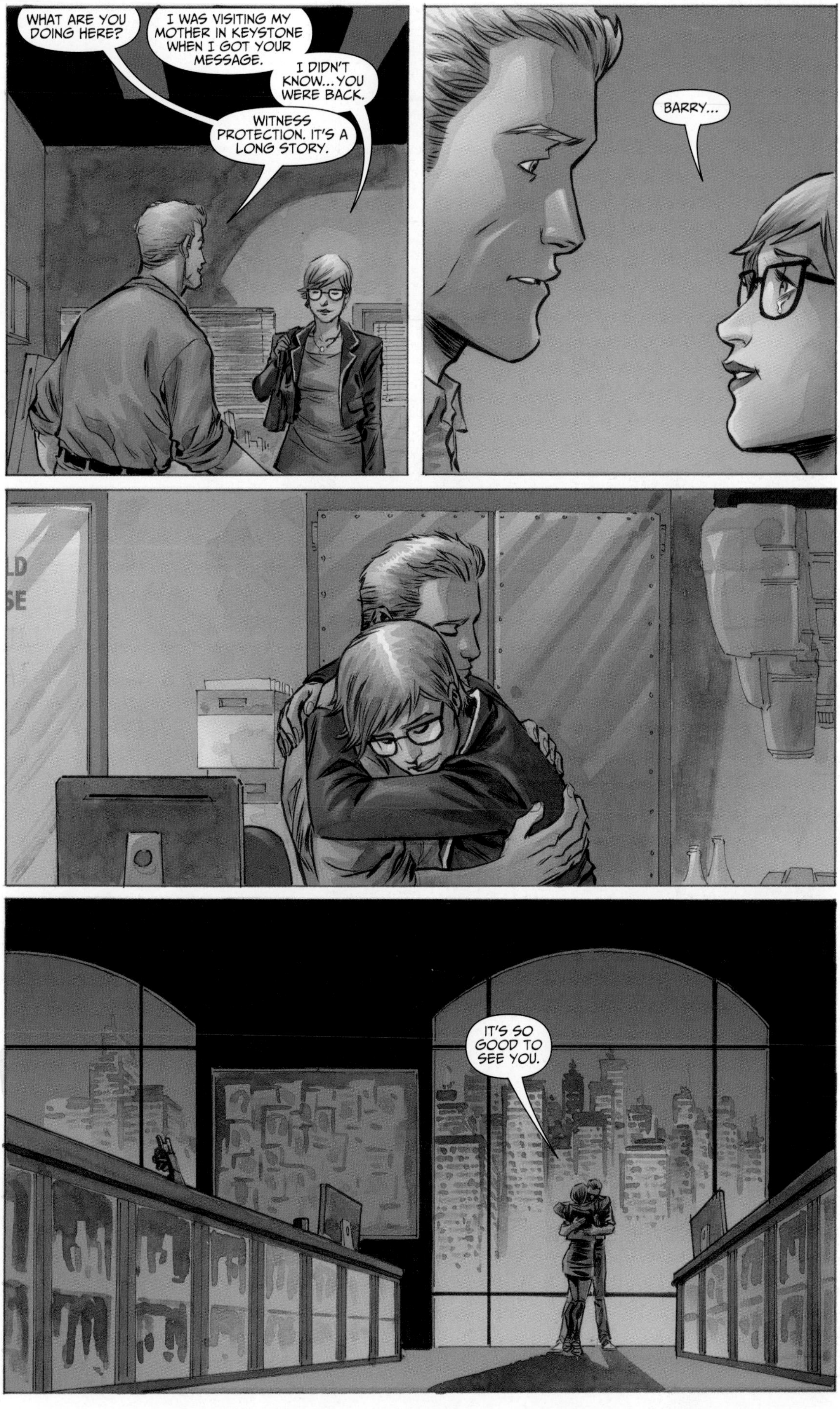
WHAT ARE YOU DOING HERE?
I WAS VISITING MY MOTHER IN KEYSTONE WHEN I GOT YOUR MESSAGE.
I DIDN'T KNOW...YOU WERE BACK.
WITNESS PROTECTION. IT'S A LONG STORY.
BARRY...
IT'S SO GOOD TO SEE YOU.

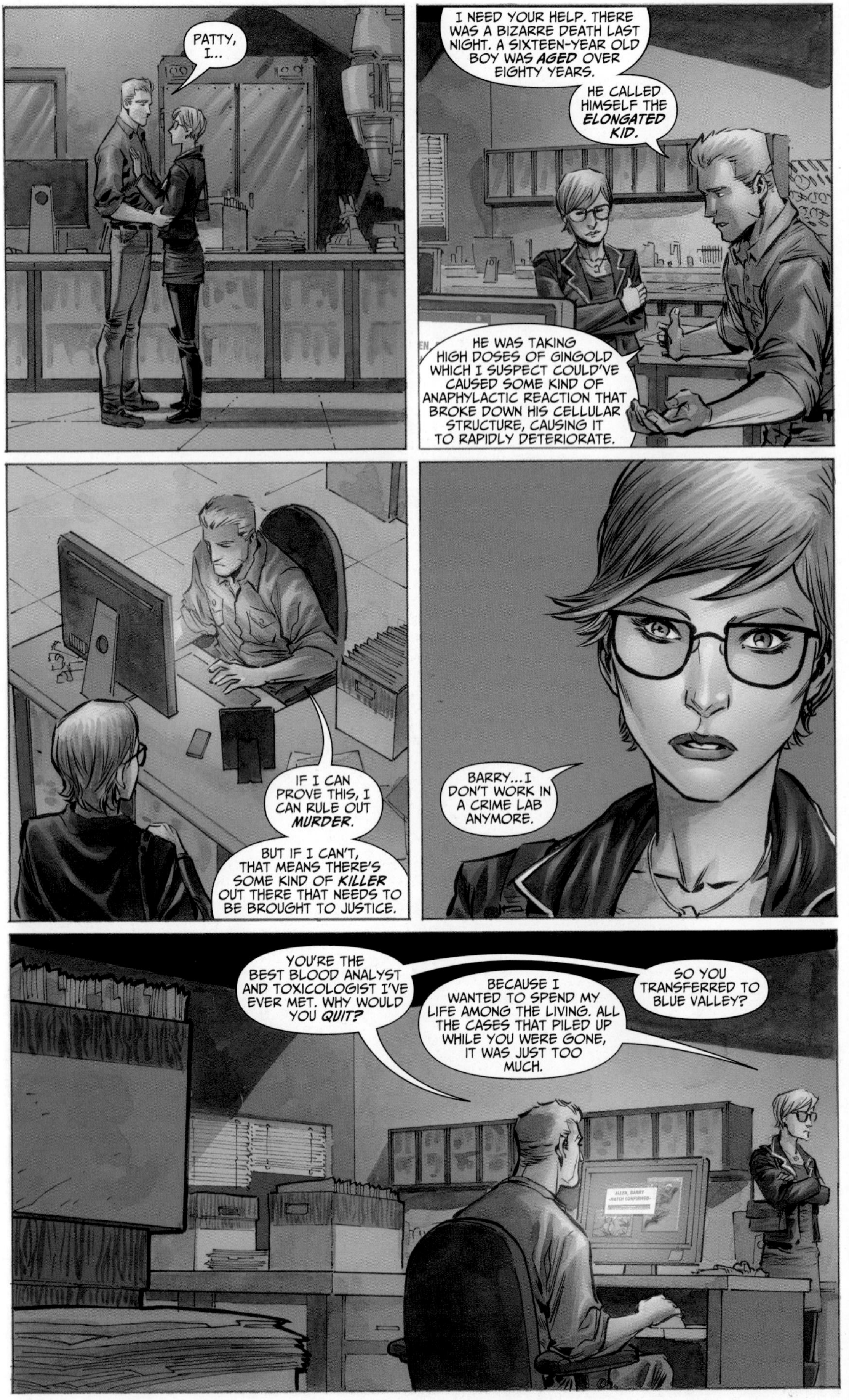
PATTY, I...
I NEED YOUR HELP. THERE WAS A BIZARRE DEATH LAST NIGHT. A SIXTEEN-YEAR OLD BOY WAS AGED OVER EIGHTY YEARS.
HE CALLED HIMSELF THE ELONGATED KID.
HE WAS TAKING HIGH DOSES OF GINGOLD WHICH I SUSPECT COULD'VE CAUSED SOME KIND OF ANAPHYLACTIC REACTION THAT BROKE DOWN HIS CELLULAR STRUCTURE, CAUSING IT TO RAPIDLY DETERIORATE.
IF I CAN PROVE THIS, I CAN RULE OUT MURDER.
BUT IF I CAN'T, THAT MEANS THERE'S SOME KIND OF KILLER OUT THERE THAT NEEDS TO BE BROUGHT TO JUSTICE.
BARRY...I DON'T WORK IN A CRIME LAB ANYMORE.
YOU'RE THE BEST BLOOD ANALYST AND TOXICOLOGIST I'VE EVER MET. WHY WOULD YOU QUIT?
BECAUSE I WANTED TO SPEND MY LIFE AMONG THE LIVING. ALL THE CASES THAT PILED UP WHILE YOU WERE GONE, IT WAS JUST TOO MUCH.
SO YOU TRANSFERRED TO BLUE VALLEY?

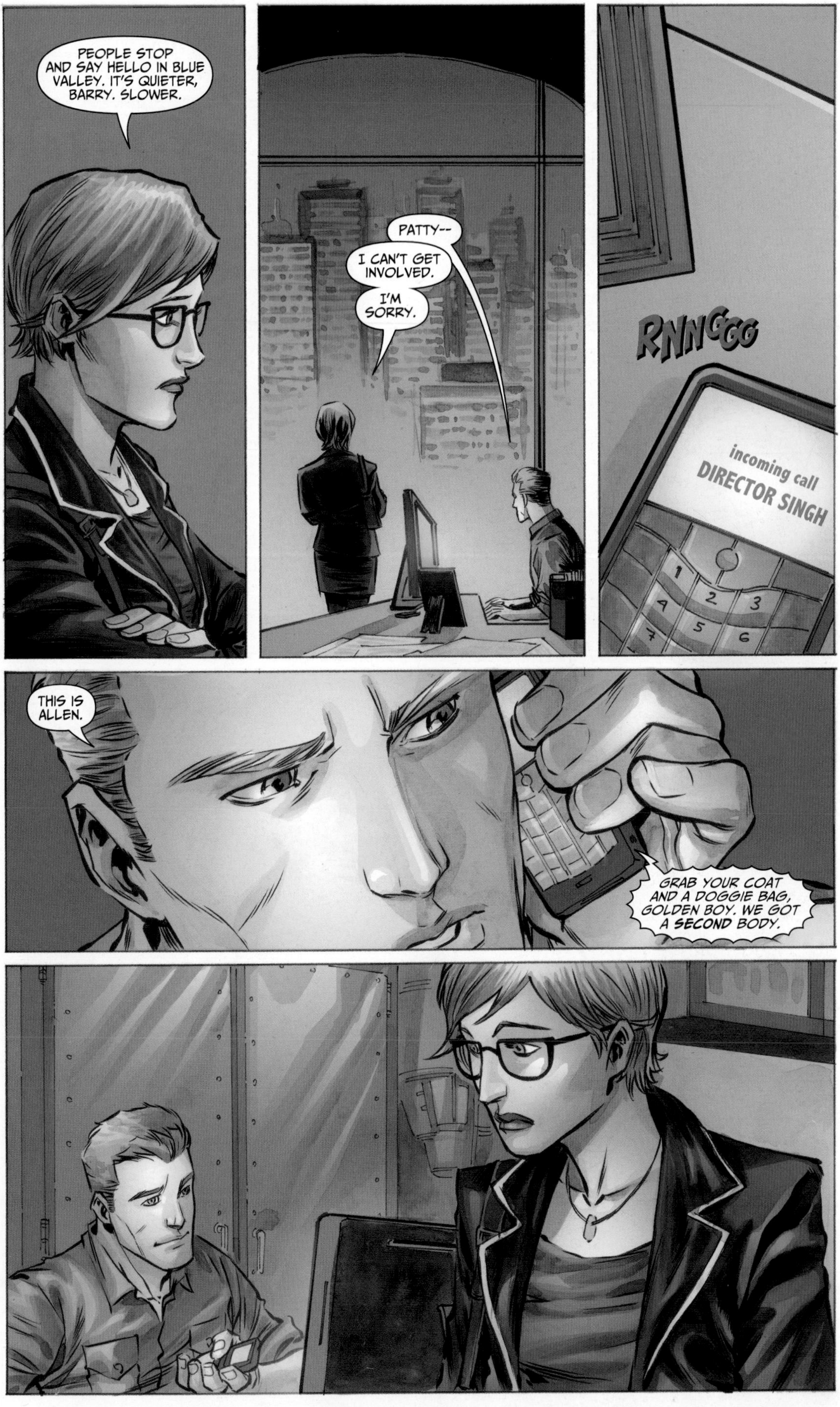
PEOPLE STOP AND SAY HELLO IN BLUE VALLEY. IT'S QUIETER, BARRY. SLOWER.
PATTY--
I CAN'T GET INVOLVED.
I'M SORRY.
RNNGGG
incoming call
DIRECTOR SINGH
THIS IS ALLEN.
GRAB YOUR COAT AND A DOGGIE BAG, GOLDEN BOY. WE GOT A SECOND BODY.

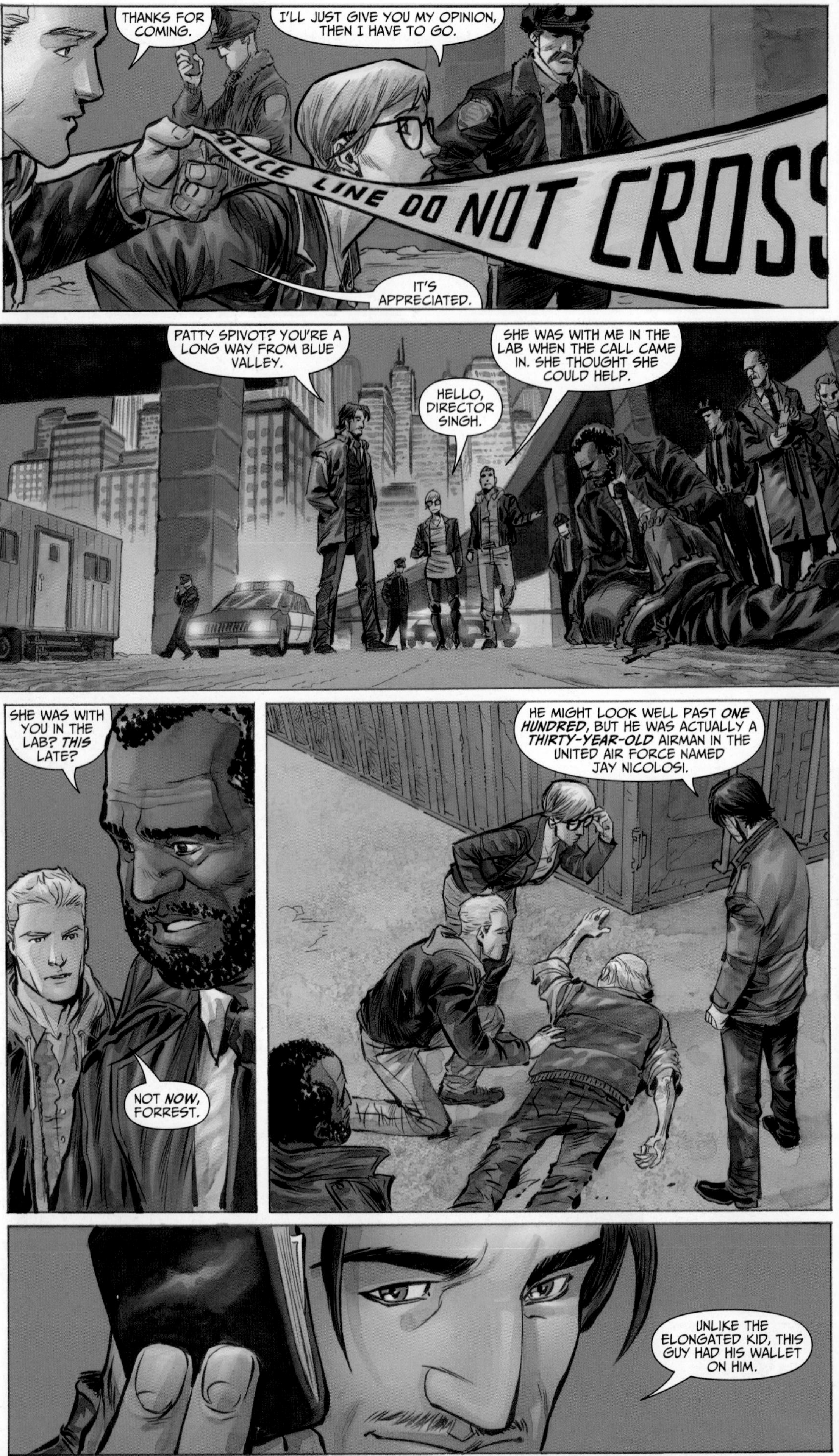
THANKS FOR COMING.
I'LL JUST GIVE YOU MY OPINION, THEN I HAVE TO GO.
POLICE LINE DO NOT CROSS
IT'S APPRECIATED.
PATTY SPIVOT? YOU'RE A LONG WAY FROM BLUE VALLEY.
HELLO, DIRECTOR SINGH.
SHE WAS WITH ME IN THE LAB WHEN THE CALL CAME IN. SHE THOUGHT SHE COULD HELP.
SHE WAS WITH YOU IN THE LAB? *THIS* LATE?
NOT *NOW*, FORREST.
HE MIGHT LOOK WELL PAST *ONE HUNDRED*, BUT HE WAS ACTUALLY A *THIRTY-YEAR-OLD* AIRMAN IN THE UNITED AIR FORCE NAMED JAY NICOLOSI.
UNLIKE THE ELONGATED KID, THIS GUY HAD HIS WALLET ON HIM.

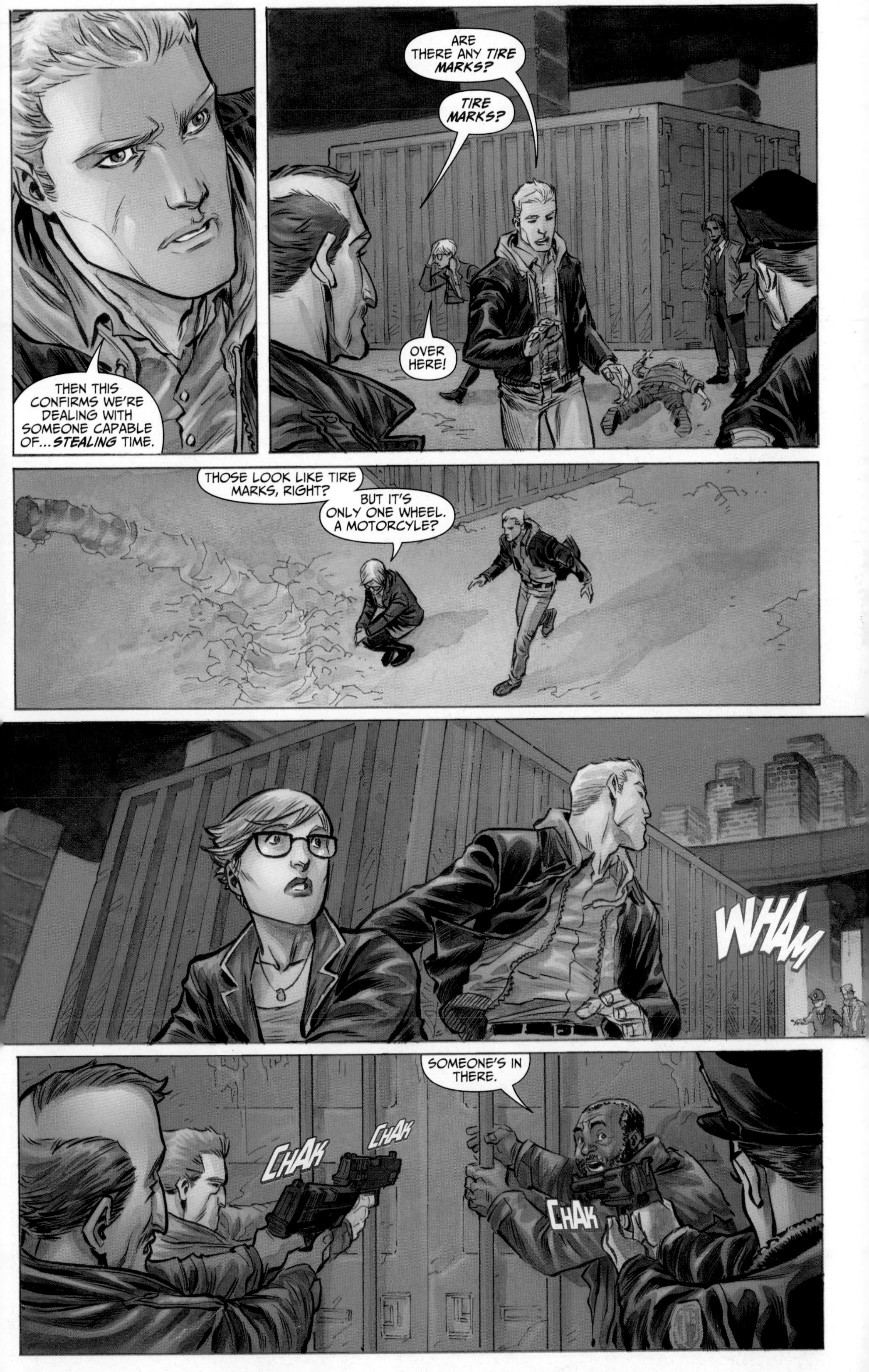
THEN THIS CONFIRMS WE'RE DEALING WITH SOMEONE CAPABLE OF...STEALING TIME.
ARE THERE ANY TIRE MARKS?
TIRE MARKS?
OVER HERE!
THOSE LOOK LIKE TIRE MARKS, RIGHT?
BUT IT'S ONLY ONE WHEEL. A MOTORCYLE?
WHAM
SOMEONE'S IN THERE.
CHAK
CHAK
CHAK

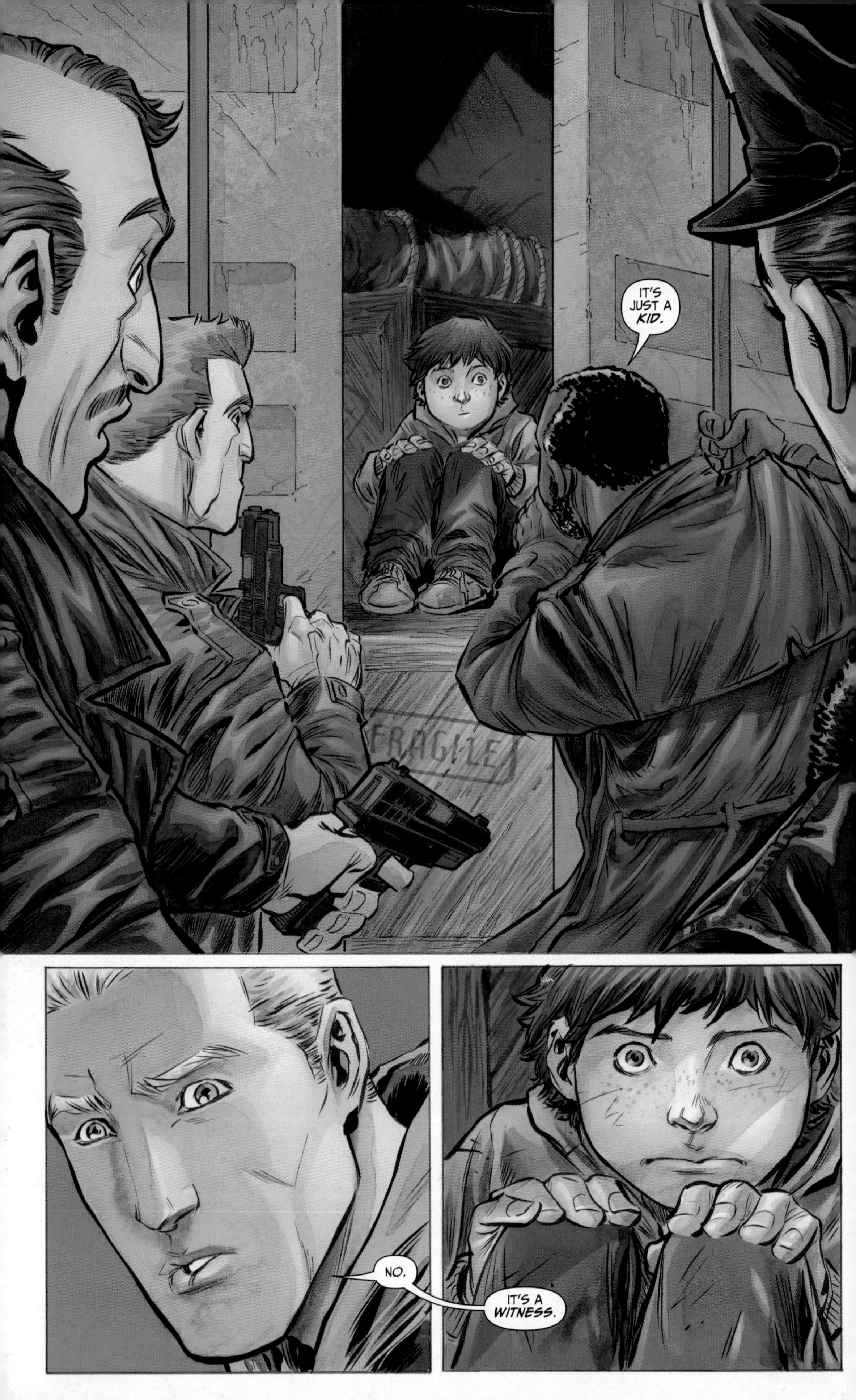
IT'S JUST A *KID*.
FRAGILE
NO.
IT'S A *WITNESS*.

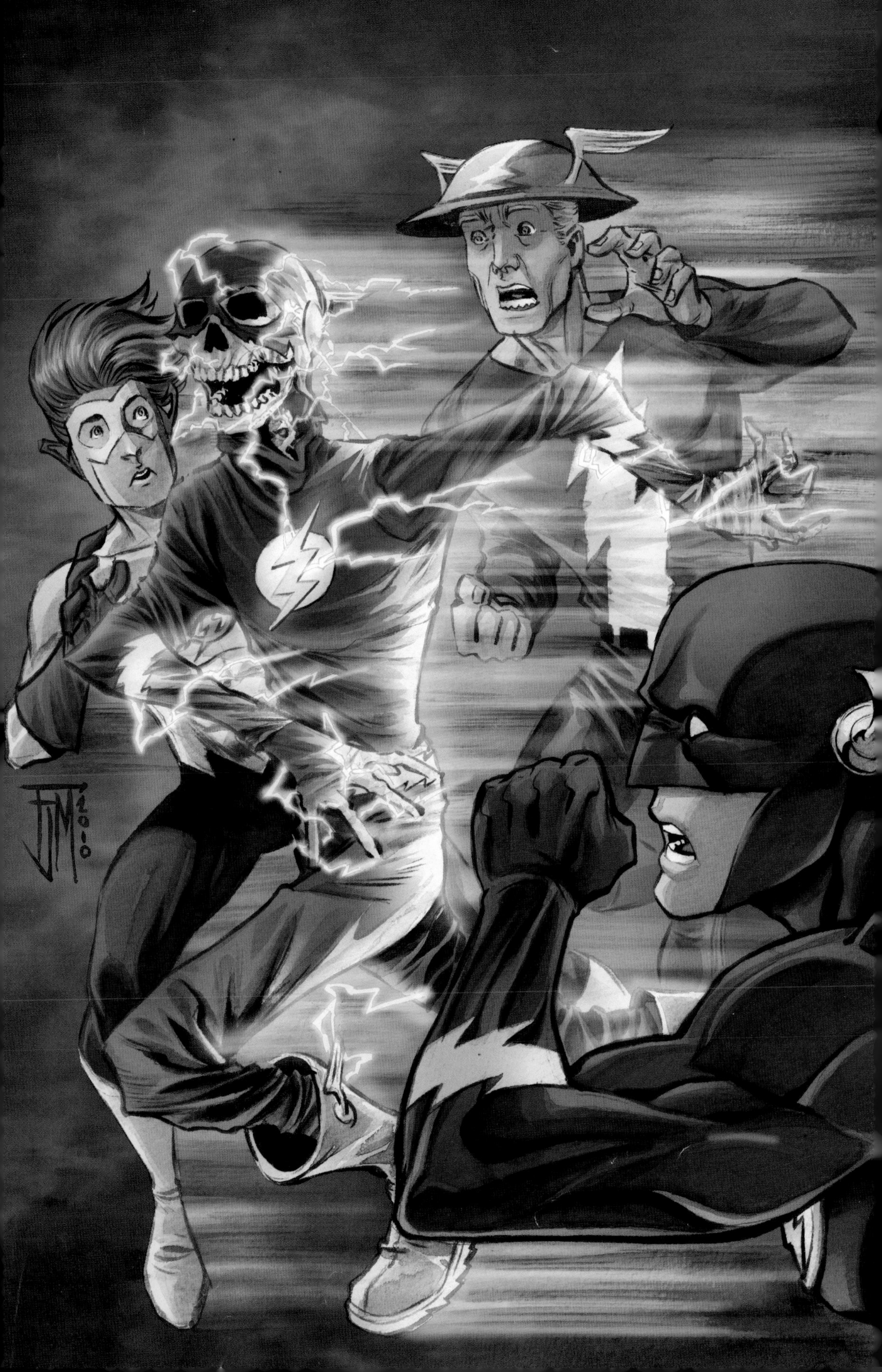
JIM 2010

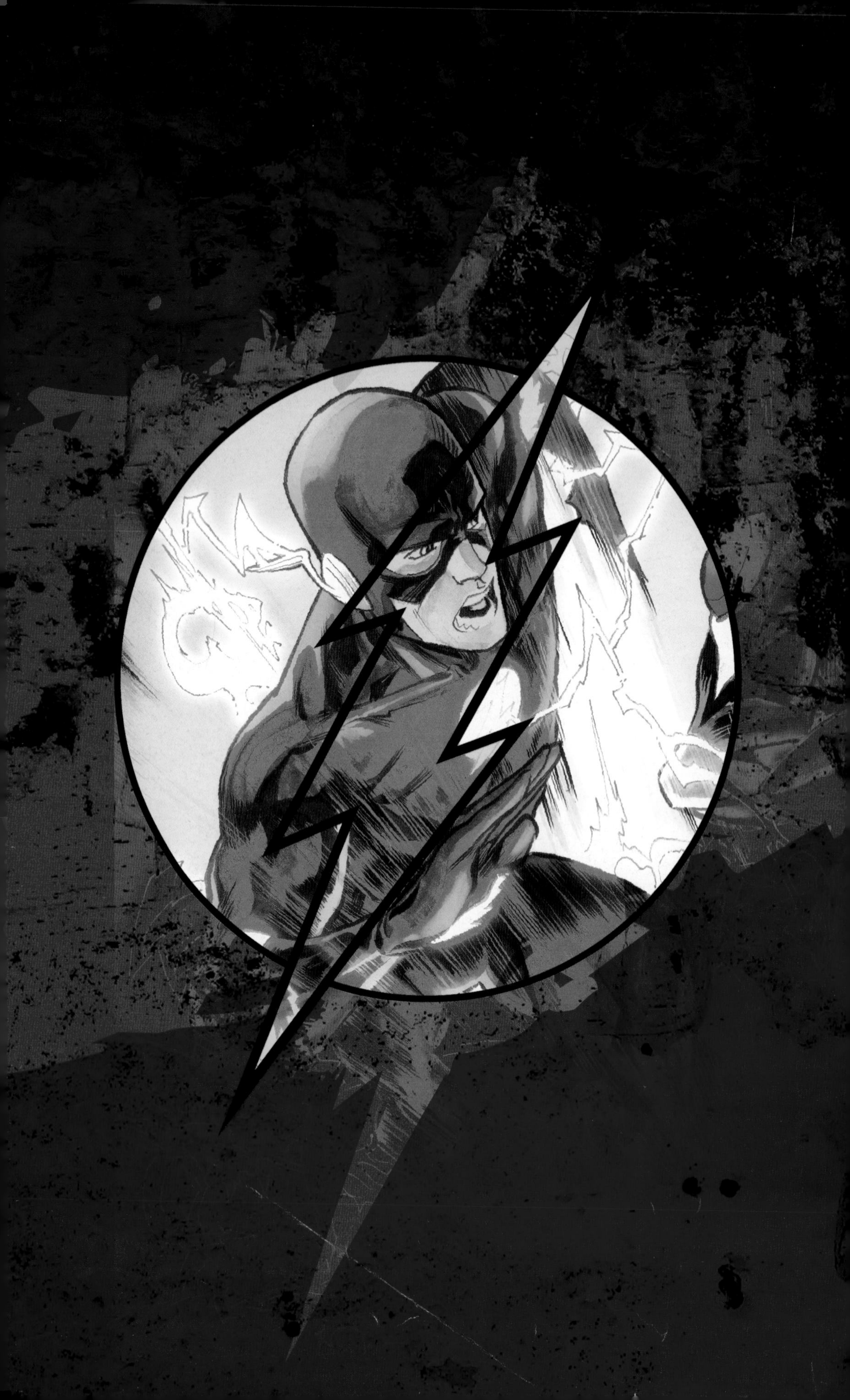

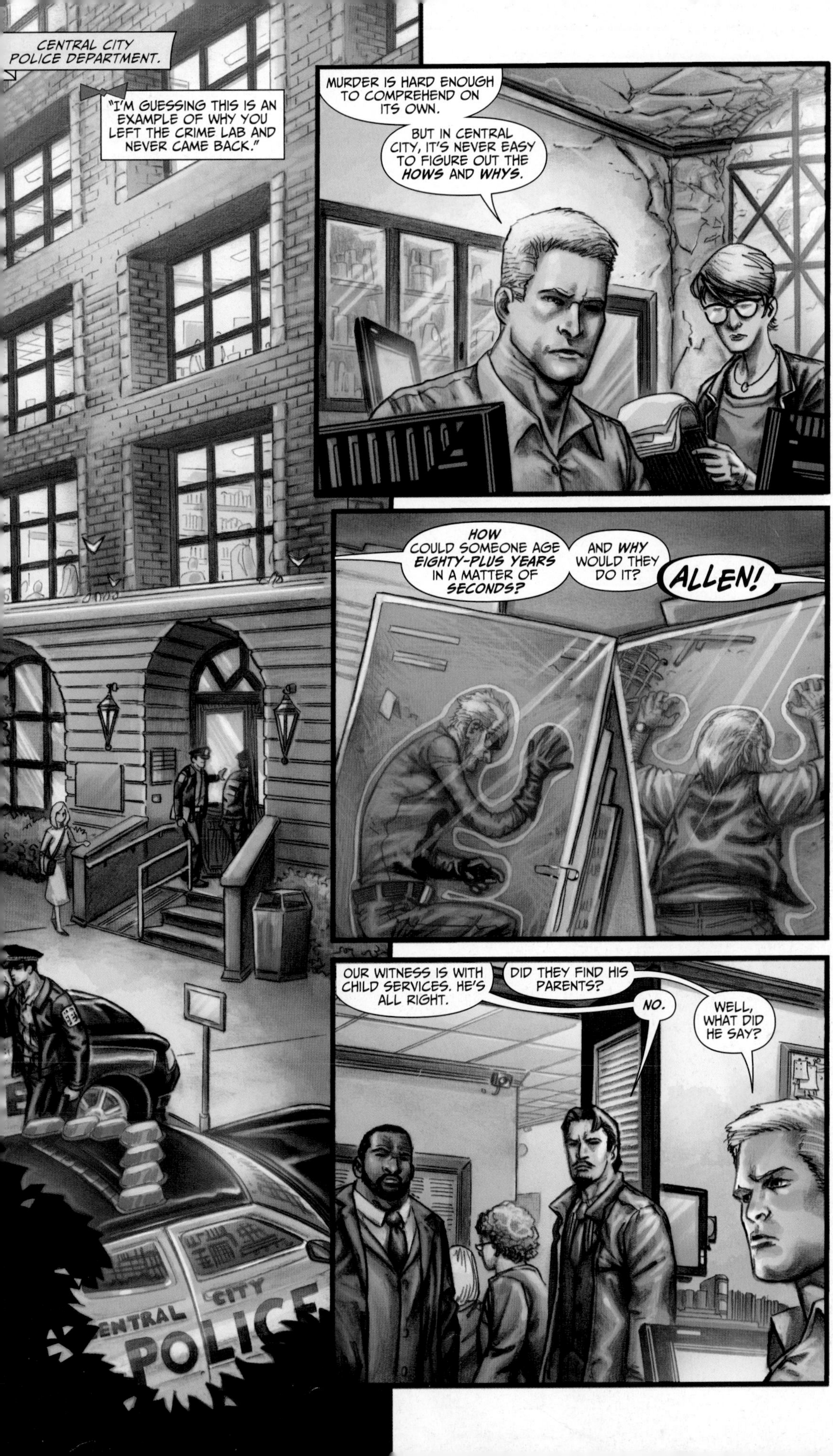
CENTRAL CITY POLICE DEPARTMENT.
"I'M GUESSING THIS IS AN EXAMPLE OF WHY YOU LEFT THE CRIME LAB AND NEVER CAME BACK."
MURDER IS HARD ENOUGH TO COMPREHEND ON ITS OWN.
BUT IN CENTRAL CITY, IT'S NEVER EASY TO FIGURE OUT THE HOWS AND WHYS.
HOW COULD SOMEONE AGE EIGHTY-PLUS YEARS IN A MATTER OF SECONDS?
AND WHY WOULD THEY DO IT?
ALLEN!
OUR WITNESS IS WITH CHILD SERVICES. HE'S ALL RIGHT.
DID THEY FIND HIS PARENTS?
NO.
WELL, WHAT DID HE SAY?
CENTRAL CITY POLICE

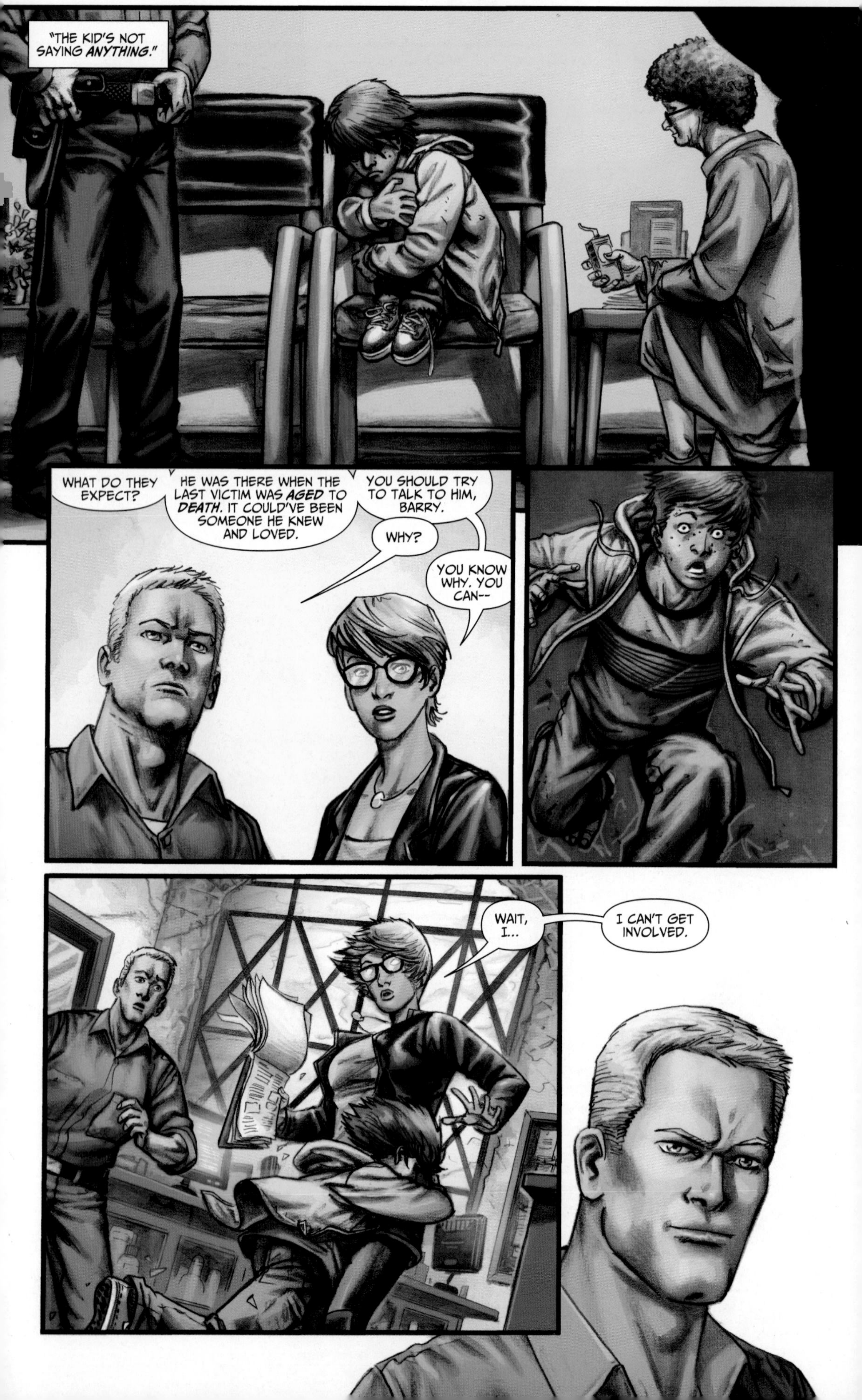
"THE KID'S NOT SAYING *ANYTHING*."
WHAT DO THEY EXPECT?
HE WAS THERE WHEN THE LAST VICTIM WAS *AGED* TO *DEATH*. IT COULD'VE BEEN SOMEONE HE KNEW AND LOVED.
YOU SHOULD TRY TO TALK TO HIM, BARRY.
WHY?
YOU KNOW WHY. YOU CAN--
WAIT, I...
I CAN'T GET INVOLVED.

I KNOW I'M ASKING A LOT HERE, PATTY, BUT IT'S ONLY BECAUSE I KNOW YOU CAN HELP.

THIS BOY OBVIOUSLY SEES THE *KINDNESS* IN YOUR EYES.

HE SEES WHAT I DO.

I...

I'LL GO TO THE CAFETERIA AND SEE IF I CAN GET HIM TO EAT SOMETHING.

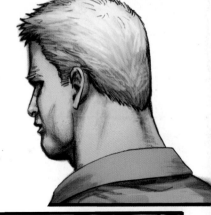

YOU REALLY THINK IT'S SMART TO HAND OVER THIS WITNESS TO A WALLFLOWER LIKE PATTY SPIVOT?

IF ANYONE CAN MAKE HIM FEEL SAFE...

"PATTY CAN."

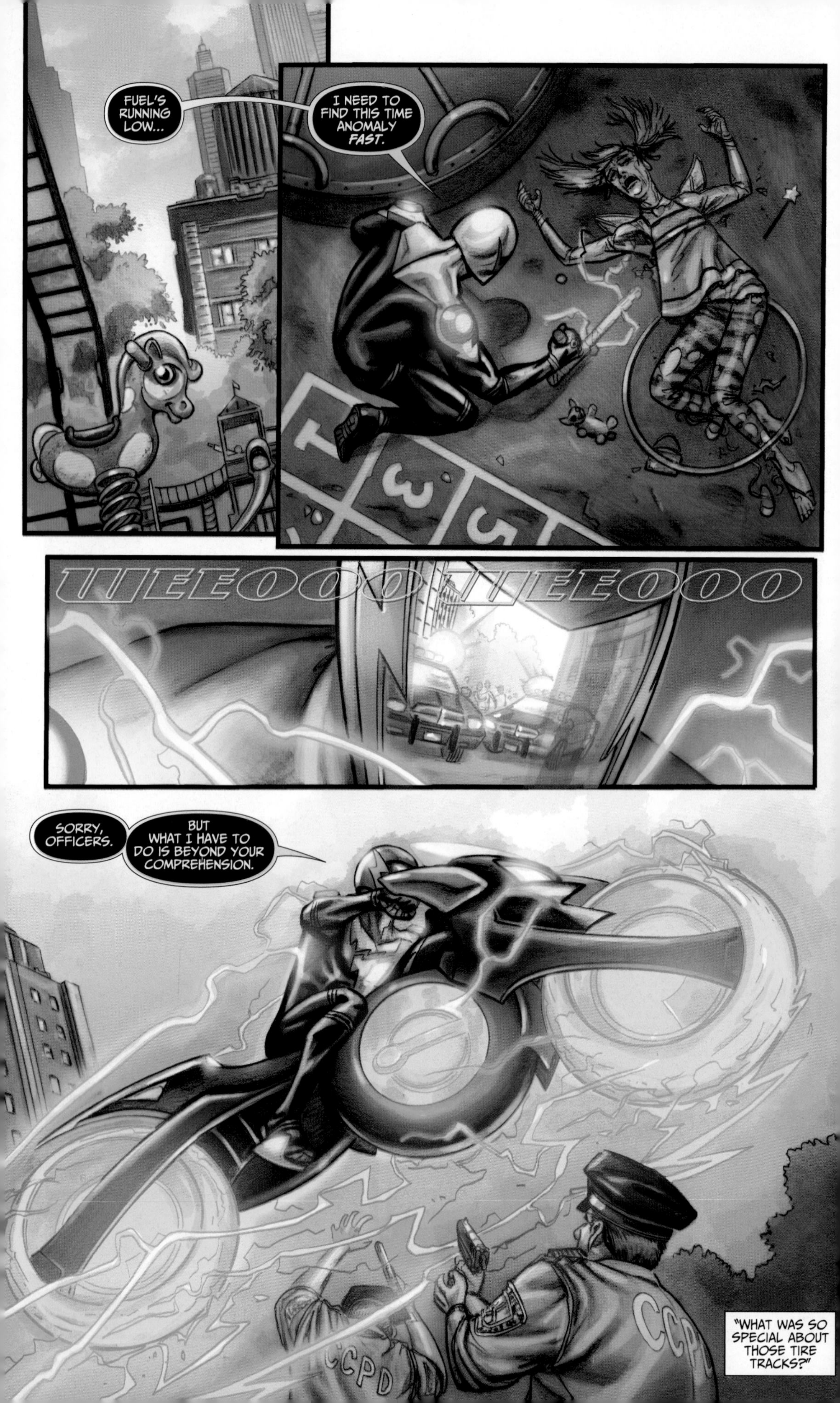

FUEL'S RUNNING LOW...
I NEED TO FIND THIS TIME ANOMALY FAST.
UEEOOO UEEOOO
SORRY, OFFICERS.
BUT WHAT I HAVE TO DO IS BEYOND YOUR COMPREHENSION.
"WHAT WAS SO SPECIAL ABOUT THOSE TIRE TRACKS?"
CCPD

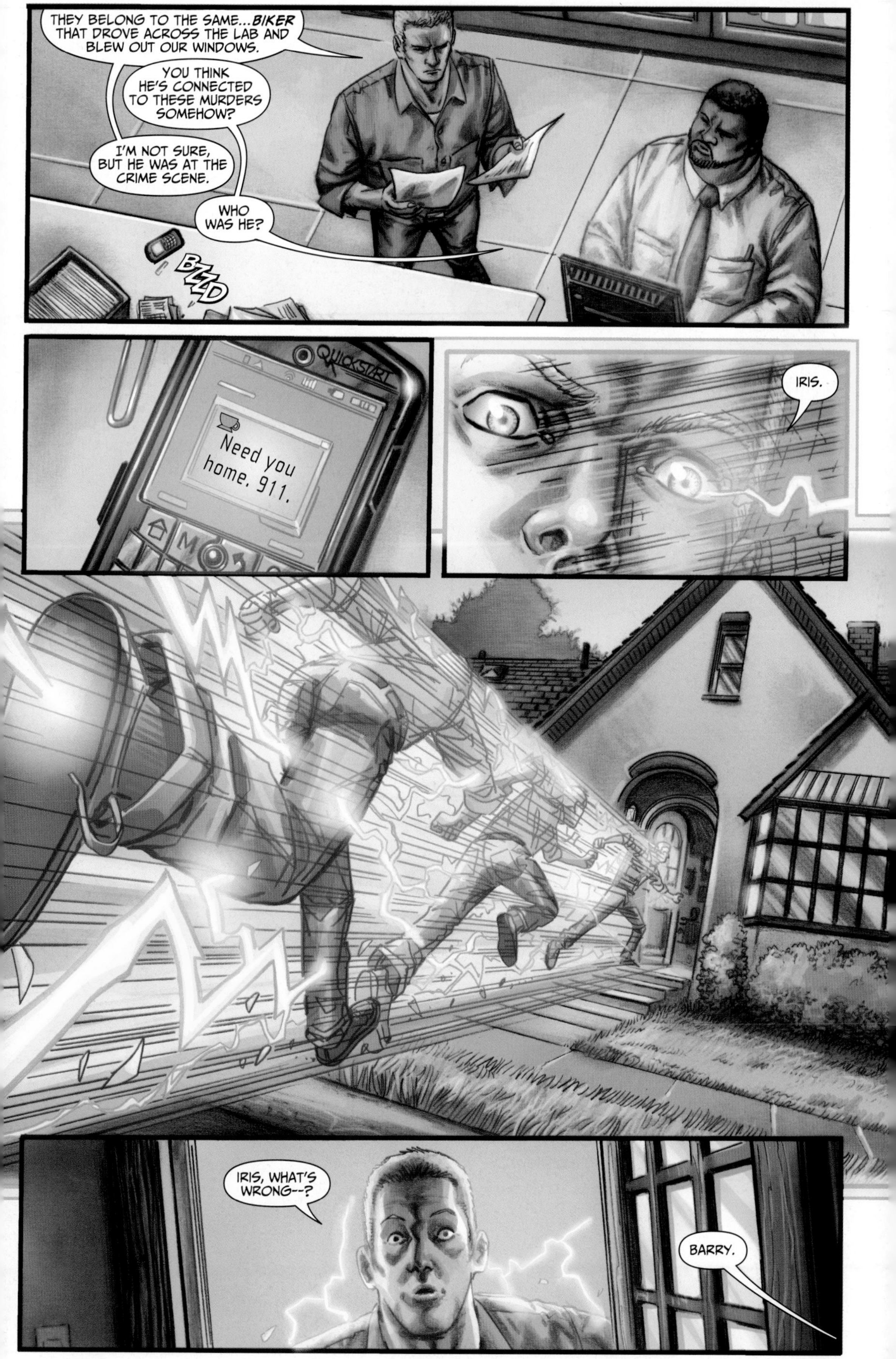
THEY BELONG TO THE SAME...BIKER THAT DROVE ACROSS THE LAB AND BLEW OUT OUR WINDOWS.
YOU THINK HE'S CONNECTED TO THESE MURDERS SOMEHOW?
I'M NOT SURE, BUT HE WAS AT THE CRIME SCENE.
WHO WAS HE?
BZZD
QUICKSTART
Need you home. 911.
IRIS.
IRIS, WHAT'S WRONG--?
BARRY.

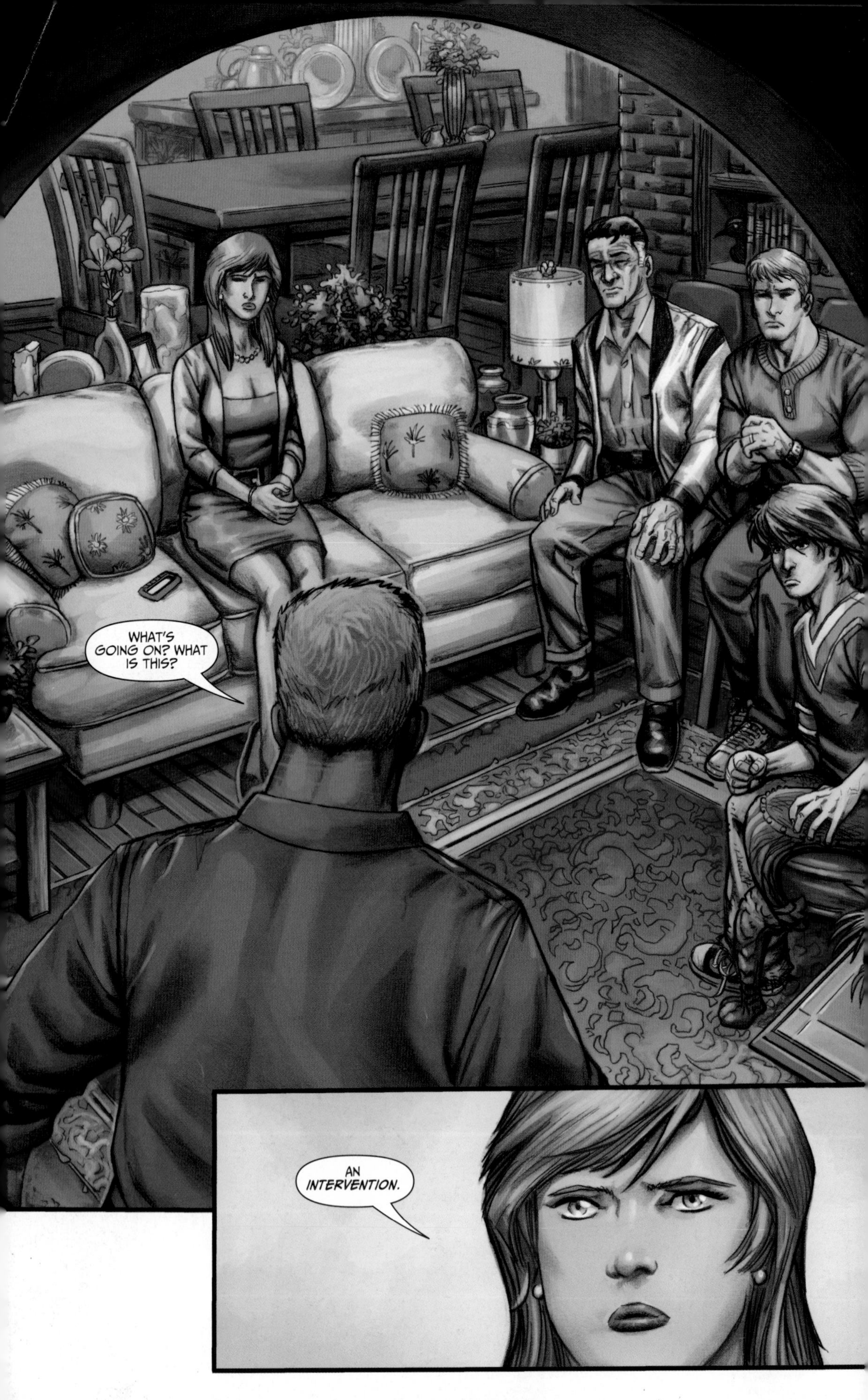
WHAT'S GOING ON? WHAT IS THIS?
AN *INTERVENTION.*

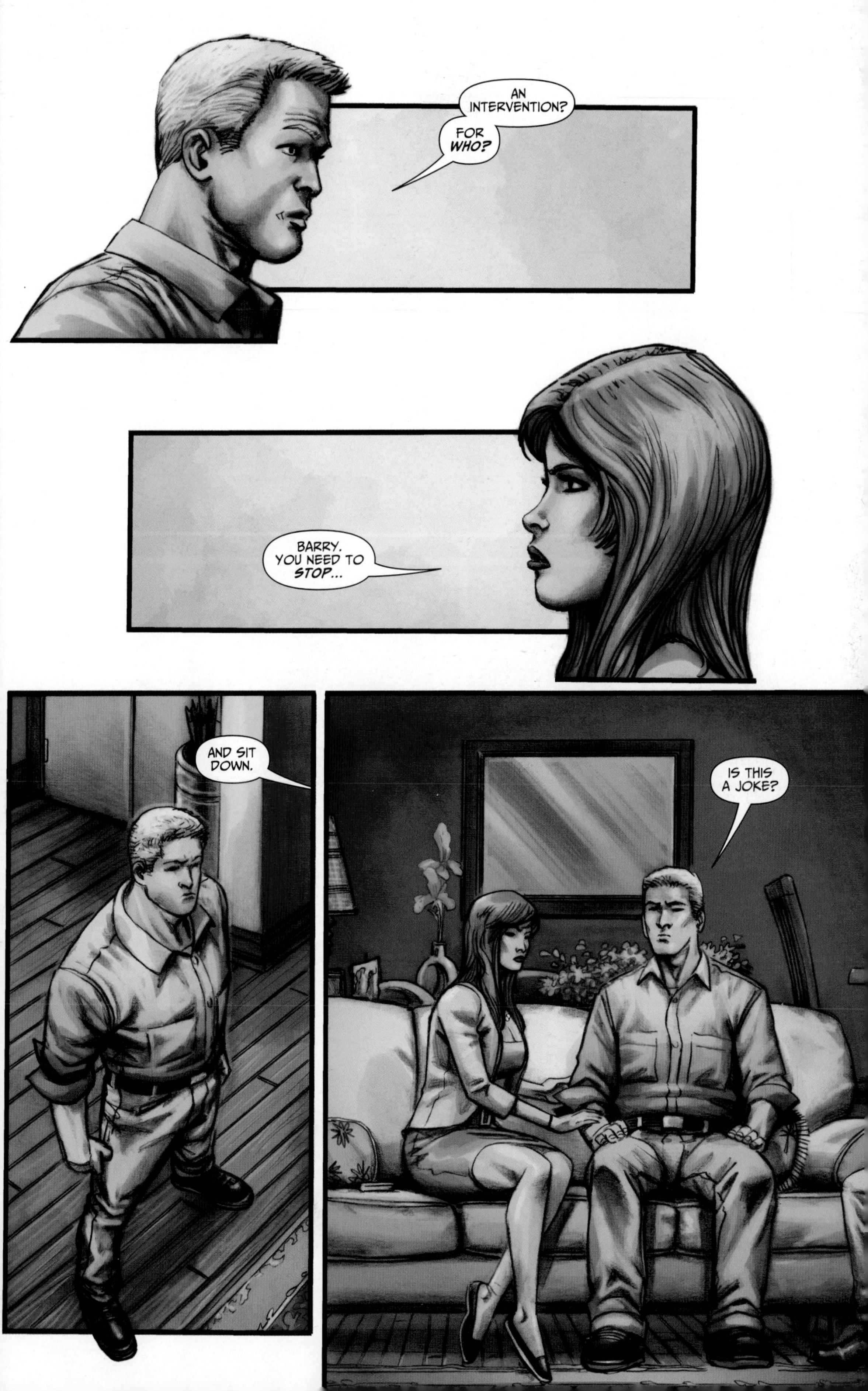
AN INTERVENTION?
FOR WHO?
BARRY. YOU NEED TO STOP...
AND SIT DOWN.
IS THIS A JOKE?

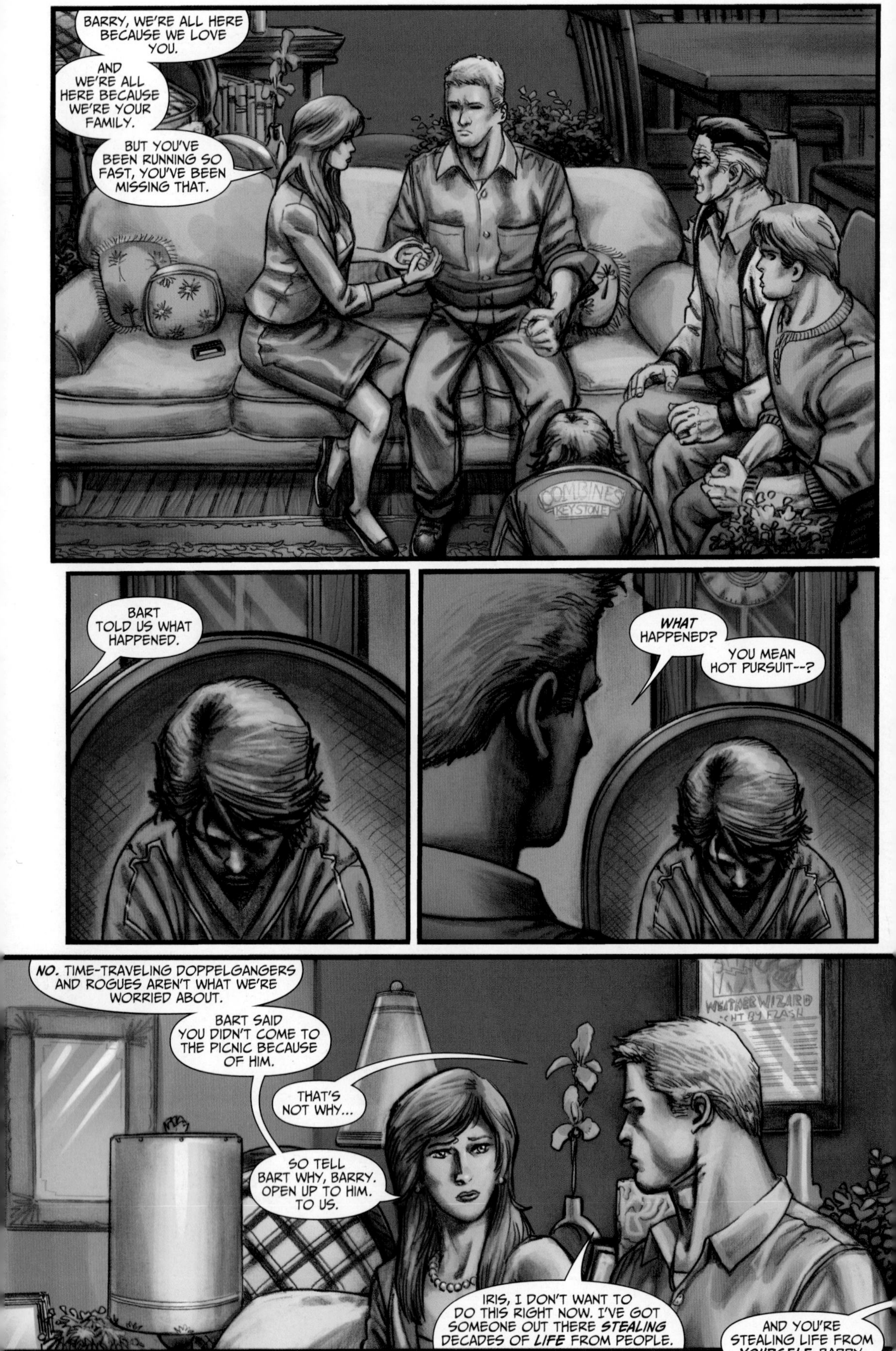
BARRY, WE'RE ALL HERE BECAUSE WE LOVE YOU.
AND WE'RE ALL HERE BECAUSE WE'RE YOUR FAMILY.
BUT YOU'VE BEEN RUNNING SO FAST, YOU'VE BEEN MISSING THAT.
COMBINES
KEYSTONE
BART TOLD US WHAT HAPPENED.
WHAT HAPPENED?
YOU MEAN HOT PURSUIT--?
NO. TIME-TRAVELING DOPPELGANGERS AND ROGUES AREN'T WHAT WE'RE WORRIED ABOUT.
BART SAID YOU DIDN'T COME TO THE PICNIC BECAUSE OF HIM.
THAT'S NOT WHY...
SO TELL BART WHY, BARRY. OPEN UP TO HIM. TO US.
IRIS, I DON'T WANT TO DO THIS RIGHT NOW. I'VE GOT SOMEONE OUT THERE STEALING DECADES OF LIFE FROM PEOPLE.
AND YOU'RE STEALING LIFE FROM YOURSELF, BARRY.

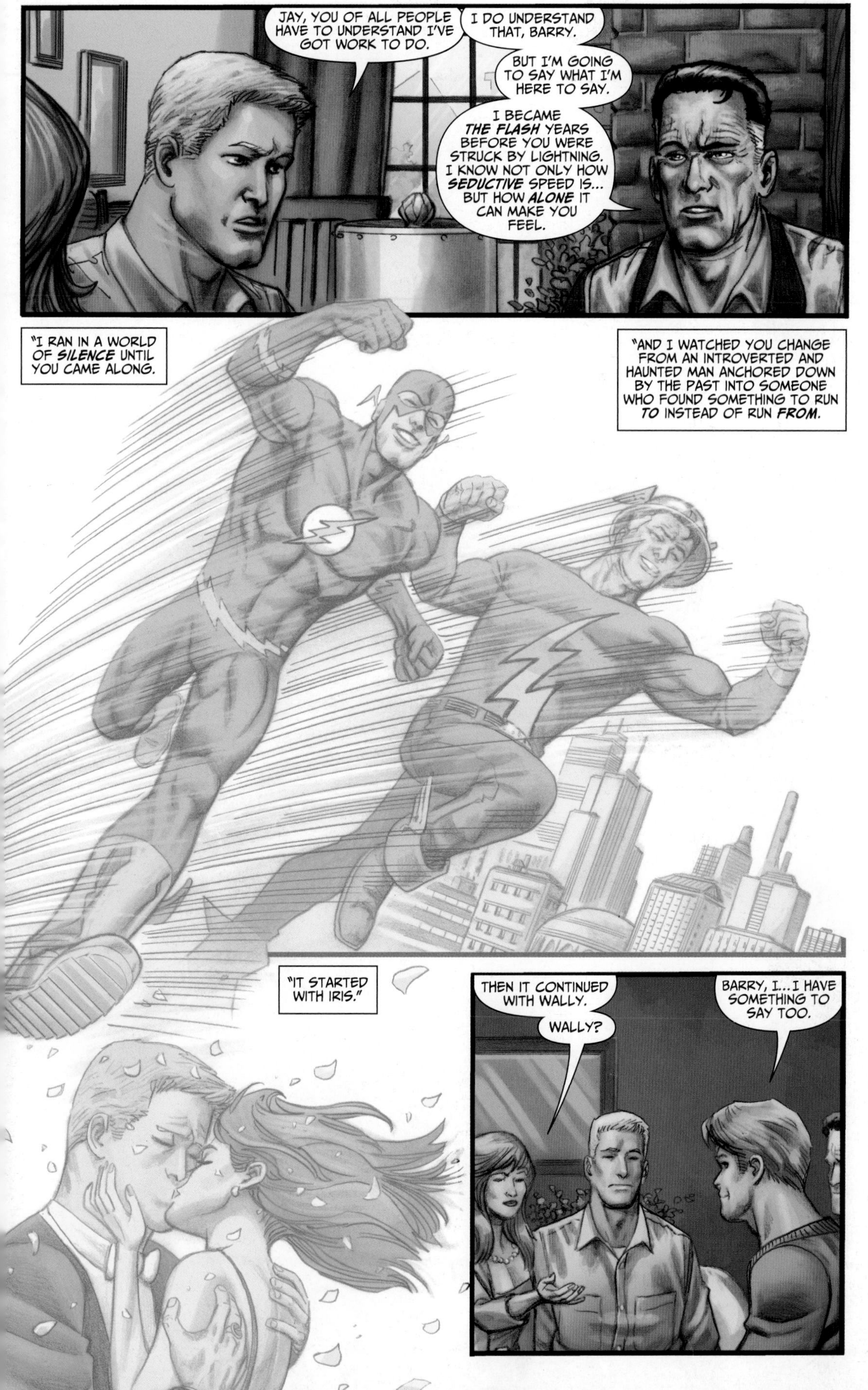
JAY, YOU OF ALL PEOPLE HAVE TO UNDERSTAND I'VE GOT WORK TO DO.
I DO UNDERSTAND THAT, BARRY.
BUT I'M GOING TO SAY WHAT I'M HERE TO SAY.
I BECAME THE FLASH YEARS BEFORE YOU WERE STRUCK BY LIGHTNING. I KNOW NOT ONLY HOW SEDUCTIVE SPEED IS... BUT HOW ALONE IT CAN MAKE YOU FEEL.
"I RAN IN A WORLD OF SILENCE UNTIL YOU CAME ALONG.
"AND I WATCHED YOU CHANGE FROM AN INTROVERTED AND HAUNTED MAN ANCHORED DOWN BY THE PAST INTO SOMEONE WHO FOUND SOMETHING TO RUN TO INSTEAD OF RUN FROM.
"IT STARTED WITH IRIS."
THEN IT CONTINUED WITH WALLY.
WALLY?
BARRY, I...I HAVE SOMETHING TO SAY TOO.

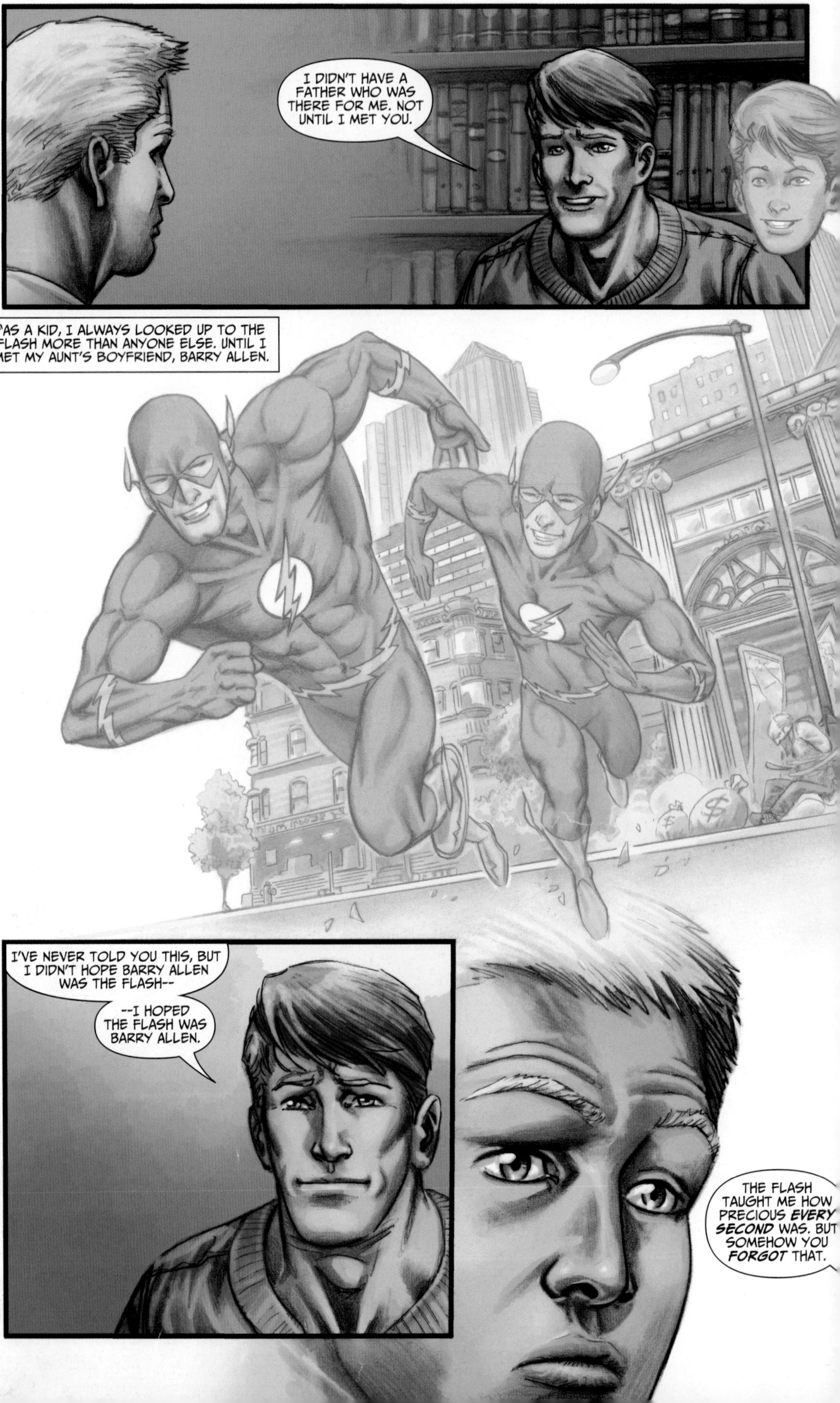
I DIDN'T HAVE A FATHER WHO WAS THERE FOR ME. NOT UNTIL I MET YOU.
"AS A KID, I ALWAYS LOOKED UP TO THE FLASH MORE THAN ANYONE ELSE. UNTIL I MET MY AUNT'S BOYFRIEND, BARRY ALLEN.
I'VE NEVER TOLD YOU THIS, BUT I DIDN'T HOPE BARRY ALLEN WAS THE FLASH--
--I HOPED THE FLASH WAS BARRY ALLEN.
THE FLASH TAUGHT ME HOW PRECIOUS *EVERY SECOND* WAS. BUT SOMEHOW YOU *FORGOT* THAT.

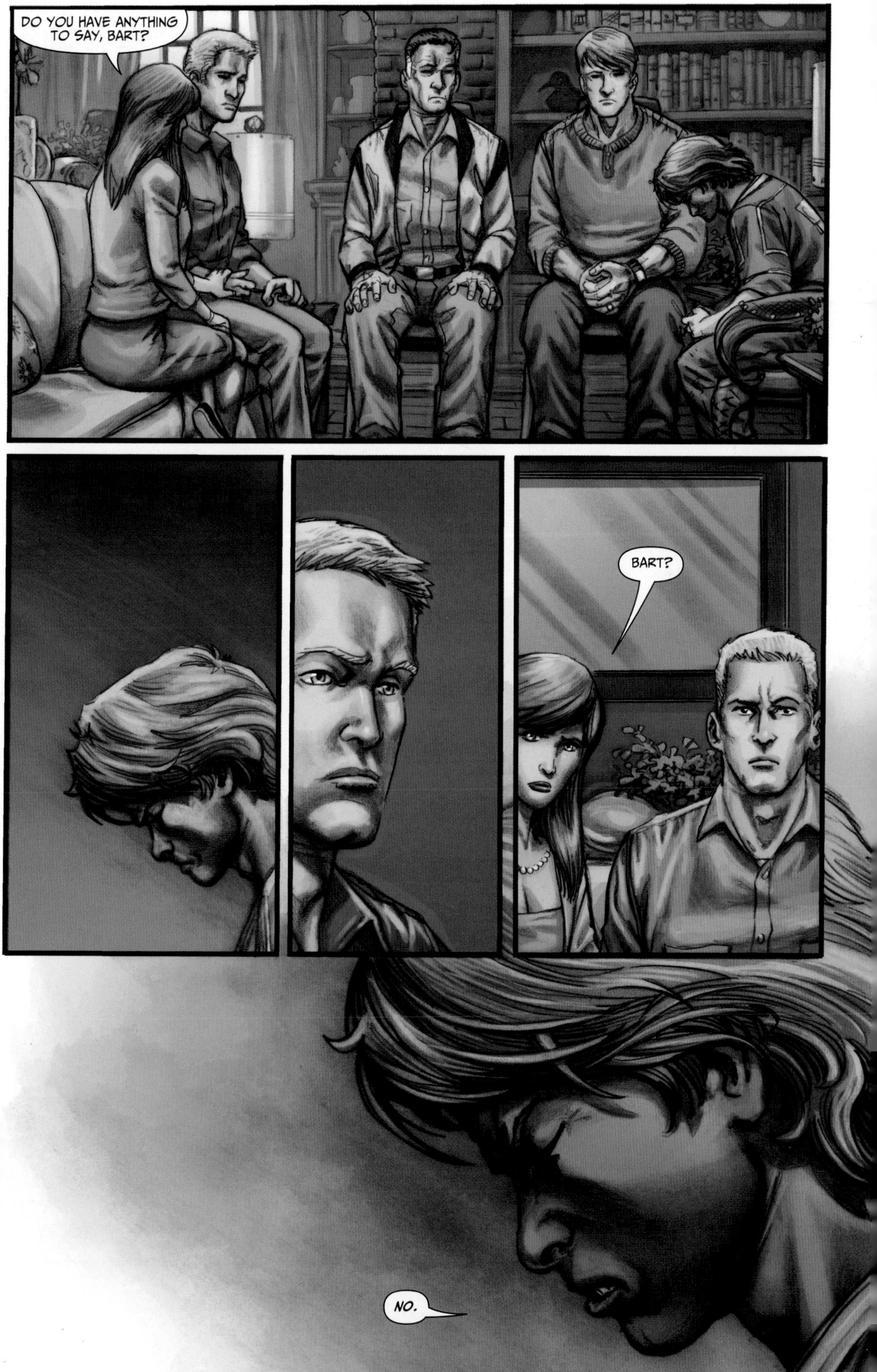
DO YOU HAVE ANYTHING TO SAY, BART?
BART?
NO.

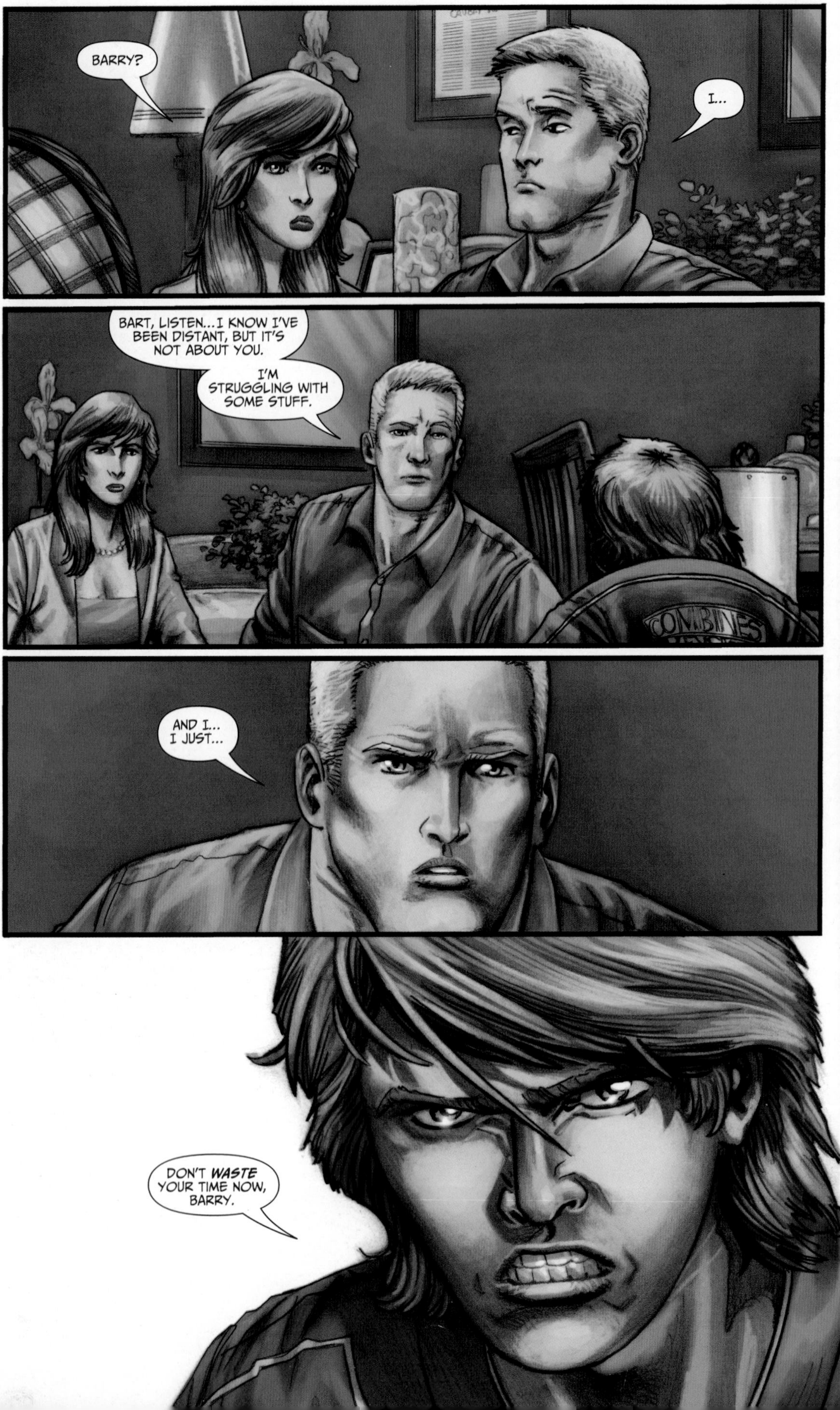
BARRY?
I...
BART, LISTEN...I KNOW I'VE BEEN DISTANT, BUT IT'S NOT ABOUT YOU.
I'M STRUGGLING WITH SOME STUFF.
COMBINES
AND I... I JUST...
DON'T WASTE YOUR TIME NOW, BARRY.

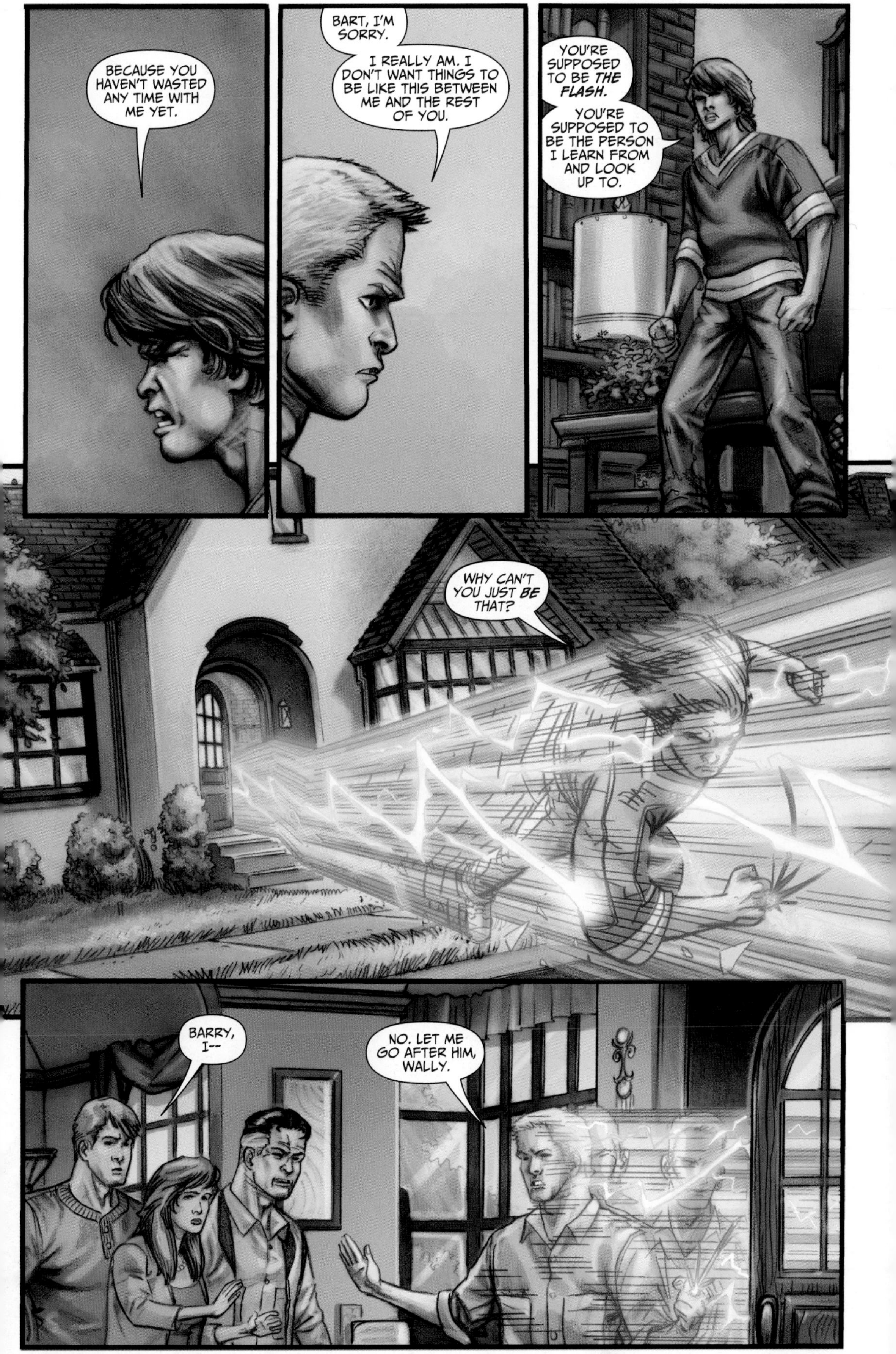
BECAUSE YOU HAVEN'T WASTED ANY TIME WITH ME YET.
BART, I'M SORRY.
I REALLY AM. I DON'T WANT THINGS TO BE LIKE THIS BETWEEN ME AND THE REST OF YOU.
YOU'RE SUPPOSED TO BE THE FLASH.
YOU'RE SUPPOSED TO BE THE PERSON I LEARN FROM AND LOOK UP TO.
WHY CAN'T YOU JUST BE THAT?
BARRY, I--
NO. LET ME GO AFTER HIM, WALLY.

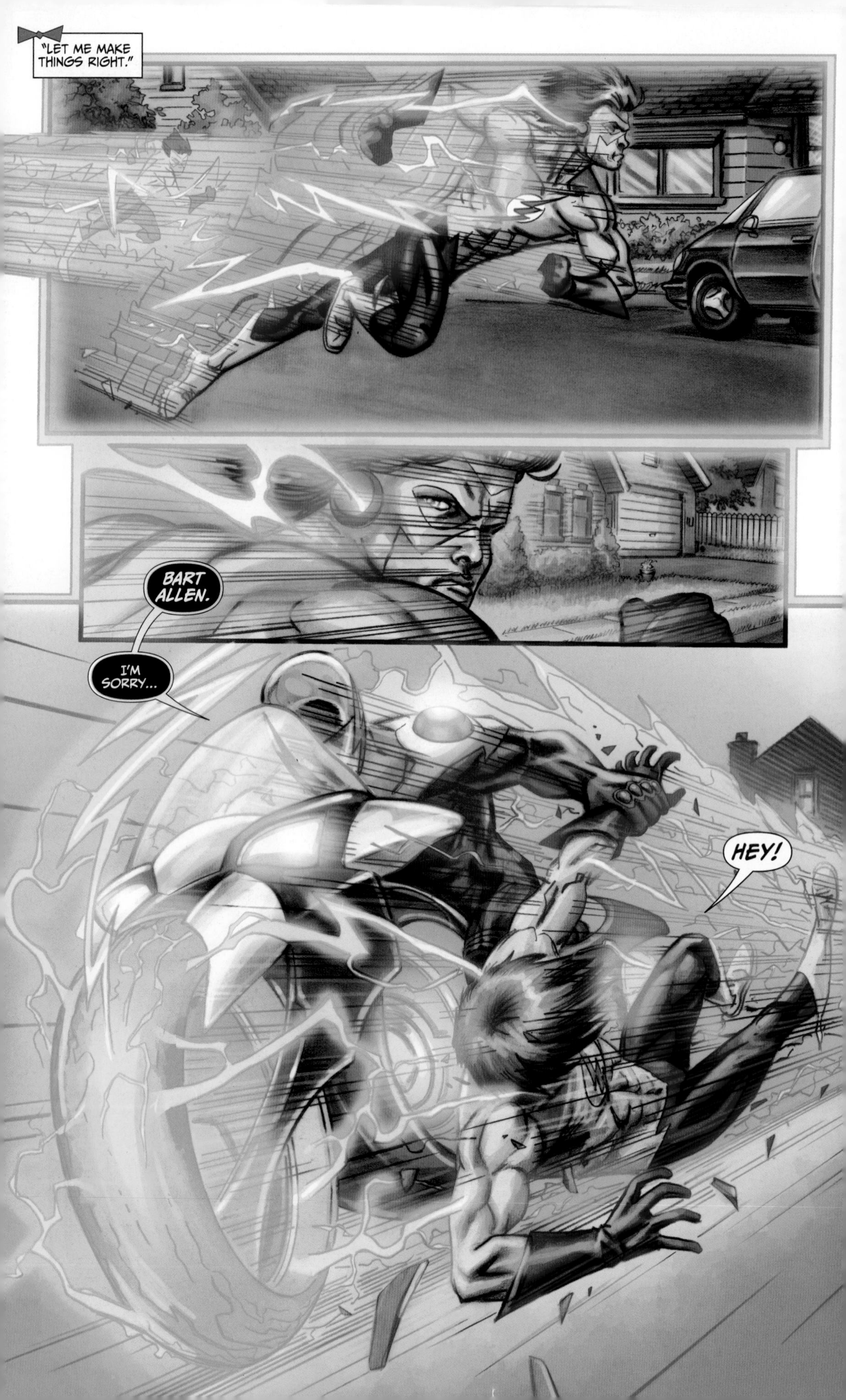
"LET ME MAKE THINGS RIGHT."
BART ALLEN.
I'M SORRY...
HEY!

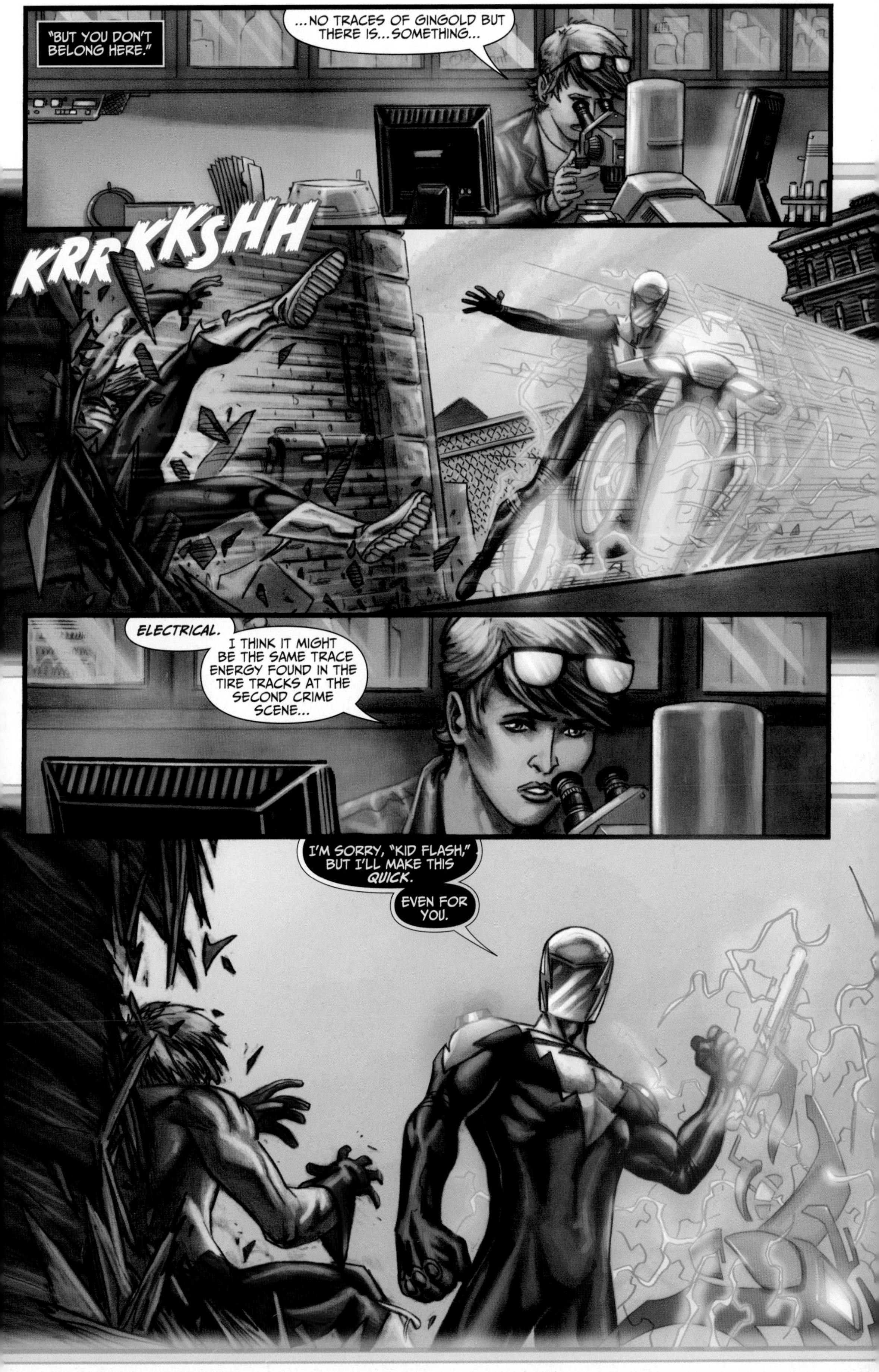
"BUT YOU DON'T BELONG HERE."
...NO TRACES OF GINGOLD BUT THERE IS...SOMETHING...
KRRKKSHH
ELECTRICAL.
I THINK IT MIGHT BE THE SAME TRACE ENERGY FOUND IN THE TIRE TRACKS AT THE SECOND CRIME SCENE...
I'M SORRY, "KID FLASH," BUT I'LL MAKE THIS QUICK.
EVEN FOR YOU.

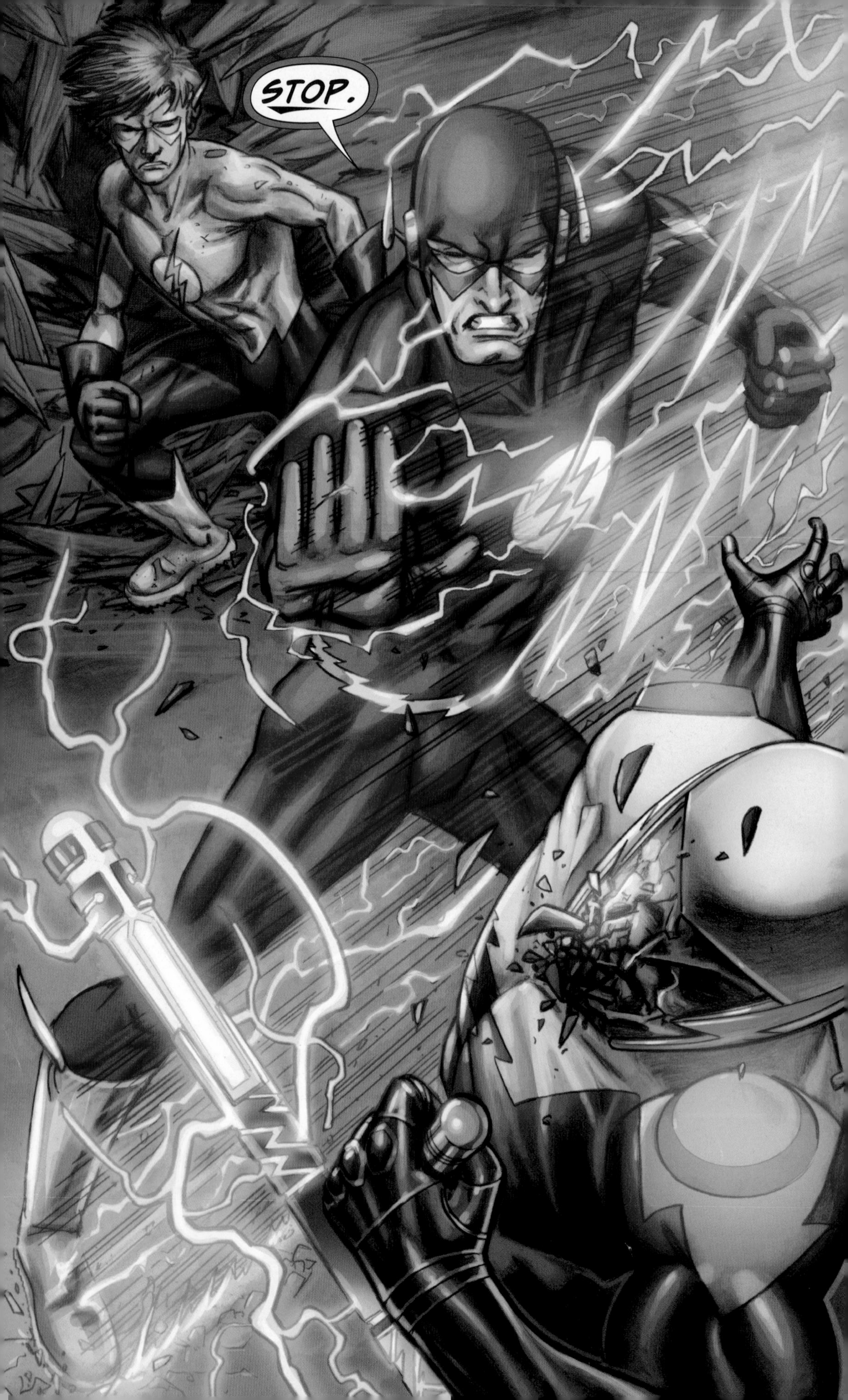
STOP.

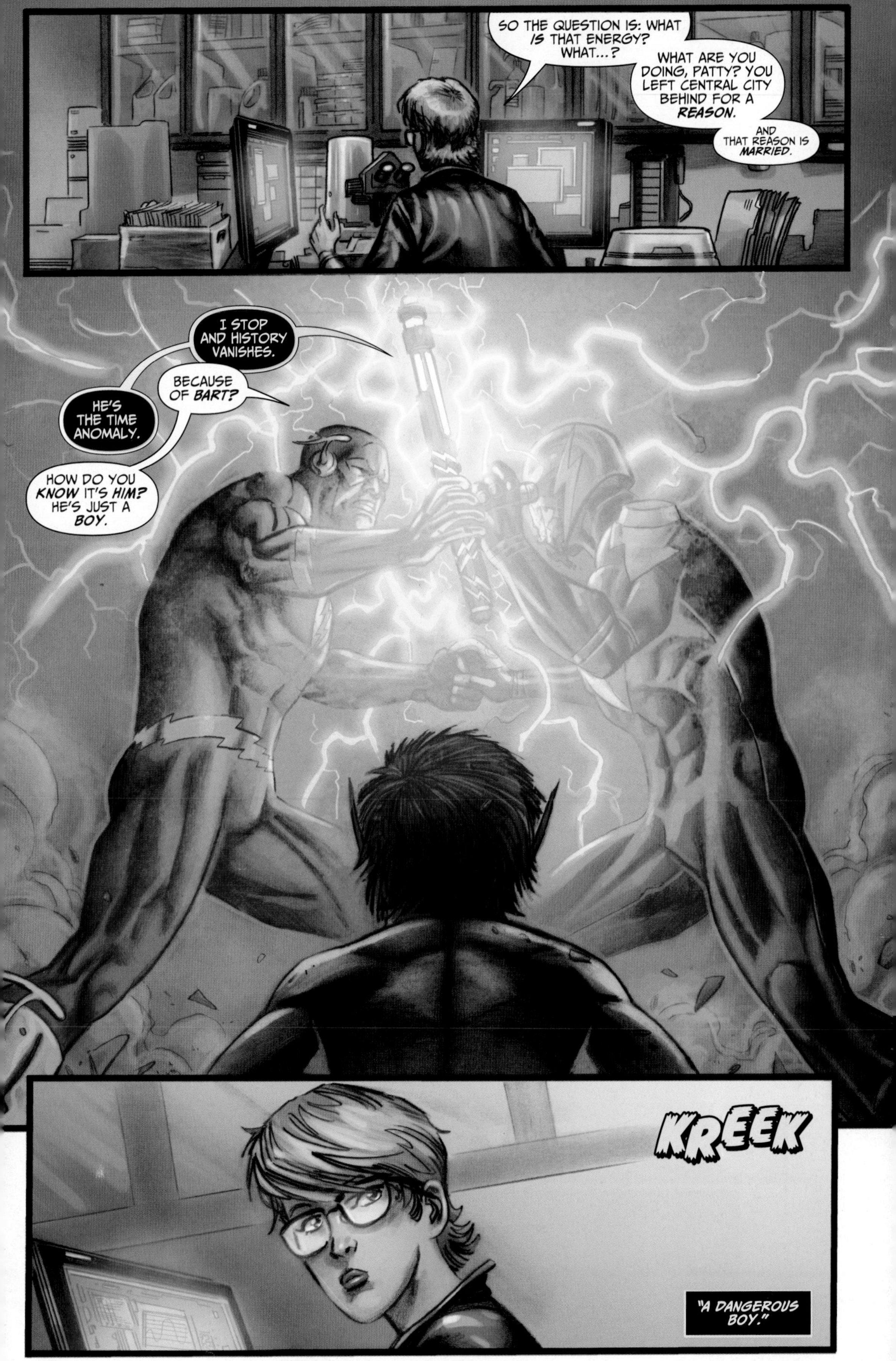

SO THE QUESTION IS: WHAT IS THAT ENERGY? WHAT...?
WHAT ARE YOU DOING, PATTY? YOU LEFT CENTRAL CITY BEHIND FOR A REASON.
AND THAT REASON IS MARRIED.
I STOP AND HISTORY VANISHES.
BECAUSE OF BART?
HE'S THE TIME ANOMALY.
HOW DO YOU KNOW IT'S HIM? HE'S JUST A BOY.
KREEK
"A DANGEROUS BOY."

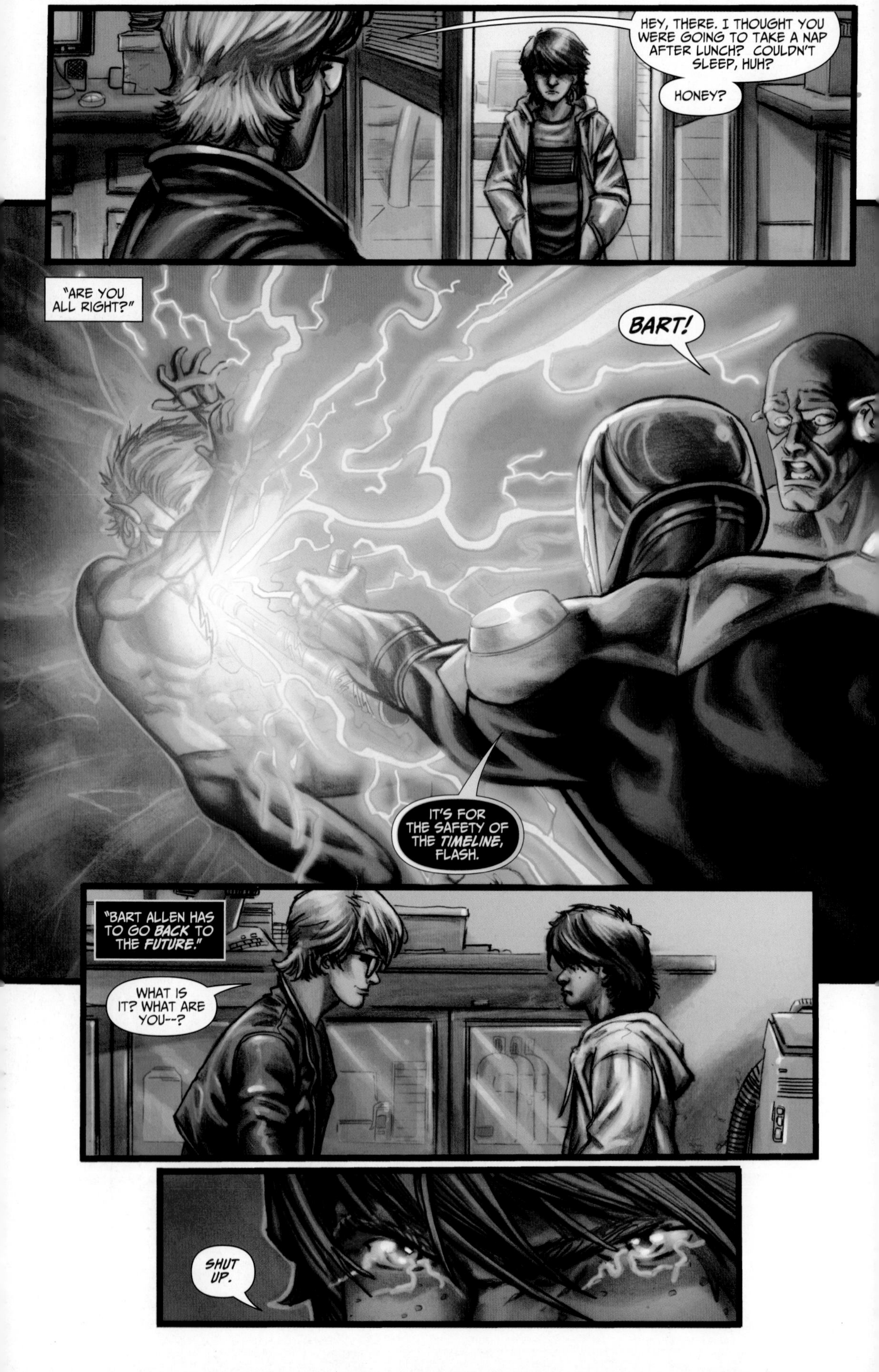
HEY, THERE. I THOUGHT YOU WERE GOING TO TAKE A NAP AFTER LUNCH? COULDN'T SLEEP, HUH?
HONEY?
"ARE YOU ALL RIGHT?"
BART!
IT'S FOR THE SAFETY OF THE TIMELINE, FLASH.
"BART ALLEN HAS TO GO BACK TO THE FUTURE."
WHAT IS IT? WHAT ARE YOU--?
SHUT UP.

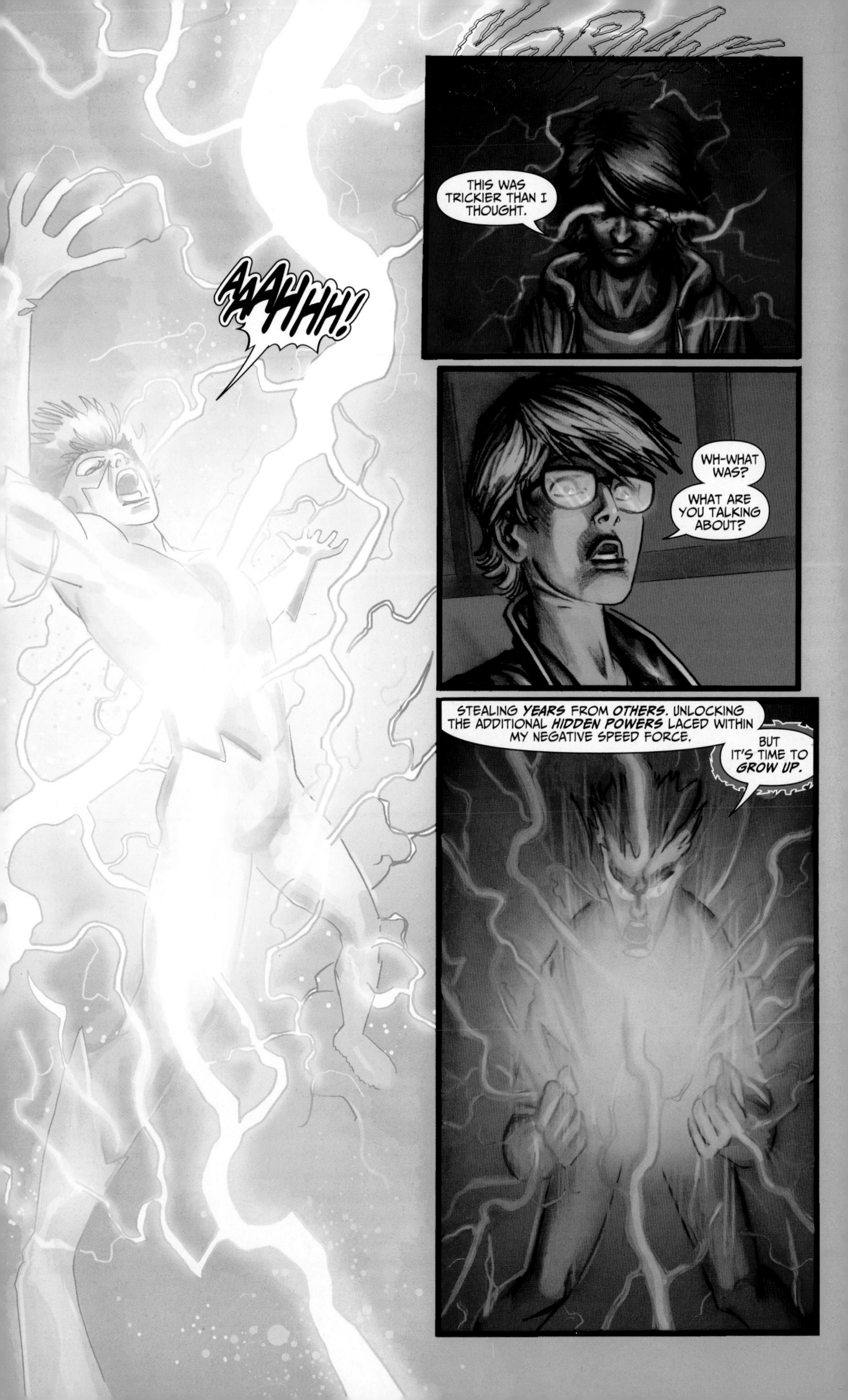
AAAHHHH!
THIS WAS TRICKIER THAN I THOUGHT.
WH-WHAT WAS?
WHAT ARE YOU TALKING ABOUT?
STEALING *YEARS* FROM *OTHERS*. UNLOCKING THE ADDITIONAL *HIDDEN POWERS* LACED WITHIN MY NEGATIVE SPEED FORCE.
BUT IT'S TIME TO *GROW UP*.

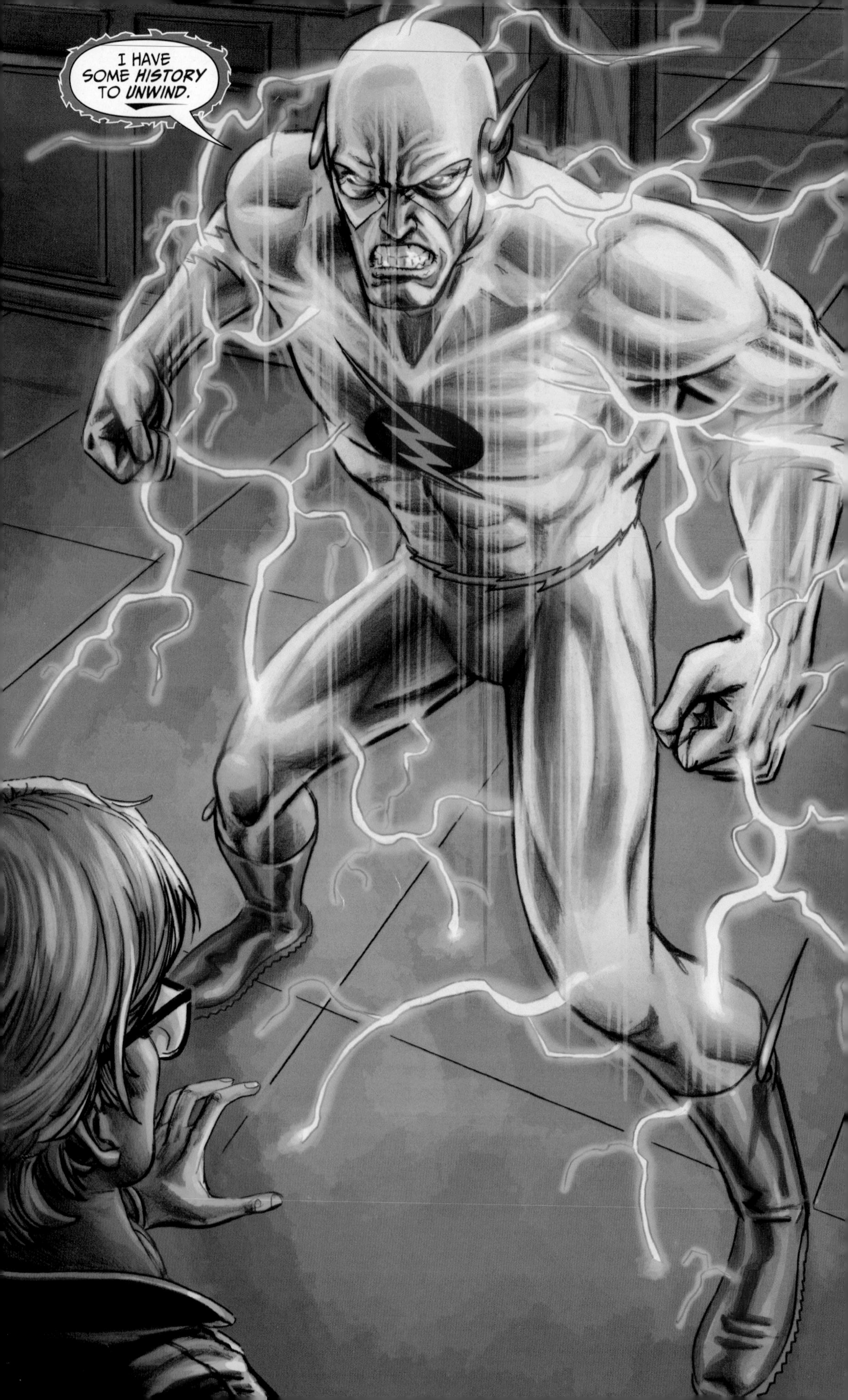
I HAVE SOME HISTORY TO UNWIND.

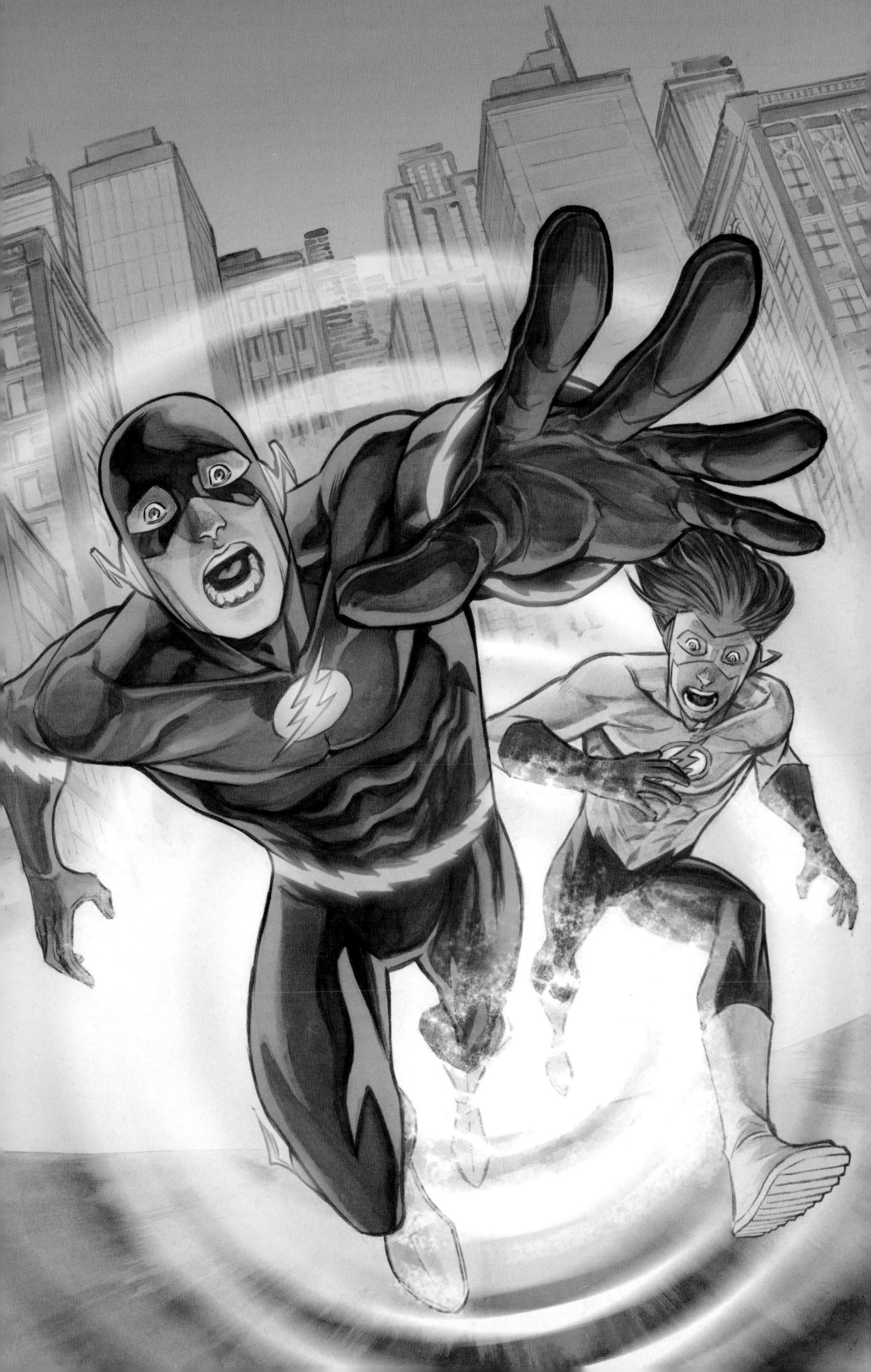

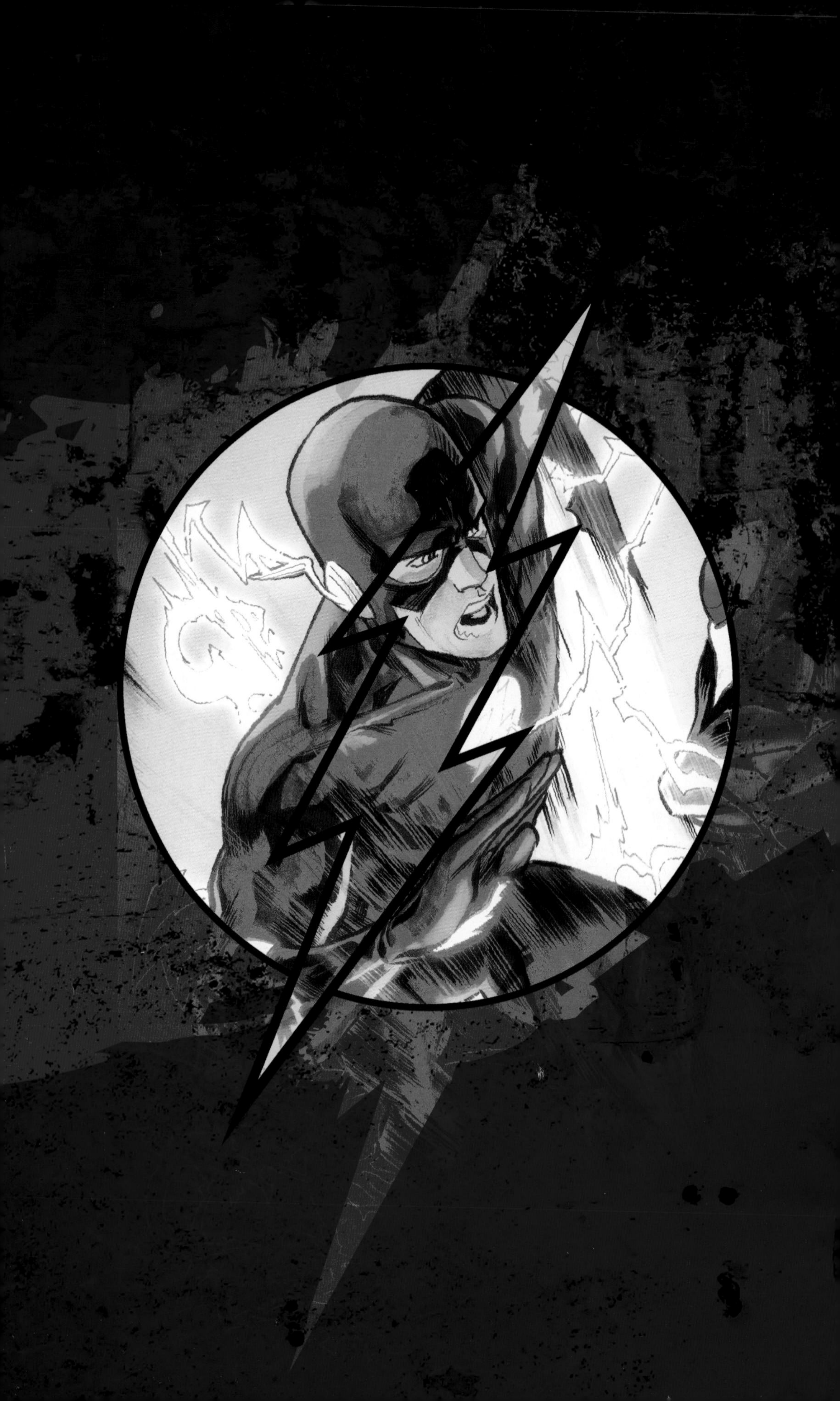

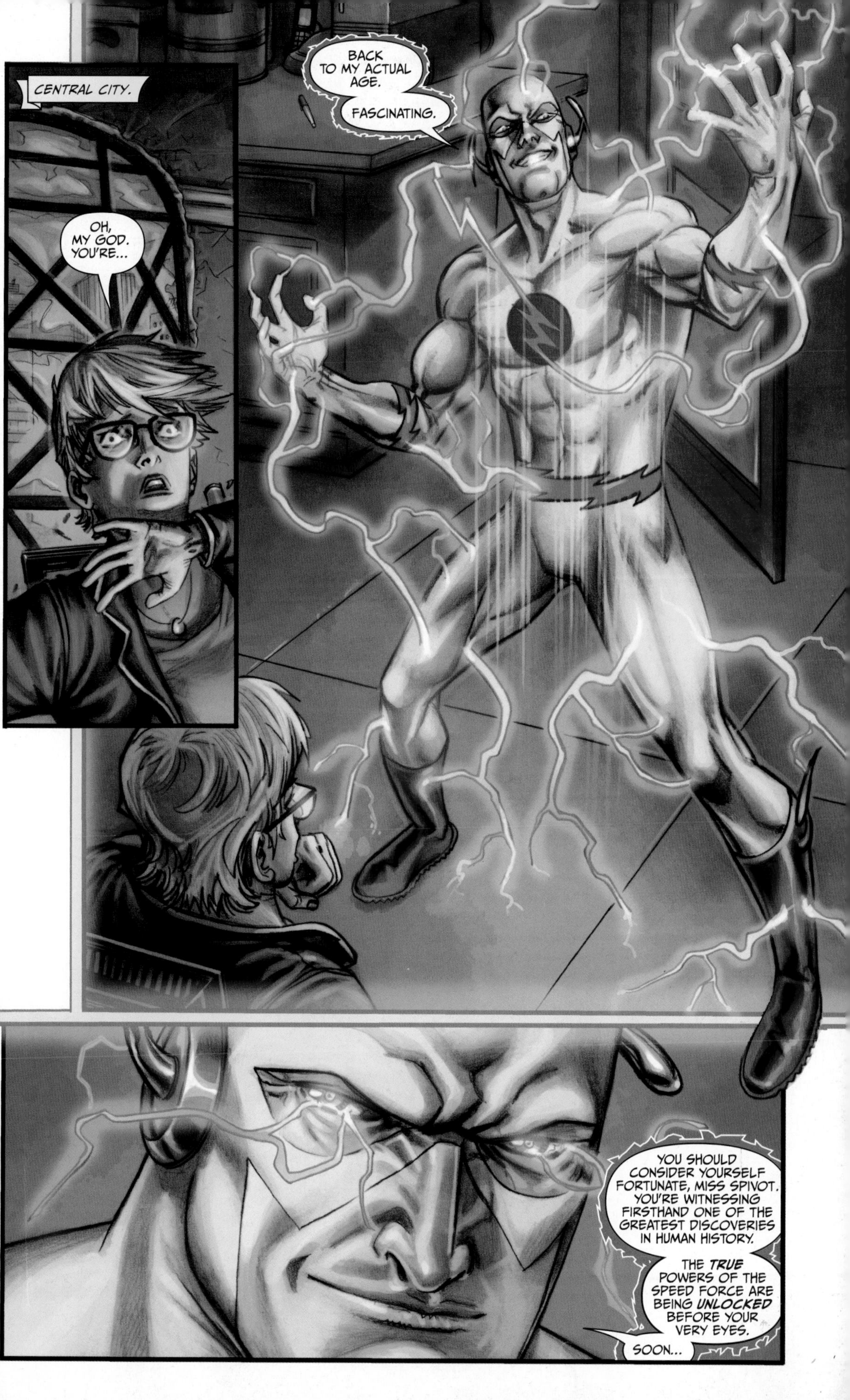
CENTRAL CITY.
BACK TO MY ACTUAL AGE.
FASCINATING.
OH, MY GOD. YOU'RE...
YOU SHOULD CONSIDER YOURSELF FORTUNATE, MISS SPIVOT. YOU'RE WITNESSING FIRSTHAND ONE OF THE GREATEST DISCOVERIES IN HUMAN HISTORY.
THE *TRUE* POWERS OF THE SPEED FORCE ARE BEING *UNLOCKED* BEFORE YOUR VERY EYES.
SOON...

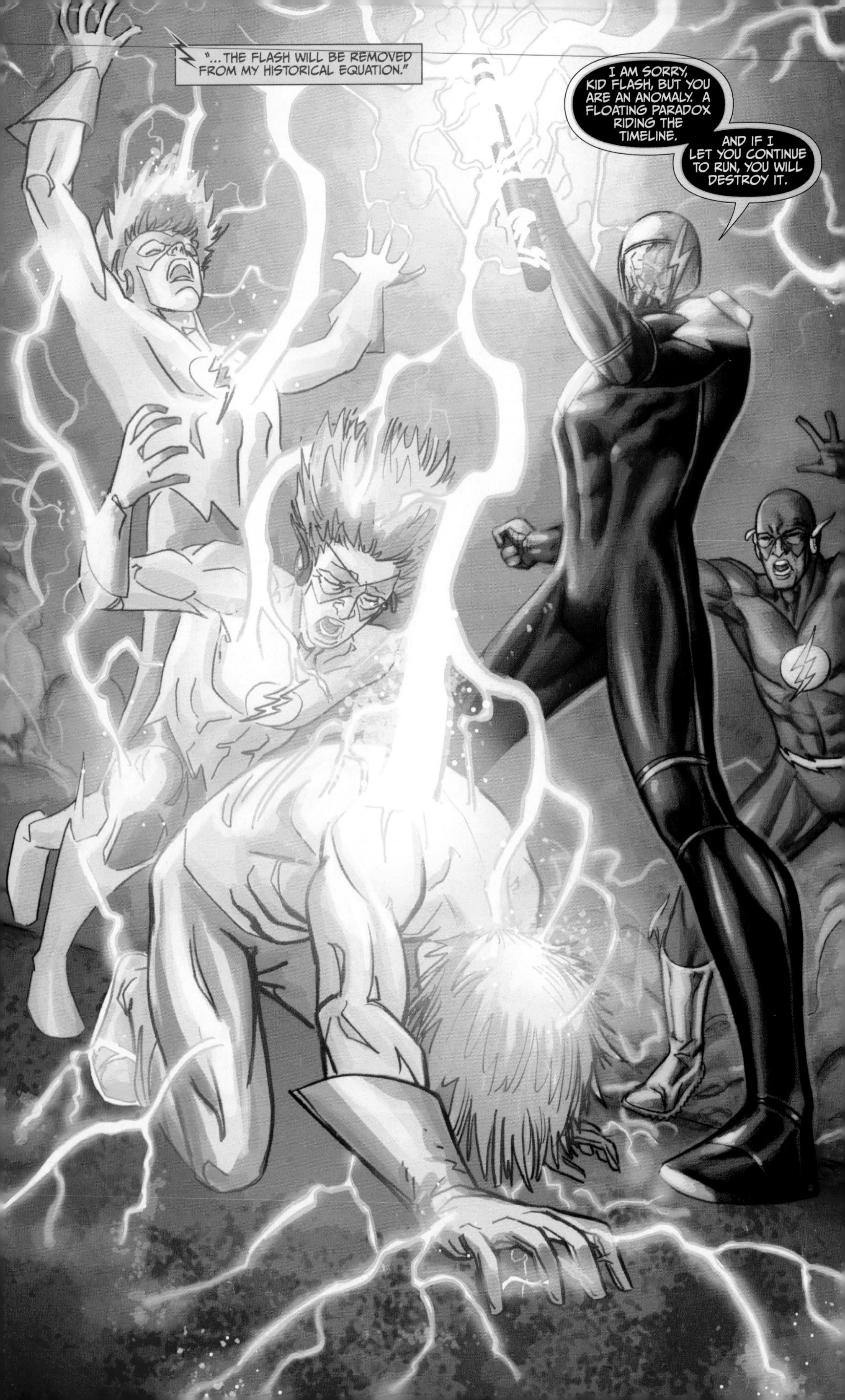
"...THE FLASH WILL BE REMOVED FROM MY HISTORICAL EQUATION."
I AM SORRY, KID FLASH, BUT YOU ARE AN ANOMALY. A FLOATING PARADOX RIDING THE TIMELINE.
AND IF I LET YOU CONTINUE TO RUN, YOU WILL DESTROY IT.

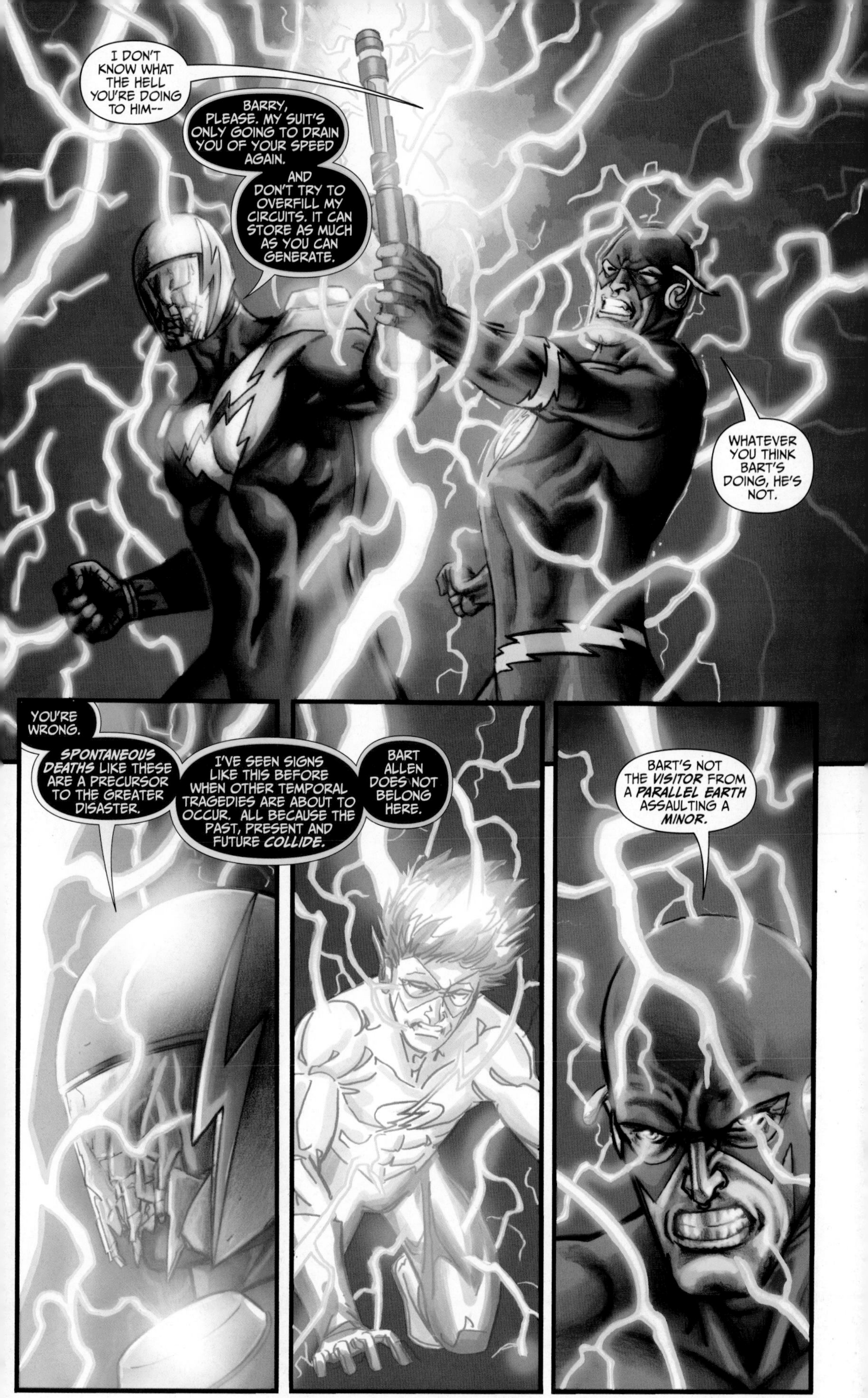

I DON'T KNOW WHAT THE HELL YOU'RE DOING TO HIM--
BARRY, PLEASE. MY SUIT'S ONLY GOING TO DRAIN YOU OF YOUR SPEED AGAIN.
AND DON'T TRY TO OVERFILL MY CIRCUITS. IT CAN STORE AS MUCH AS YOU CAN GENERATE.
WHATEVER YOU THINK BART'S DOING, HE'S NOT.
YOU'RE WRONG.
SPONTANEOUS DEATHS LIKE THESE ARE A PRECURSOR TO THE GREATER DISASTER.
I'VE SEEN SIGNS LIKE THIS BEFORE WHEN OTHER TEMPORAL TRAGEDIES ARE ABOUT TO OCCUR. ALL BECAUSE THE PAST, PRESENT AND FUTURE *COLLIDE*.
BART ALLEN DOES NOT BELONG HERE.
BART'S NOT THE *VISITOR* FROM A *PARALLEL EARTH* ASSAULTING A *MINOR*.

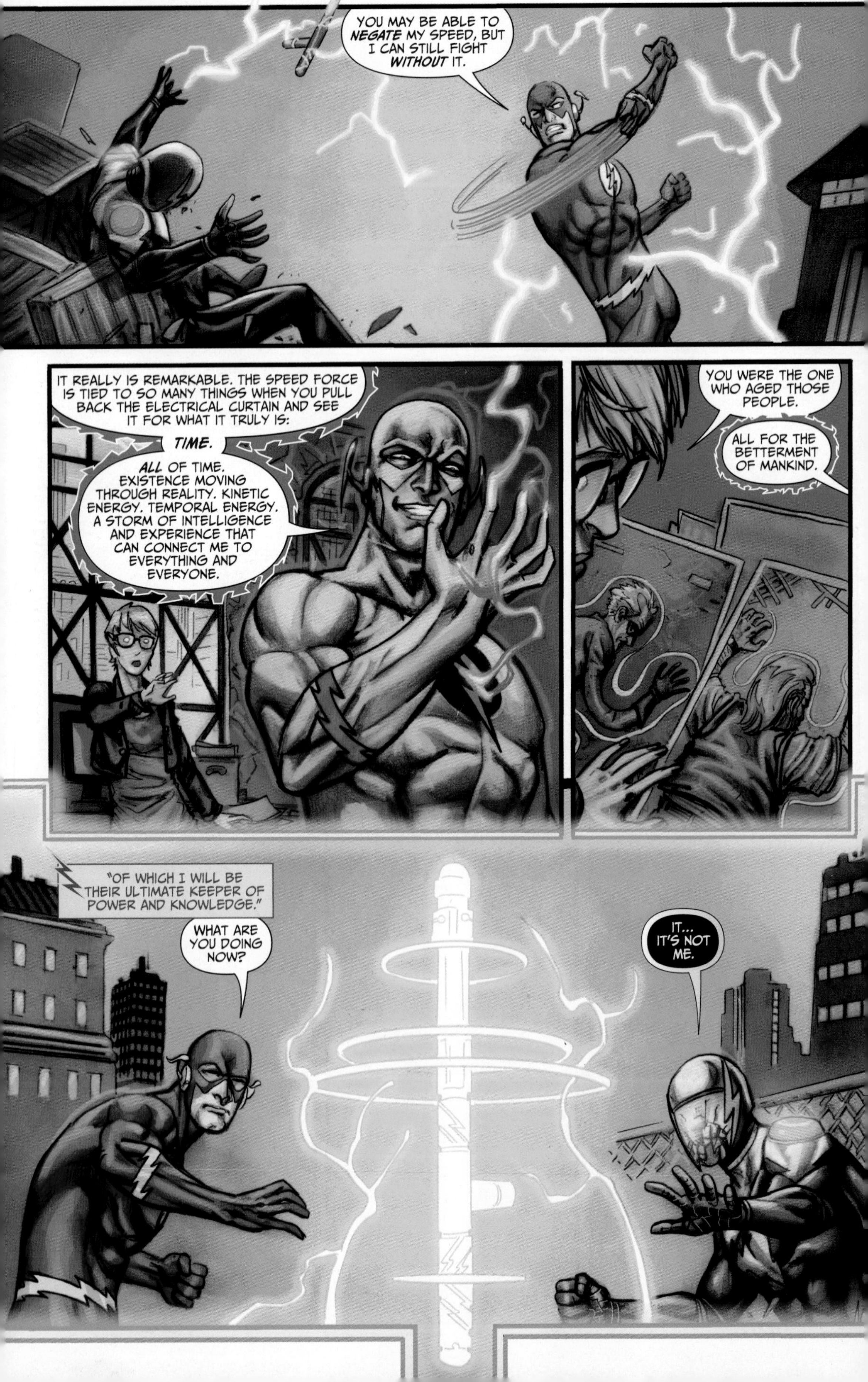

YOU MAY BE ABLE TO NEGATE MY SPEED, BUT I CAN STILL FIGHT WITHOUT IT.
IT REALLY IS REMARKABLE. THE SPEED FORCE IS TIED TO SO MANY THINGS WHEN YOU PULL BACK THE ELECTRICAL CURTAIN AND SEE IT FOR WHAT IT TRULY IS:
TIME.
ALL OF TIME. EXISTENCE MOVING THROUGH REALITY. KINETIC ENERGY. TEMPORAL ENERGY. A STORM OF INTELLIGENCE AND EXPERIENCE THAT CAN CONNECT ME TO EVERYTHING AND EVERYONE.
YOU WERE THE ONE WHO AGED THOSE PEOPLE.
ALL FOR THE BETTERMENT OF MANKIND.
"OF WHICH I WILL BE THEIR ULTIMATE KEEPER OF POWER AND KNOWLEDGE."
WHAT ARE YOU DOING NOW?
IT... IT'S NOT ME.

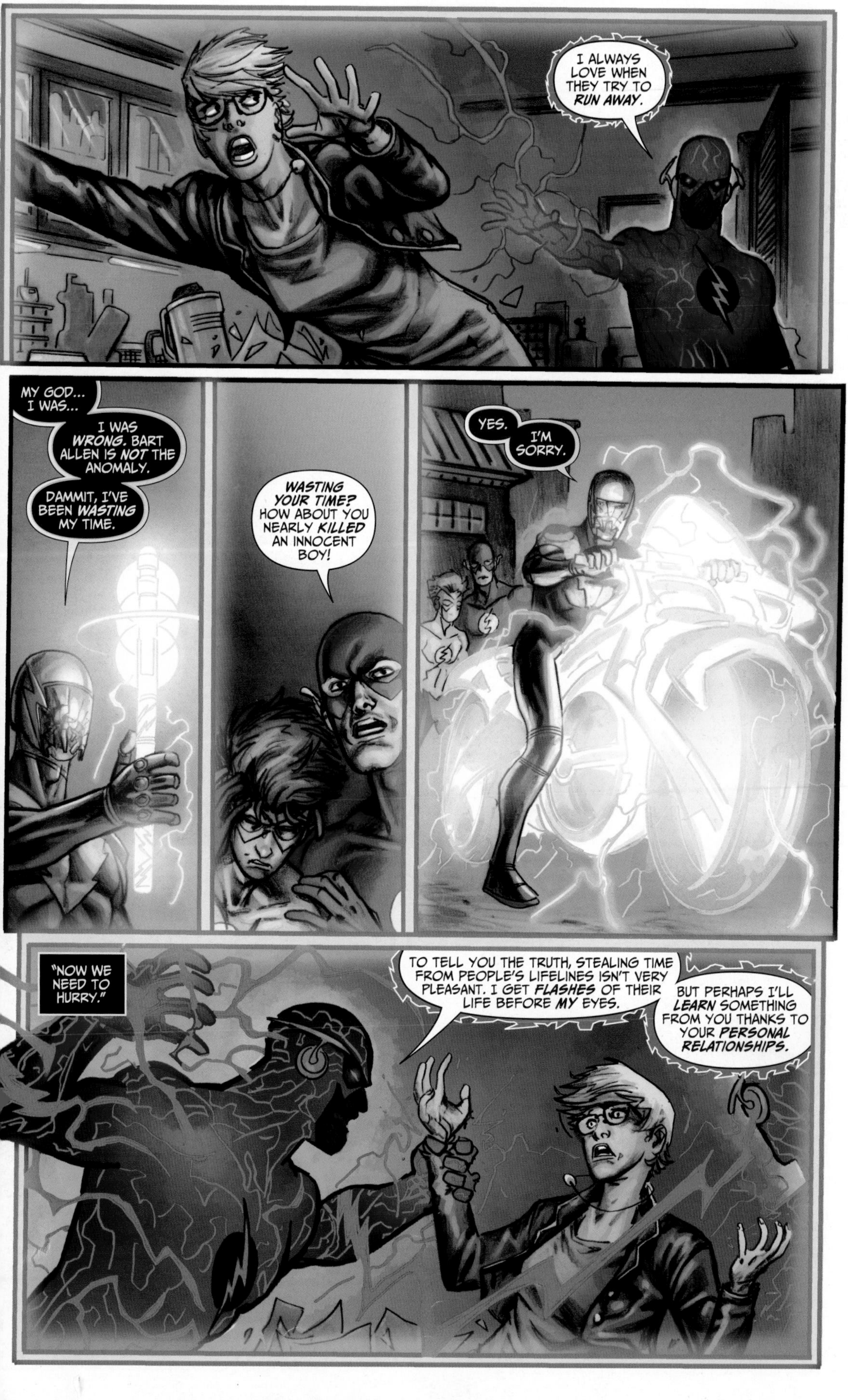

I ALWAYS LOVE WHEN THEY TRY TO RUN AWAY.
MY GOD... I WAS...
I WAS WRONG. BART ALLEN IS NOT THE ANOMALY.
DAMMIT, I'VE BEEN WASTING MY TIME.
WASTING YOUR TIME? HOW ABOUT YOU NEARLY KILLED AN INNOCENT BOY!
YES.
I'M SORRY.
"NOW WE NEED TO HURRY."
TO TELL YOU THE TRUTH, STEALING TIME FROM PEOPLE'S LIFELINES ISN'T VERY PLEASANT. I GET FLASHES OF THEIR LIFE BEFORE MY EYES.
BUT PERHAPS I'LL LEARN SOMETHING FROM YOU THANKS TO YOUR PERSONAL RELATIONSHIPS.

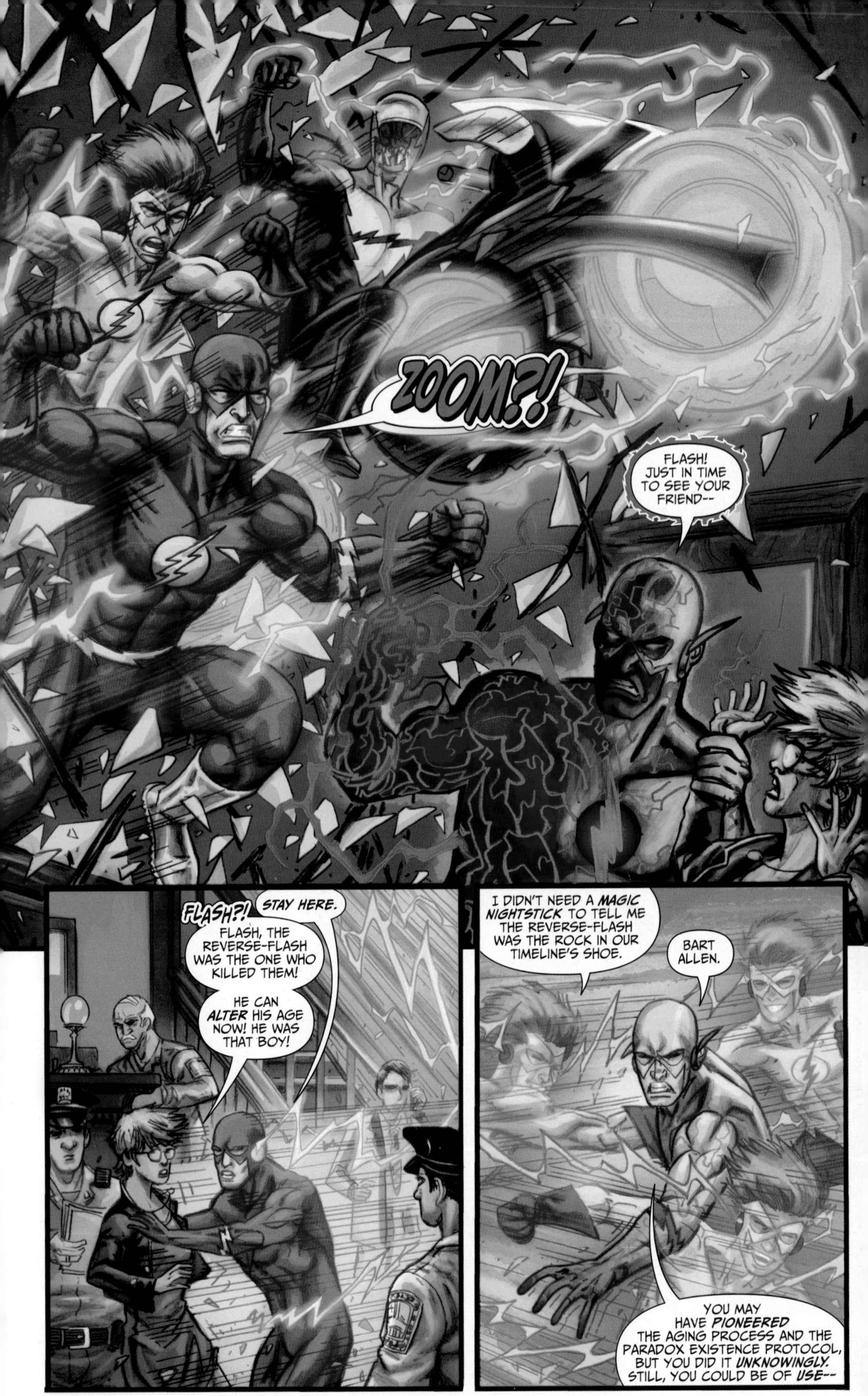
ZOOM?!
FLASH! JUST IN TIME TO SEE YOUR FRIEND--
FLASH?!
STAY HERE.
FLASH, THE REVERSE-FLASH WAS THE ONE WHO KILLED THEM!
HE CAN ALTER HIS AGE NOW! HE WAS THAT BOY!
I DIDN'T NEED A MAGIC NIGHTSTICK TO TELL ME THE REVERSE-FLASH WAS THE ROCK IN OUR TIMELINE'S SHOE.
BART ALLEN.
YOU MAY HAVE PIONEERED THE AGING PROCESS AND THE PARADOX EXISTENCE PROTOCOL, BUT YOU DID IT UNKNOWINGLY. STILL, YOU COULD BE OF USE--

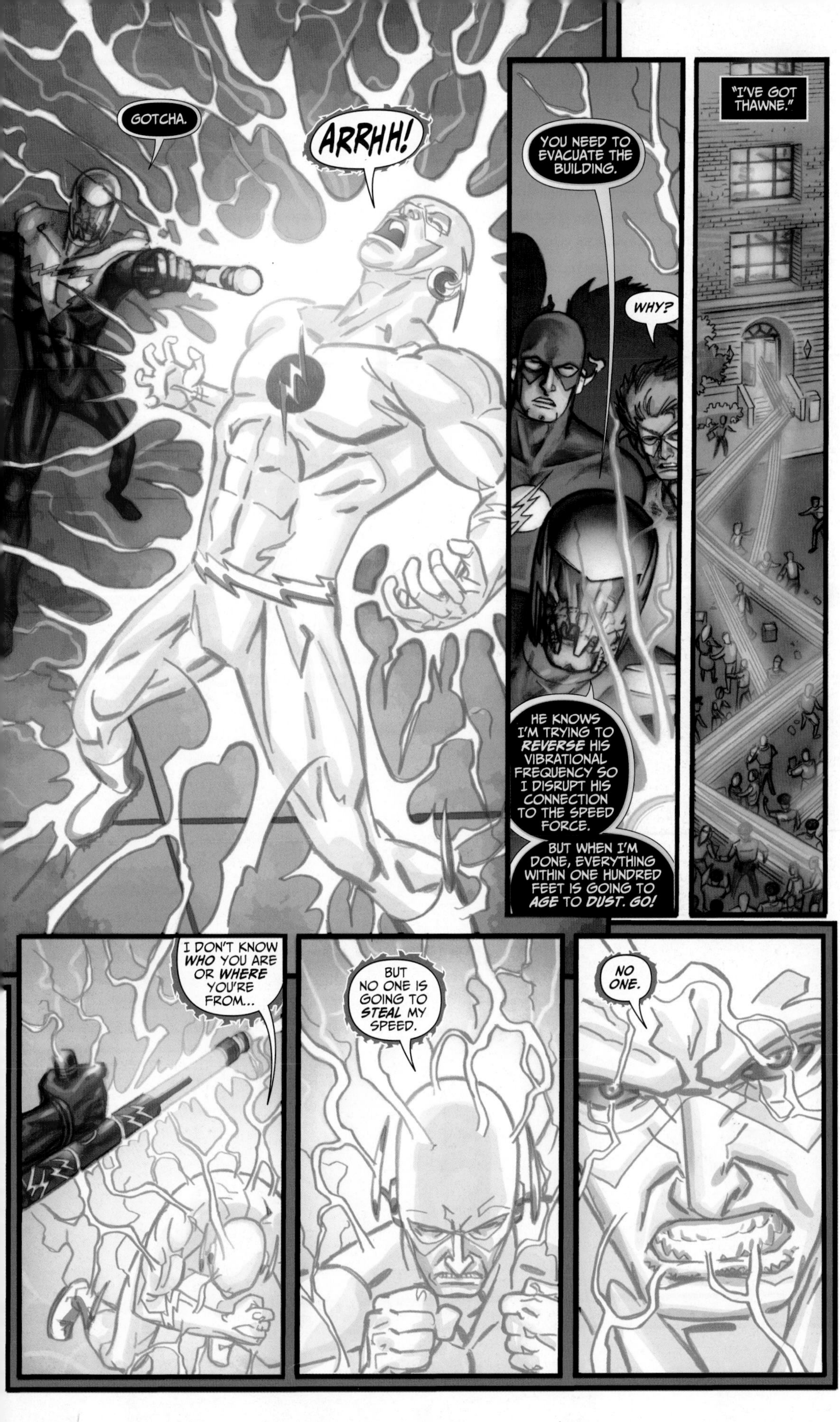
GOTCHA.
ARRHH!
YOU NEED TO EVACUATE THE BUILDING.
WHY?
HE KNOWS I'M TRYING TO REVERSE HIS VIBRATIONAL FREQUENCY SO I DISRUPT HIS CONNECTION TO THE SPEED FORCE.
BUT WHEN I'M DONE, EVERYTHING WITHIN ONE HUNDRED FEET IS GOING TO AGE TO DUST. GO!
"I'VE GOT THAWNE."
I DON'T KNOW WHO YOU ARE OR WHERE YOU'RE FROM...
BUT NO ONE IS GOING TO STEAL MY SPEED.
NO ONE.

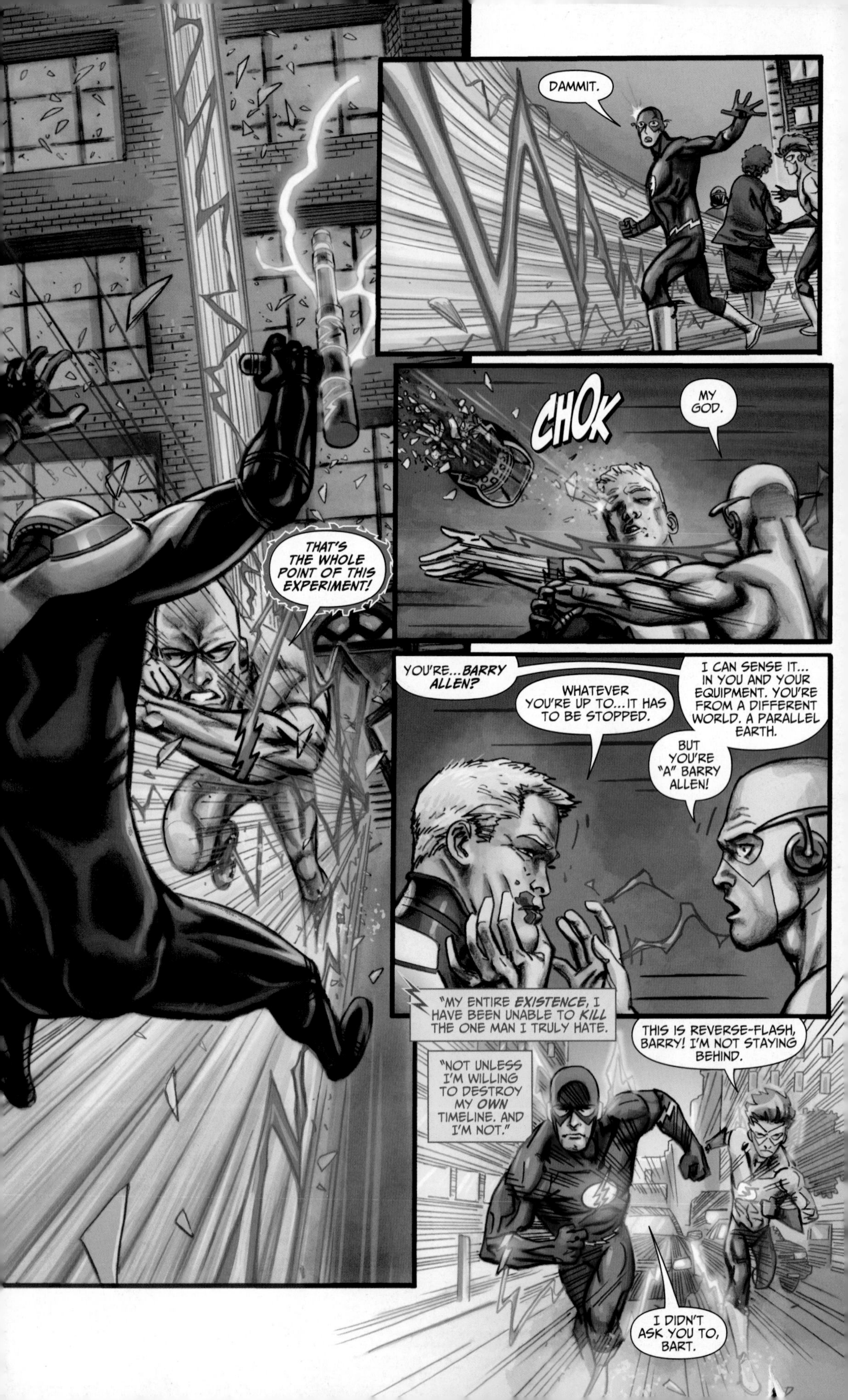
DAMMIT.
CHOK
MY GOD.
THAT'S THE WHOLE POINT OF THIS EXPERIMENT!
YOU'RE...BARRY ALLEN?
WHATEVER YOU'RE UP TO...IT HAS TO BE STOPPED.
I CAN SENSE IT... IN YOU AND YOUR EQUIPMENT. YOU'RE FROM A DIFFERENT WORLD. A PARALLEL EARTH.
BUT YOU'RE "A" BARRY ALLEN!
"MY ENTIRE EXISTENCE, I HAVE BEEN UNABLE TO KILL THE ONE MAN I TRULY HATE.
"NOT UNLESS I'M WILLING TO DESTROY MY OWN TIMELINE. AND I'M NOT."
THIS IS REVERSE-FLASH, BARRY! I'M NOT STAYING BEHIND.
I DIDN'T ASK YOU TO, BART.

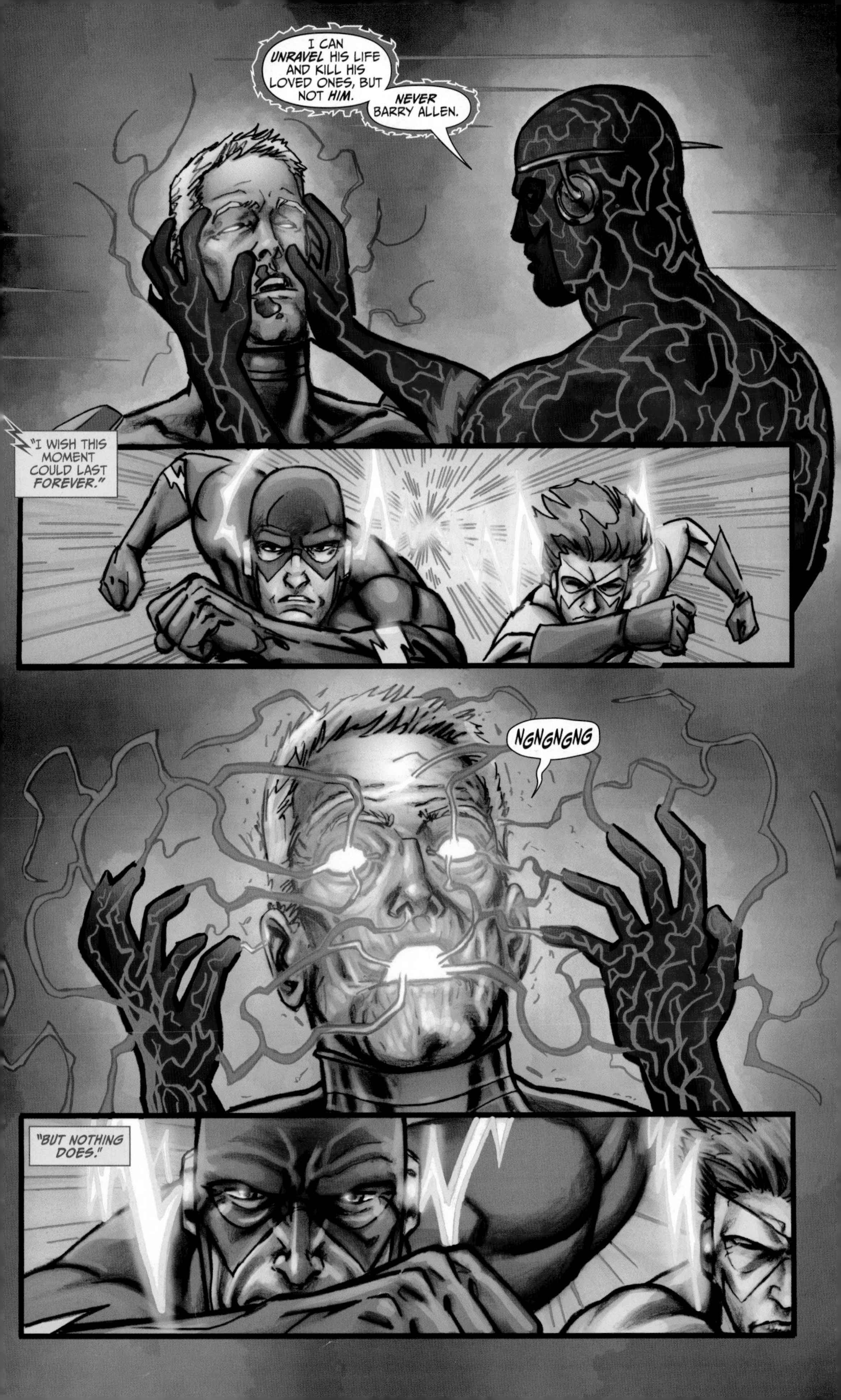
I CAN UNRAVEL HIS LIFE AND KILL HIS LOVED ONES, BUT NOT HIM.
NEVER BARRY ALLEN.
"I WISH THIS MOMENT COULD LAST FOREVER."
NGNGNGNG
"BUT NOTHING DOES."

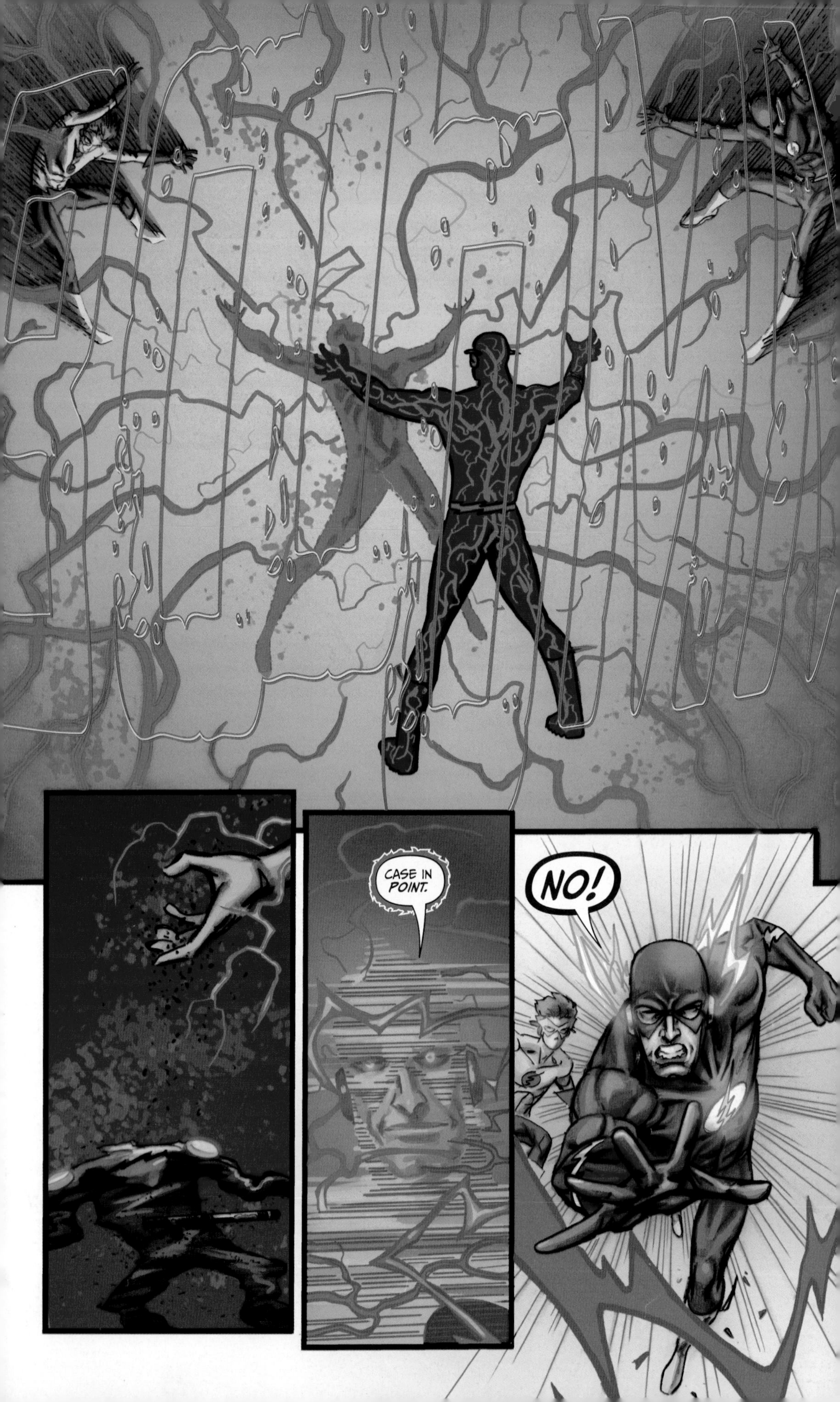
CASE IN POINT.
NO!

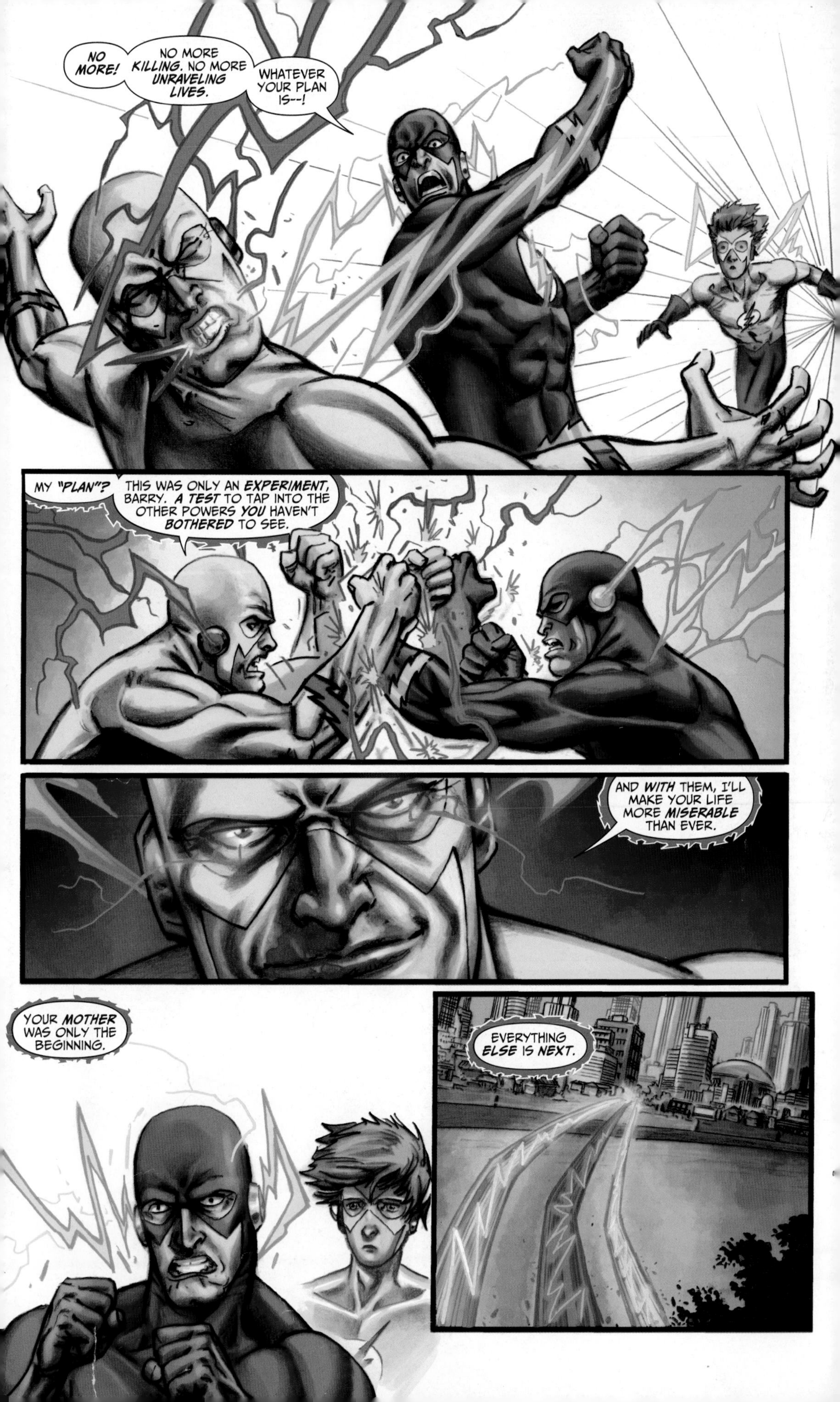
NO MORE!
NO MORE KILLING. NO MORE UNRAVELING LIVES.
WHATEVER YOUR PLAN IS--!
MY "PLAN"?
THIS WAS ONLY AN EXPERIMENT, BARRY. A TEST TO TAP INTO THE OTHER POWERS YOU HAVEN'T BOTHERED TO SEE.
AND WITH THEM, I'LL MAKE YOUR LIFE MORE MISERABLE THAN EVER.
YOUR MOTHER WAS ONLY THE BEGINNING.
EVERYTHING ELSE IS NEXT.

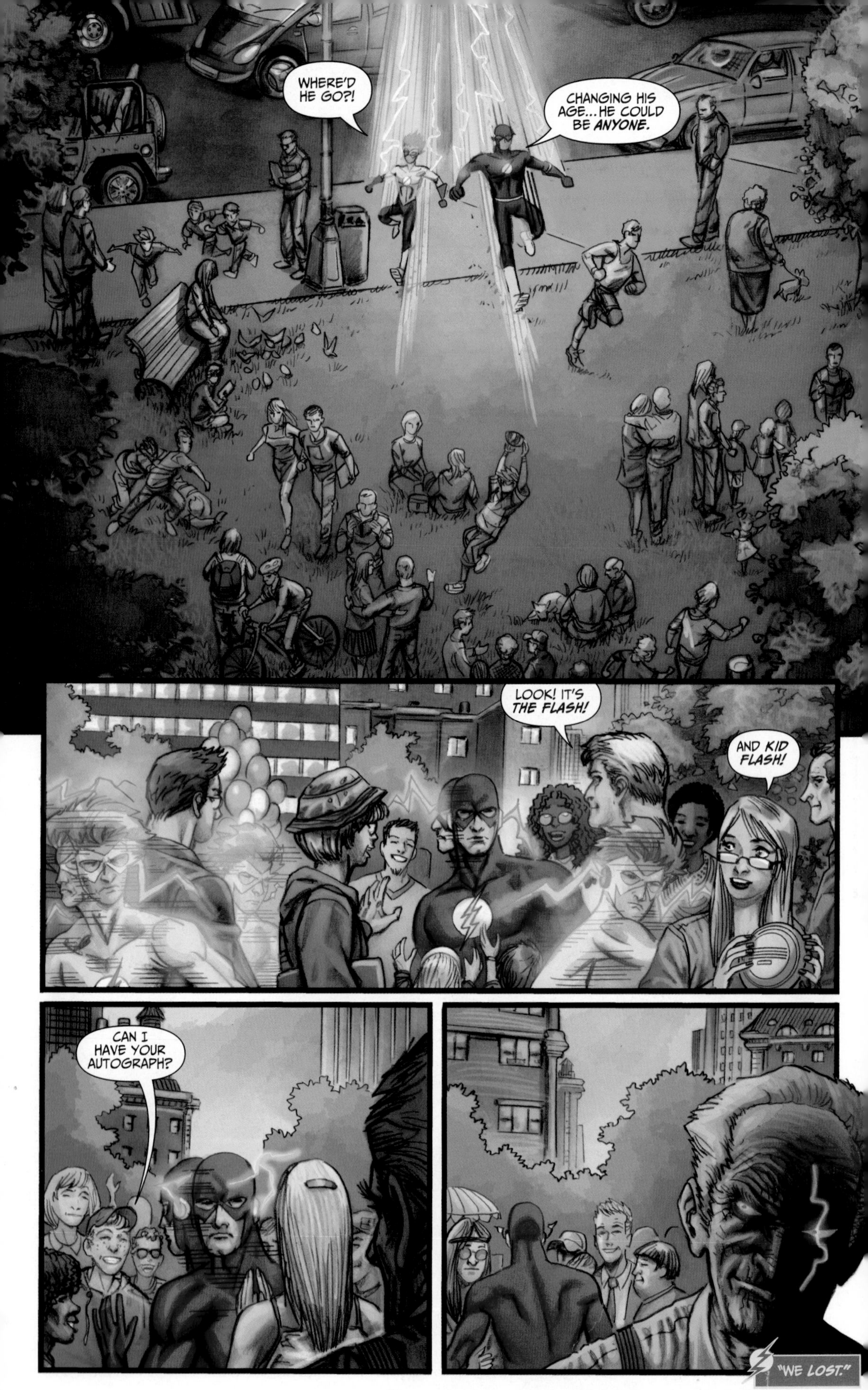
WHERE'D HE GO?!
CHANGING HIS AGE...HE COULD BE ANYONE.
LOOK! IT'S THE FLASH!
AND KID FLASH!
CAN I HAVE YOUR AUTOGRAPH?
"WE LOST."

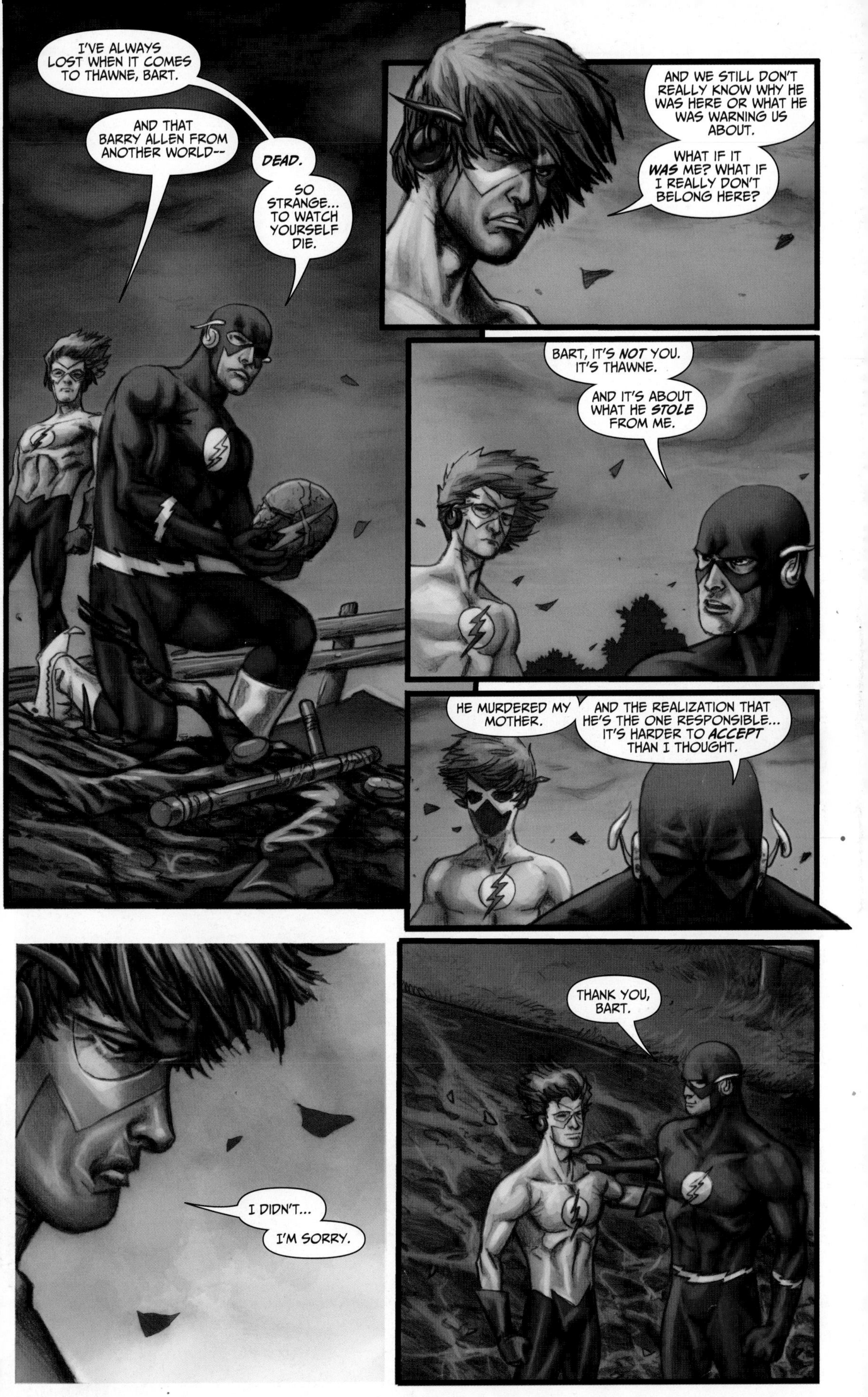
I'VE ALWAYS LOST WHEN IT COMES TO THAWNE, BART.
AND THAT BARRY ALLEN FROM ANOTHER WORLD--
DEAD.
SO STRANGE... TO WATCH YOURSELF DIE.
AND WE STILL DON'T REALLY KNOW WHY HE WAS HERE OR WHAT HE WAS WARNING US ABOUT.
WHAT IF IT WAS ME? WHAT IF I REALLY DON'T BELONG HERE?
BART, IT'S NOT YOU. IT'S THAWNE.
AND IT'S ABOUT WHAT HE STOLE FROM ME.
HE MURDERED MY MOTHER.
AND THE REALIZATION THAT HE'S THE ONE RESPONSIBLE... IT'S HARDER TO ACCEPT THAN I THOUGHT.
I DIDN'T...
I'M SORRY.
THANK YOU, BART.

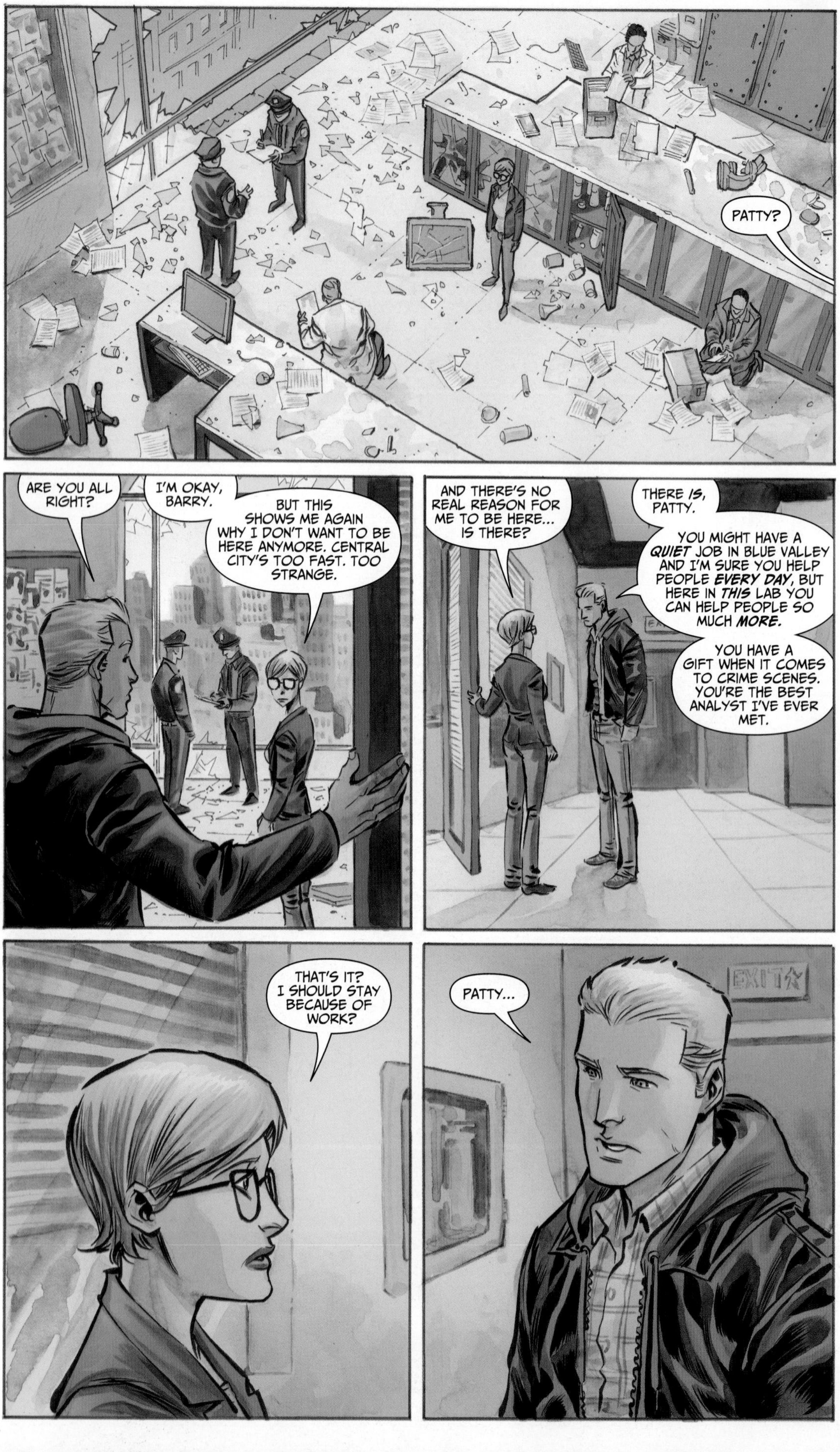
PATTY?
ARE YOU ALL RIGHT?
I'M OKAY, BARRY.
BUT THIS SHOWS ME AGAIN WHY I DON'T WANT TO BE HERE ANYMORE. CENTRAL CITY'S TOO FAST. TOO STRANGE.
AND THERE'S NO REAL REASON FOR ME TO BE HERE... IS THERE?
THERE IS, PATTY.
YOU MIGHT HAVE A QUIET JOB IN BLUE VALLEY AND I'M SURE YOU HELP PEOPLE EVERY DAY, BUT HERE IN THIS LAB YOU CAN HELP PEOPLE SO MUCH MORE.
YOU HAVE A GIFT WHEN IT COMES TO CRIME SCENES. YOU'RE THE BEST ANALYST I'VE EVER MET.
THAT'S IT? I SHOULD STAY BECAUSE OF WORK?
PATTY...
EXIT

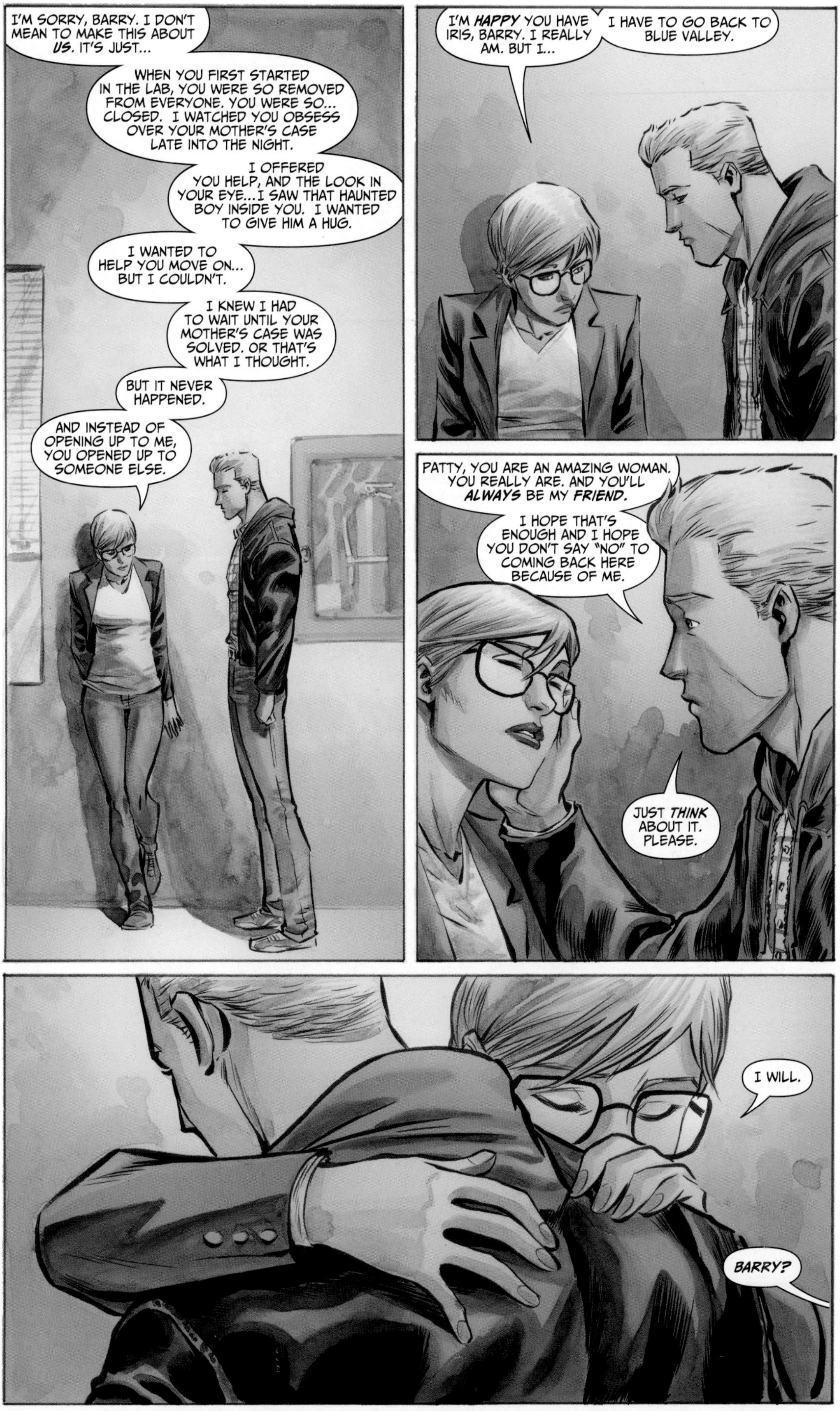

I'M SORRY, BARRY. I DON'T MEAN TO MAKE THIS ABOUT *US*. IT'S JUST...
WHEN YOU FIRST STARTED IN THE LAB, YOU WERE SO REMOVED FROM EVERYONE. YOU WERE SO... CLOSED. I WATCHED YOU OBSESS OVER YOUR MOTHER'S CASE LATE INTO THE NIGHT.
I OFFERED YOU HELP, AND THE LOOK IN YOUR EYE...I SAW THAT HAUNTED BOY INSIDE YOU. I WANTED TO GIVE HIM A HUG.
I WANTED TO HELP YOU MOVE ON... BUT I COULDN'T.
I KNEW I HAD TO WAIT UNTIL YOUR MOTHER'S CASE WAS SOLVED. OR THAT'S WHAT I THOUGHT.
BUT IT NEVER HAPPENED.
AND INSTEAD OF OPENING UP TO ME, YOU OPENED UP TO SOMEONE ELSE.
I'M *HAPPY* YOU HAVE IRIS, BARRY. I REALLY AM. BUT I...
I HAVE TO GO BACK TO BLUE VALLEY.
PATTY, YOU ARE AN AMAZING WOMAN. YOU REALLY ARE. AND YOU'LL *ALWAYS* BE MY *FRIEND.*
I HOPE THAT'S ENOUGH AND I HOPE YOU DON'T SAY "NO" TO COMING BACK HERE BECAUSE OF ME.
JUST *THINK* ABOUT IT. PLEASE.
I WILL.
BARRY?

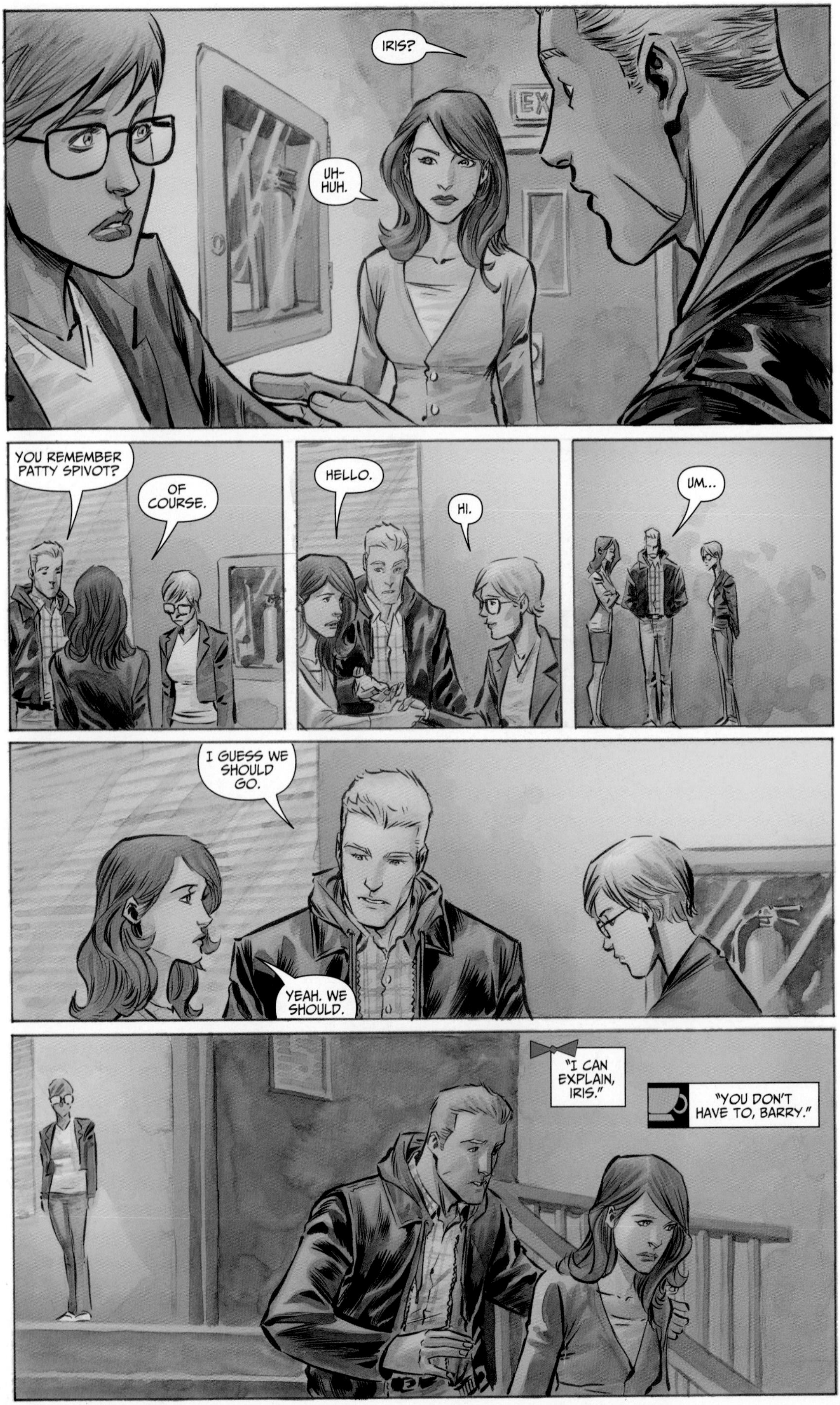
IRIS?
UH-HUH.
YOU REMEMBER PATTY SPIVOT?
OF COURSE.
HELLO.
HI.
UM...
I GUESS WE SHOULD GO.
YEAH. WE SHOULD.
"I CAN EXPLAIN, IRIS."
"YOU DON'T HAVE TO, BARRY."

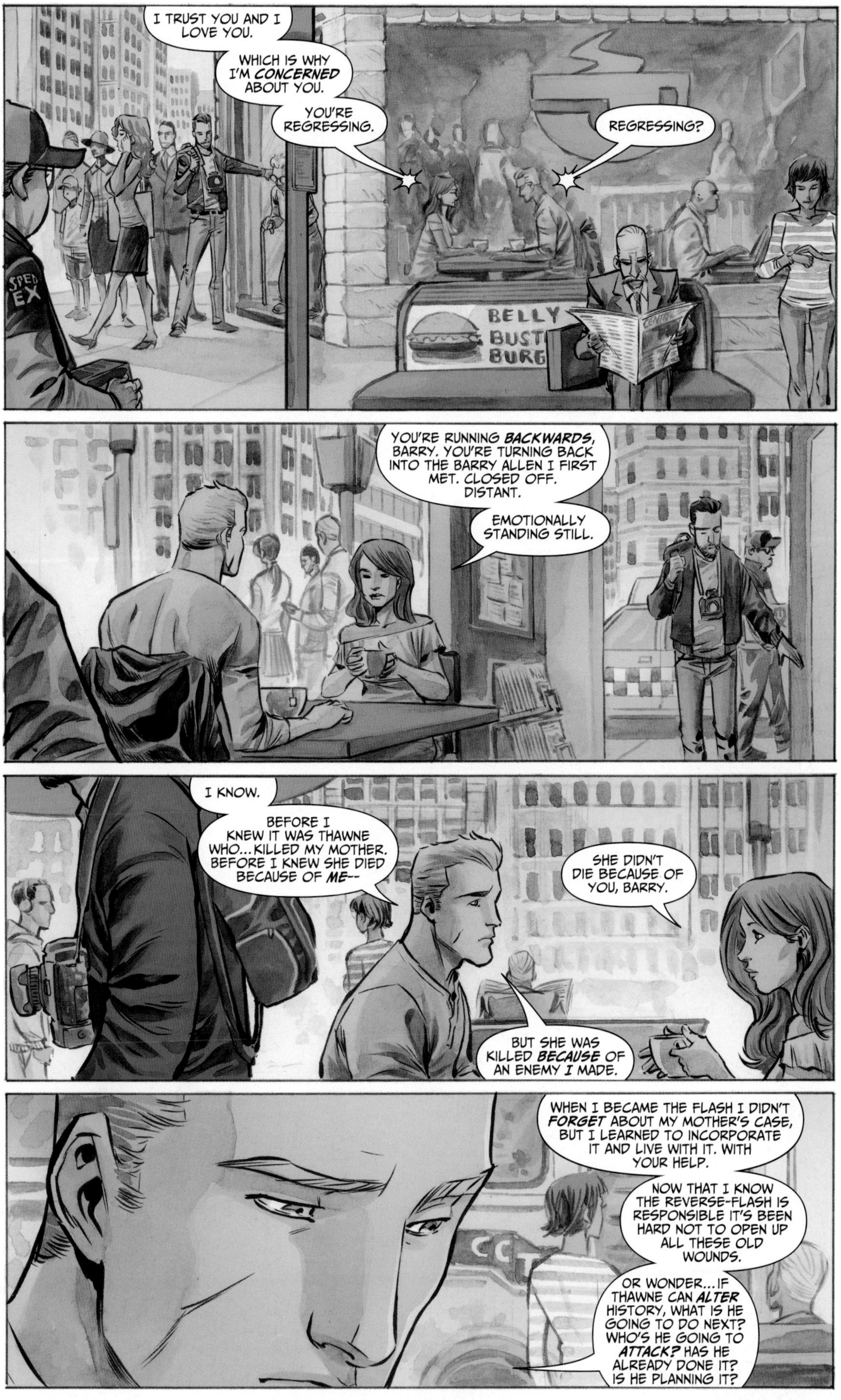
I TRUST YOU AND I LOVE YOU.
WHICH IS WHY I'M *CONCERNED* ABOUT YOU.
YOU'RE REGRESSING.
REGRESSING?
BELLY BUST BURG
YOU'RE RUNNING *BACKWARDS,* BARRY. YOU'RE TURNING BACK INTO THE BARRY ALLEN I FIRST MET. CLOSED OFF. DISTANT.
EMOTIONALLY STANDING STILL.
I KNOW.
BEFORE I KNEW IT WAS THAWNE WHO...KILLED MY MOTHER. BEFORE I KNEW SHE DIED BECAUSE OF *ME*--
SHE DIDN'T DIE BECAUSE OF YOU, BARRY.
BUT SHE WAS KILLED *BECAUSE* OF AN ENEMY *I* MADE.
WHEN I BECAME THE FLASH I DIDN'T *FORGET* ABOUT MY MOTHER'S CASE, BUT I LEARNED TO INCORPORATE IT AND LIVE WITH IT. WITH YOUR HELP.
NOW THAT I KNOW THE REVERSE-FLASH IS RESPONSIBLE IT'S BEEN HARD NOT TO OPEN UP ALL THESE OLD WOUNDS.
OR WONDER...IF THAWNE CAN *ALTER* HISTORY, WHAT IS HE GOING TO DO NEXT? WHO'S HE GOING TO *ATTACK?* HAS HE ALREADY DONE IT? IS HE PLANNING IT?

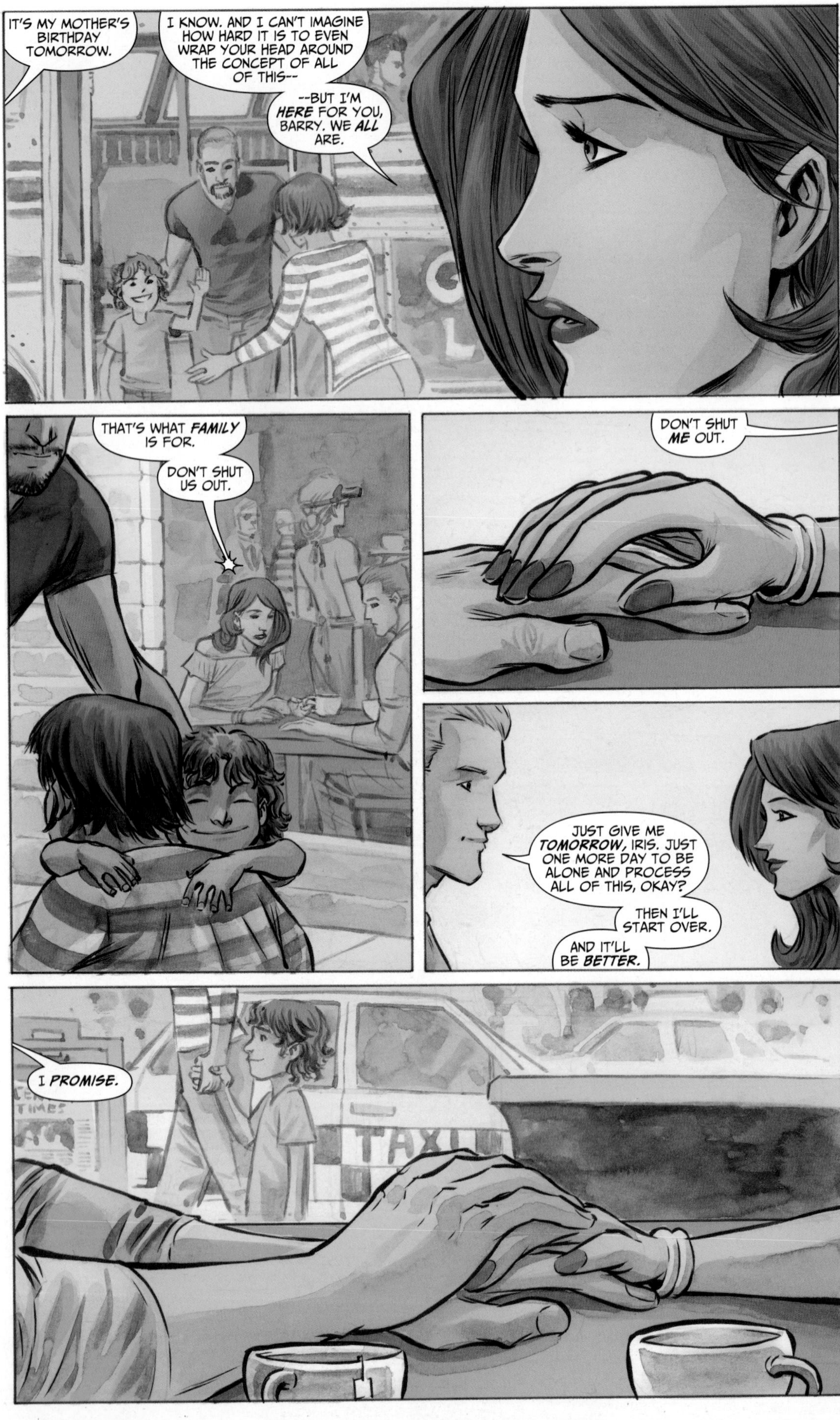
IT'S MY MOTHER'S BIRTHDAY TOMORROW.
I KNOW. AND I CAN'T IMAGINE HOW HARD IT IS TO EVEN WRAP YOUR HEAD AROUND THE CONCEPT OF ALL OF THIS--
--BUT I'M *HERE* FOR YOU, BARRY. WE *ALL* ARE.
THAT'S WHAT *FAMILY* IS FOR.
DON'T SHUT US OUT.
DON'T SHUT *ME* OUT.
JUST GIVE ME *TOMORROW*, IRIS. JUST ONE MORE DAY TO BE ALONE AND PROCESS ALL OF THIS, OKAY?
THEN I'LL START OVER.
AND IT'LL BE *BETTER*.
I *PROMISE*.
TAXI

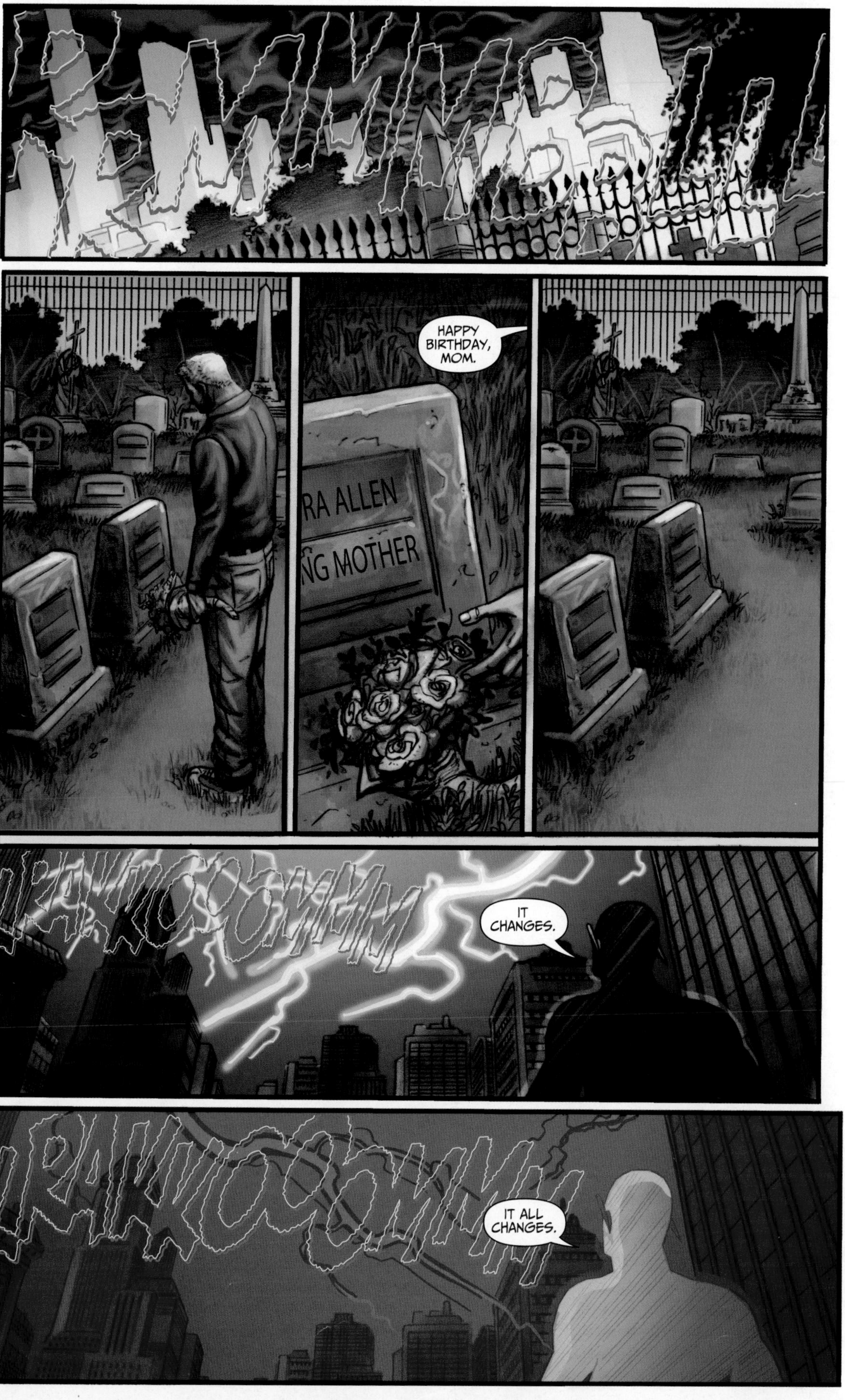
HAPPY BIRTHDAY, MOM.
RA ALLEN
NG MOTHER
IT CHANGES.
IT ALL CHANGES.

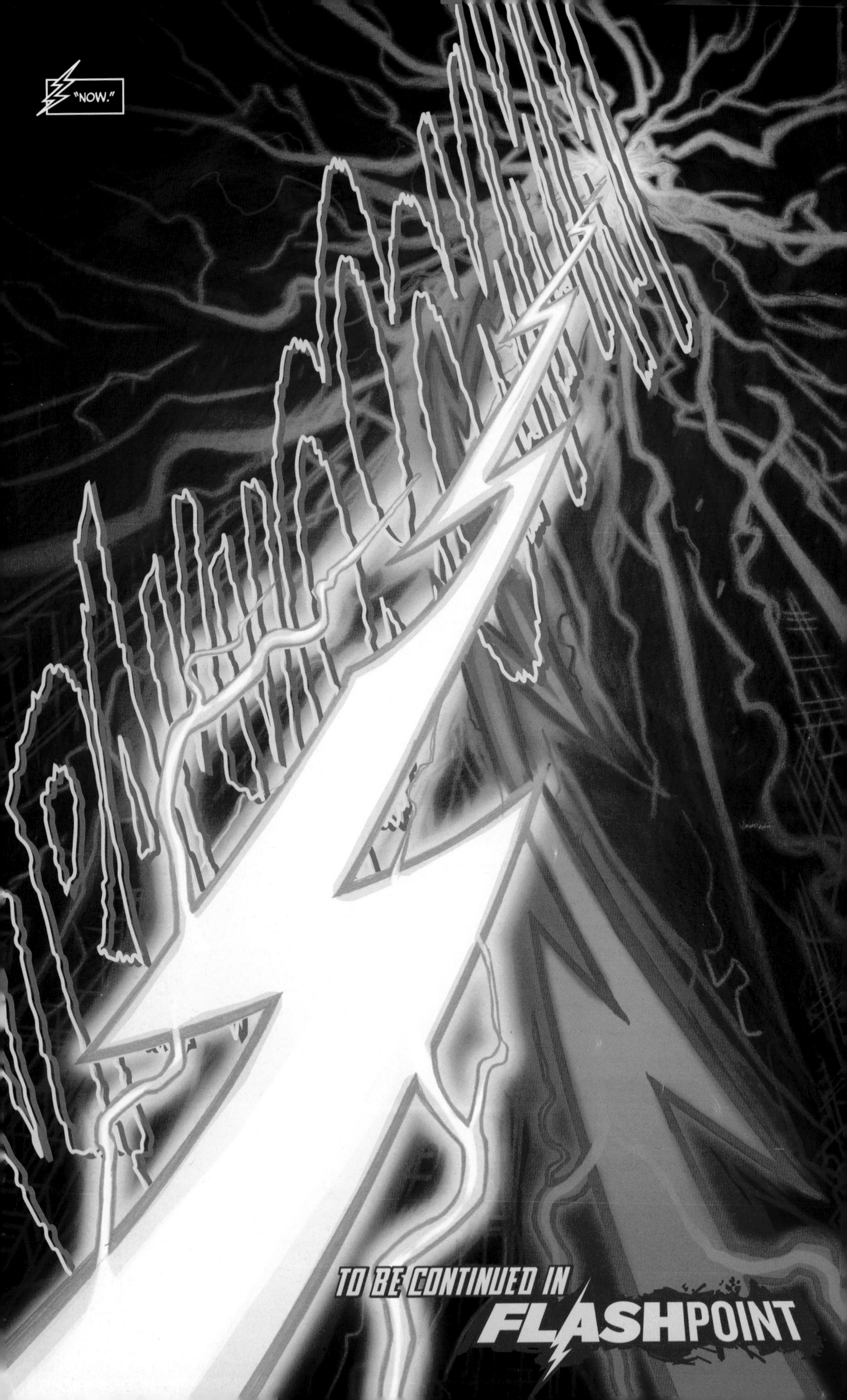
"NOW."
TO BE CONTINUED IN
FLASHPOINT

The FLASH

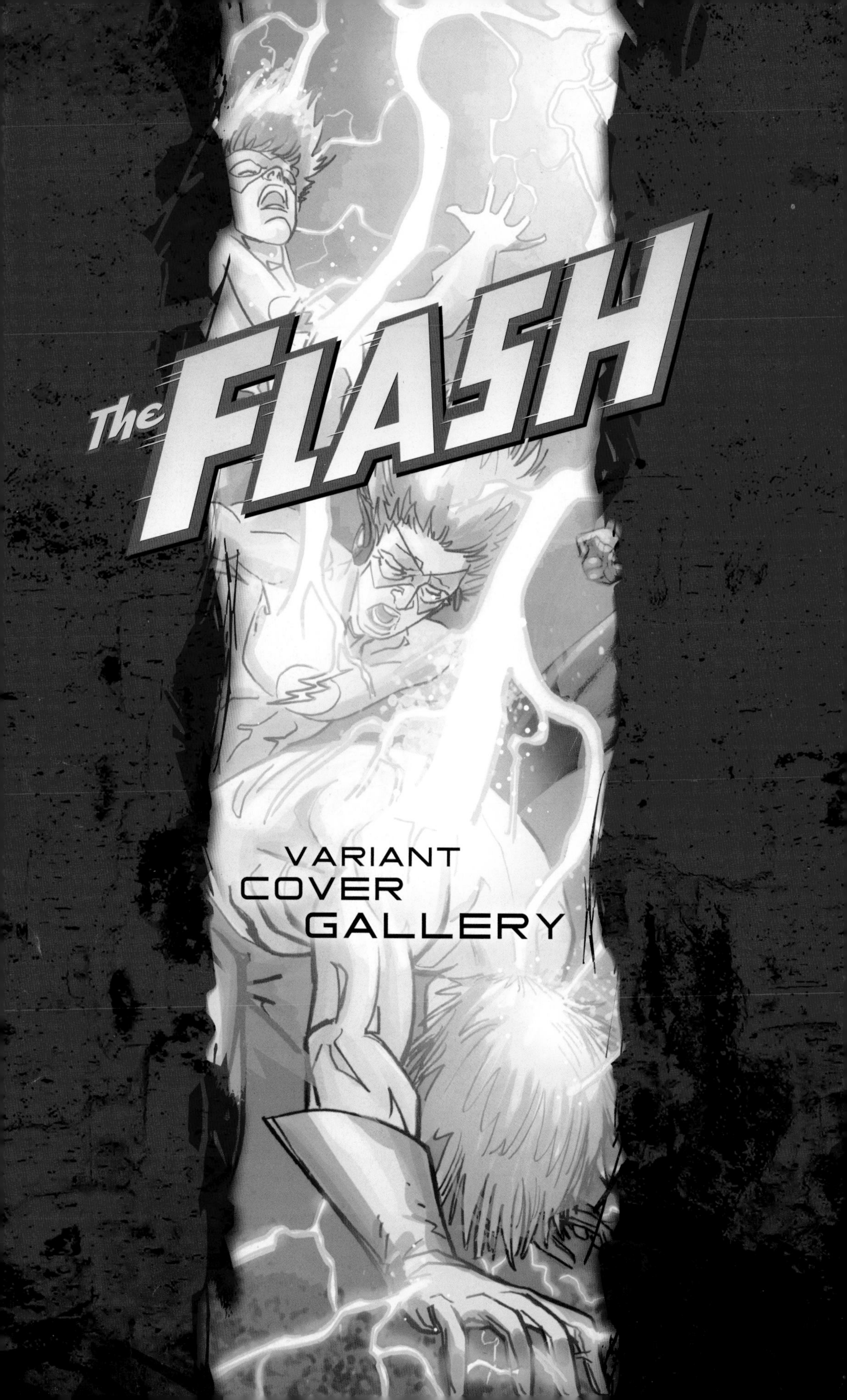

VARIANT COVER GALLERY

THE FLASH 8
by Stanley "Art Germ" Lau

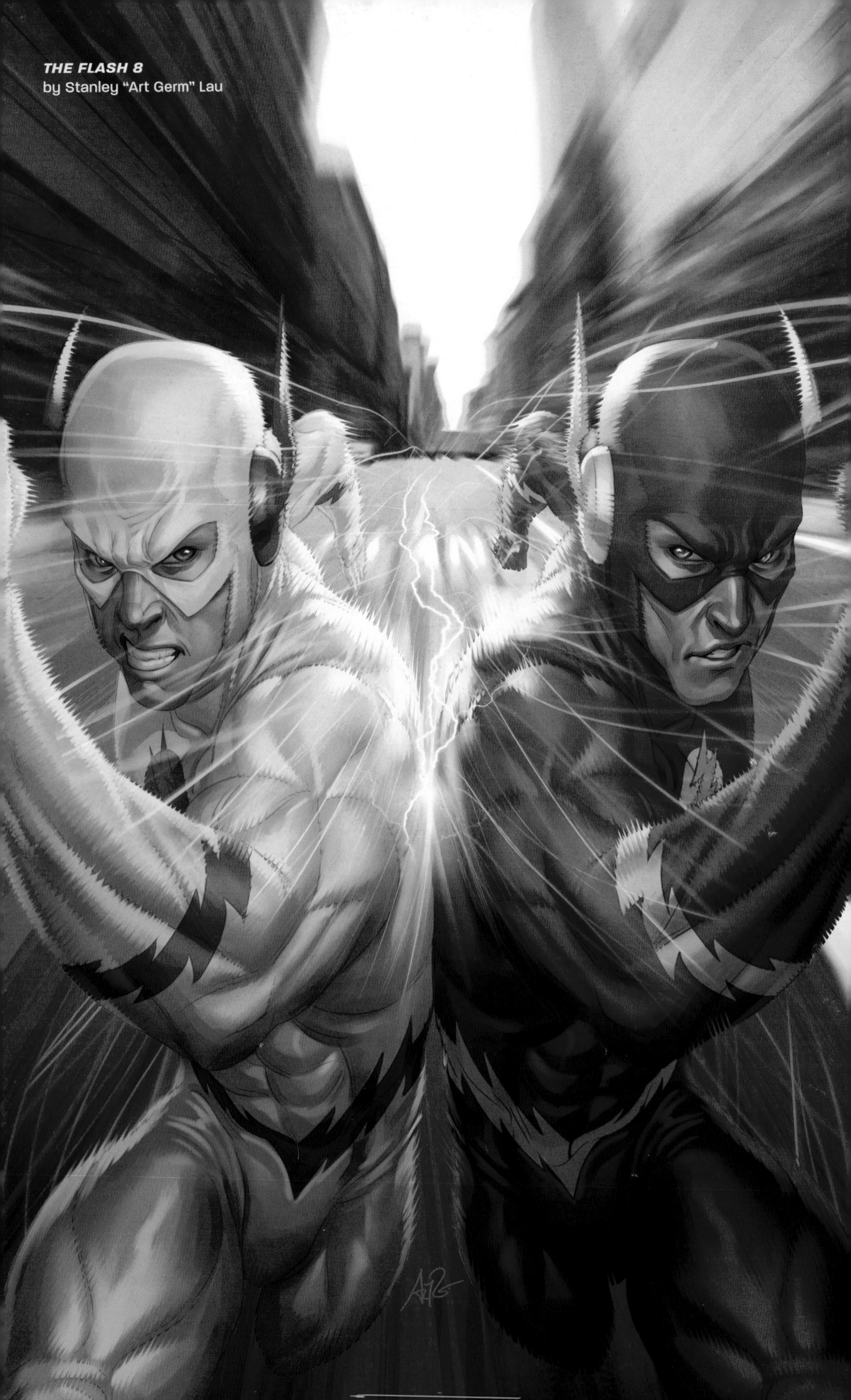

THE FLASH 9 by Tyler Kirkham, Batt and Nei Ruffino

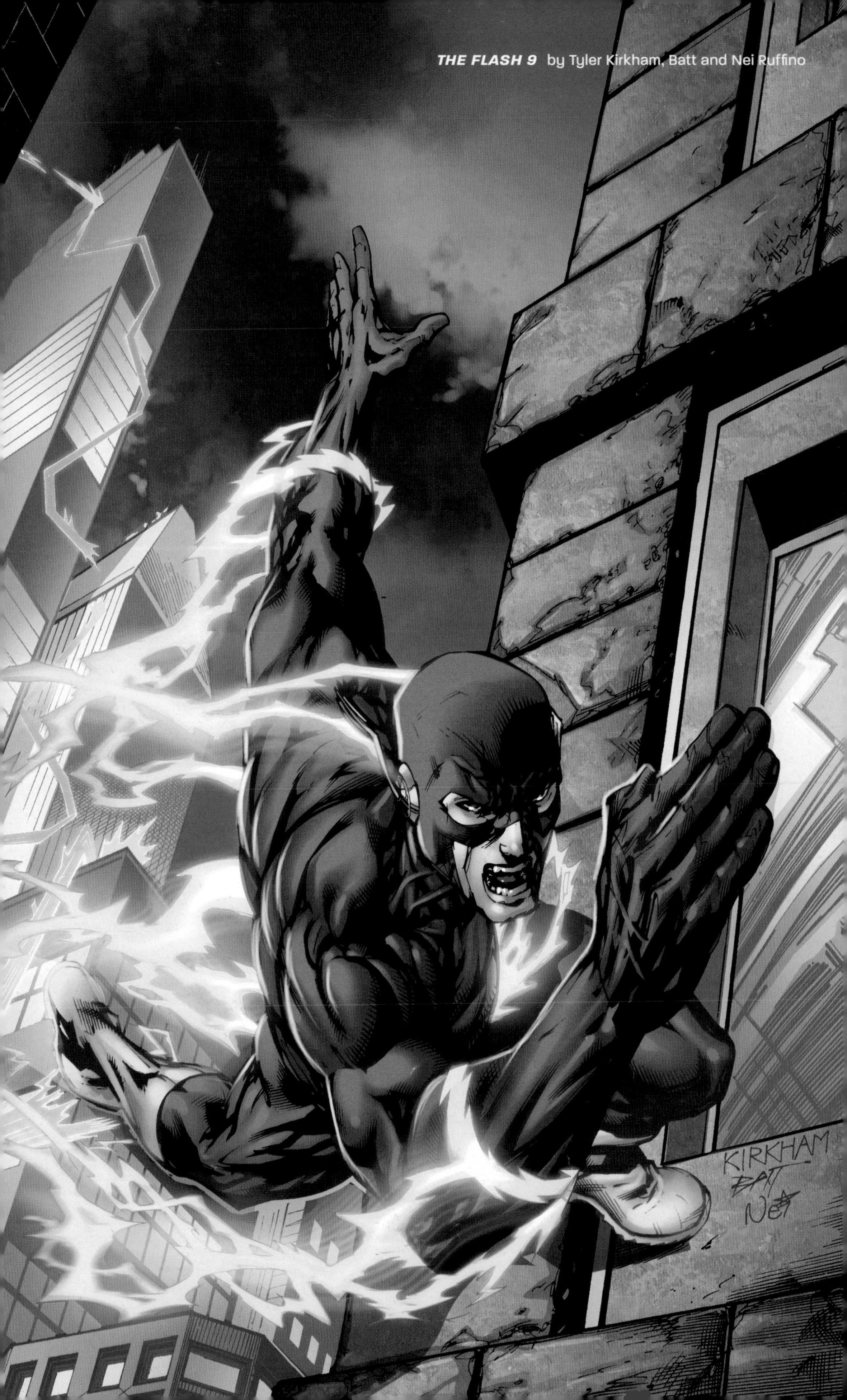
KIRKHAM
BATT
NEI

THE FLASH 10 by Ed Benes and Rob Hunter with Brian Buccellato

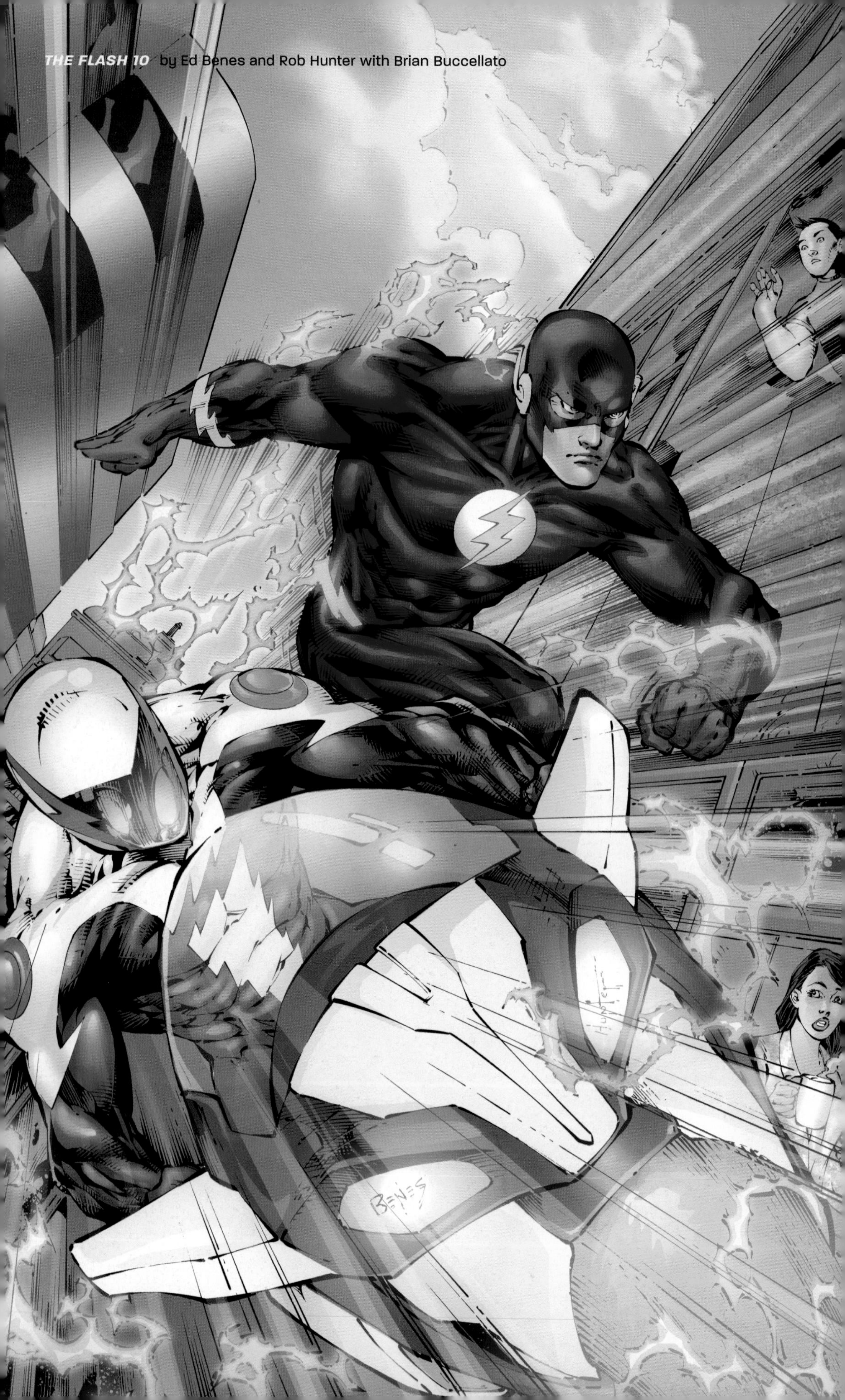
BENES

THE FLASH 11 by Scott Kolins with Michael Atiyeh

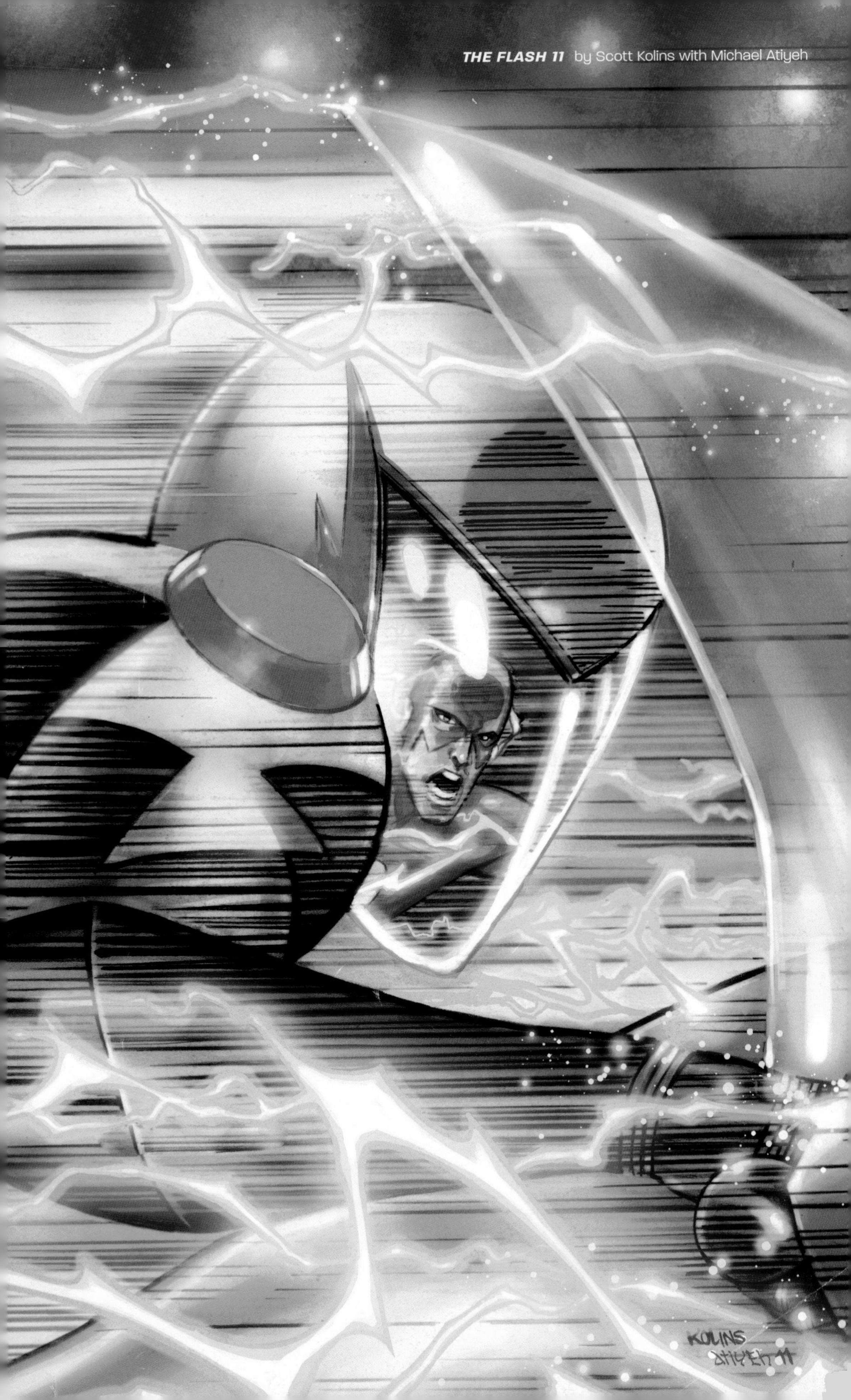
KOLINS
ATIYEH 11

THE FLASH 12 by Francis Portela with Javier Mena

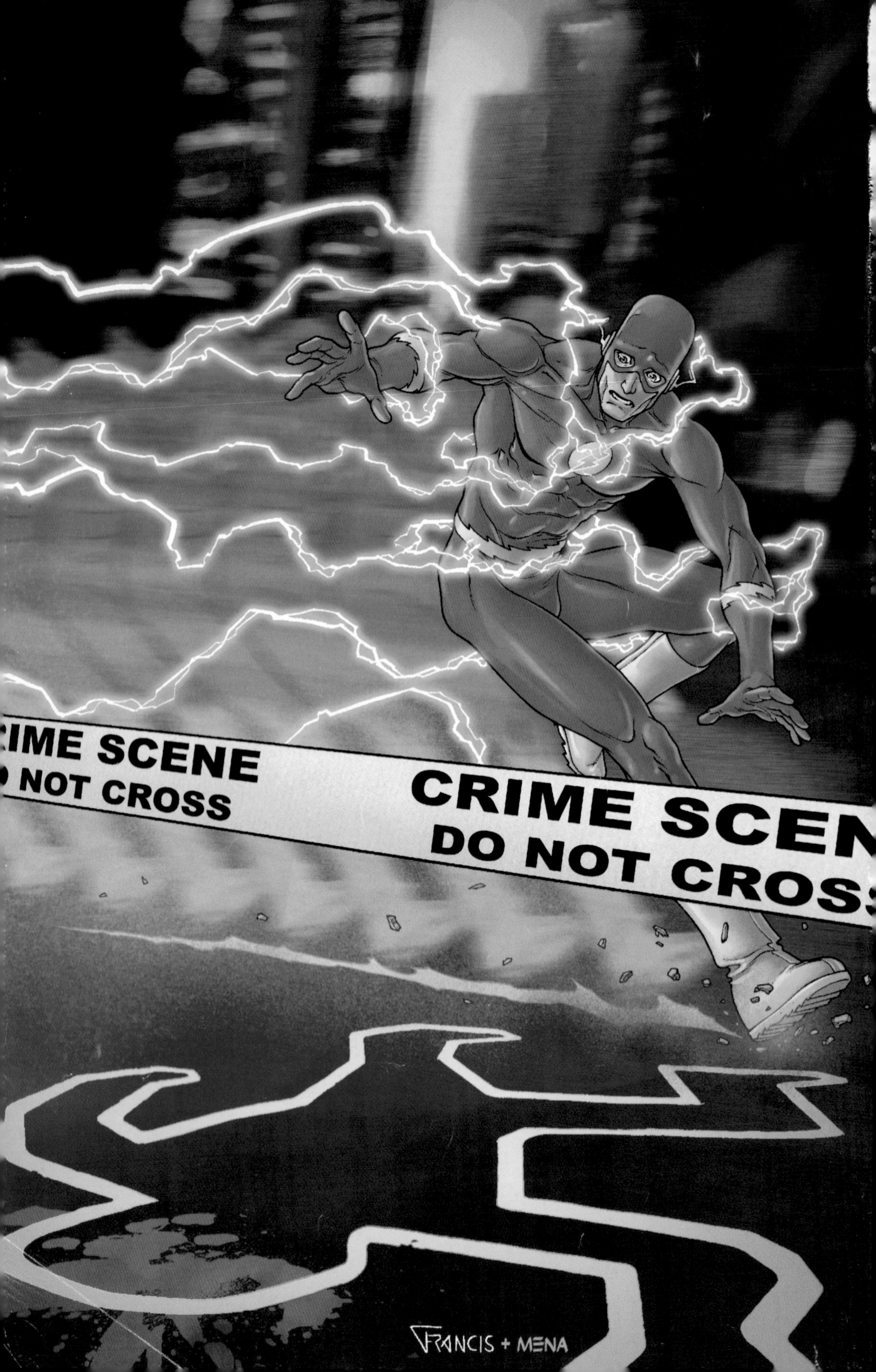
IME SCENE
NOT CROSS
CRIME SCEN
DO NOT CROS
FRANCIS + MENA